"Rosie's life is an incredible story a  able odds through God's grace. He inspire you no matter what mount.

-Travis Cox, Ministry Leader Celebrate Recovery, Cottonwood Church, California State Representative for Celebrate Recovery

---

"Imagine both parents dying and being orphaned at 19 with four younger siblings. And imagine that right before your father dies you make a promise to take care of the younger kids. It's an incredible sacrifice and responsibility, but it's also a dangerous prescription for codependency. Through God's grace, strength, and help, as well as an incredible ministry called Celebrate Recovery, Rosie has not only overcome an overwhelming challenge, but learned to live free from having to "fix" everything."

-Gene Petrini, Assistant Pastor, Cottonwood Church

"Rosie, You have always been such a wonderful supporter for both Jill Watson and me. We have treasured your friendship and the encouragement you showed us as we pressed forward in pursuit of our Olympic and World medals. Your positive attitude and belief in us helped sustain us. We are grateful for your friendship then as now. Your (Rosie's) story is motivational and inspirational. A true pioneer."

-Peter Oppegard, 1988 Olympic Pairs Bronze Medalist, 1987 World Pairs Bronze Medalist, World and Olympic coach, Hall of Fame skater 2004, USFS Choreographer of the Year, USFS Coach of the Year

---

"I've known Rosie a little over a decade. She's walked with me as I've faced physical challenges, spiritual attacks, the loss of a brother, and the passing of my mother. During these times she's been a great source of Christian comfort; a woman of integrity who displays The Father's LOVE & a spirit of understanding.

Two words best describe my friend, Rosie: "gentle leader." Most of us have heard the term, "Jack of all trades; master of none." Myles Munroe stated, "You become a leader when you find the thing you're supposed to master." Rosie has mastered rejection, sudden abandonment, cruelty from supposed friends, pain, sorrow, and grief. Yet she kept her eyes on Christ. In doing so, she's cultivated a heart of compassion for God's hurting people. This book will speak to those whose silent heart's cry has not been heard during things they've suffered. She truly exemplifies tenacity because she never gives up as she faces obstacles. Rosie is one who leads with strength and by example. I'm honored to call her my friend & sister."

-Gina Wilson, Psalmist

"It was the summer of 1989 that I was introduced by neighbors and mutual friends to Rose Mary George Ann Finocchi – or Rosie as she is best known. Of the two close friendships forged while living in Costa Mesa; Rosie's my oldest. One of the first things you notice about Rosie is her fully-formed smile - a smile emphasized by bright brown eyes that radiate intelligence, warmth and sincerity. After only moments of our first conversation, I realized that Rosie was different from the vain, acquisitive, aspirational and affluent 30-somethings that I'd met since moving to Southern California earlier that year. It wasn't just that she was a practicing Christian woman - but there was that. It is Rosie's inquisitiveness about people and processes, coupled with a lightning-quick ability to contemplate, comprehend and accept, people and ideas that make her a powerful yet understated presence. She has that unique ability to make everyone feel as if what they are saying is of utmost importance; and her response reveals that she not only heard but understood what was said, and what was unsaid.

I believe that God puts people in our path that He knows will help us on our life's journey. I believe that God put Rosie into my new life in California to help me maintain my Christian consciousness and to grow in my Christian life. When I told Rosie that I was a stockbroker, she shared her desire to learn about the inner workings of the market, and said that if she ever got enough money, she would become an investor. Within a few short years and against what most people would consider insurmountable odds; Rosie not only became my favorite client, but went on to become a Series 7 licensed general securities professional.

If you have ever wondered what a human force of nature looks like; check out my friend Rosie. Her personal story has something that nearly everyone can relate to. Unconditional love and an unwavering commitment to do what is right, no matter how hard, the cost or time. Self-sacrifice and the willingness to be vulnerable while at the same time moving forward to achieve lofty goals. A knowing that while others may have one up on you for any number of reasons; that if you want it bad enough, almost anything is doable. The awareness that ignorance is nothing to be ashamed of - but ignoring education is.

Rosie's life is a declaration of confidence in the fulfillment of God's promise. Her journey and recovery is proof positive that He will provide respite and resolution to all who serve Him.

-Arnette Wright Travis
Author – Wellness Advocate – Activist

"This wonderful story of the journey of Rosie Finocchi is testament to her love and perseverance in the numbing face of adversity. Rosie's steadfastness in pursuit of a better life overcame any delays in achieving success. Her love of figure skating and ultimate attainment of champion status exemplifies her sense of confidence that has sustained her path to fulfillment."

-Lorin O'Neil Caccamise,
U.S. Sectional/Midwestern Mens' Champion; 3-Time USFSA National Championships Bronze Medal; World Pro Championship Silver Medal; Principal skater Ice Capades and Ice Follies; Coach National/International Champions; Director of ice shows including USFSA show starring Champions Peggy Fleming and her contemporaies; Director of skating in Riverside and Ontario, California.

"*My Parents Orphans* is unlike any other personal account of surviving against all odds that I have ever seen. Rosie's story has given us an invaluable, spiritual harvest of the redemption of a life and insights that can very well help anyone with an abandoned Spirit. This affirming message of hope and healing is a gem to be treasured!"

-Kimberly Carlile-Celebrate Recovery-Amarillo, TX

"We live in a society where people are always saying what they can't do. Rosie's story shows how true Philippians 4:13 is that we "Can do all things through Christ who strengthens us." This is a good read and allows readers to see that with perseverance, faith in God and the truth of God's word we are all capable of becoming our best version of ourselves and Rosie has done this."

-Rochelle SmallWare,
CEO of Full Armour, a Nonprofit Corporation.

"Inspired and insightful. Rosie's story is a testament to the constant presence of God in our lives, our source of strength and courage through the difficult times, and of joyful celebration on the other side of life's difficulties."

-Kim and Mark Eliff, House Pastors, Mercy House Ministries

"Rosie is not the girl I met years ago in 1980. She has matured so much in so many ways. Her growth in the Lord, her graciousness (especially in her speaking abilities) and even her appearance, show a new Rosie. She has been like a daughter to me and I love her very much."

-Jeanne Solum Perry, Retired minister's wife

"For Rosie:

Though our chosen lives started us on different roads, our love of Figure Skating, our desire for the realization of our dreams coming true as we became USFS Adult National Figure Skating Champions, now our roads have become one.'

You will find inspiration and hope for your own journey as you read of Rosie's journey."

-Nancy Horton, USFS Adult Ladies Gold Medal Champion, USFS Adult Ladies Adult Nationals Medalist, ISI Adult Ladies National Gold Medal Champion

---

"It is very admirable that Rosie is bringing attention to the efforts of the pioneering California skaters. Rosie and her friends broke new ground or perhaps dug up what had been earlier and when it looked like Adults were going to go backwards again, they were the foundation we were able to build upon to become the now popular USFS Adult Nationals.

The United States Figure Skating/Association (USFS/USFA) Adult Ice Figure Skating movement has had an interesting and perhaps checkered history. In the seventies and eighties, a group of adults and USFSA clubs in California and a few other areas took up the challenge of providing adult competition. They had adult events and were able to get adults in Regionals and Sectionals competitions and Adult National Showcase.

The USFSA formed an Adult Skaters Advisory Committee and Adult Nationals Committee and I was asked to Chair. Eventually we reached our goal and the First Adult Nationals was held.

There is a lot more to the history that is to be written. But our efforts to have an Adult Nationals were based on many of the earlier pioneering efforts from the California adult skaters, officials and skating clubs.

Her personal story shows triumph over adversity. While watching a video she shared about her life my eyes were in tears. It also touches very close to me as my life has been very challenging and it was necessary to overcome much adversity in my life . . . but her story is close to my heart.

As someone else mentioned online it should be made into a movie. I would agree."

-Joe Kaplenk, Author and composer, Sports video Analysis and Adult competition advocate in multiple sports as a competitor, coach and an official in ice, roller, and inline figure skating and the United Skates Ski Association, the Olympic organization, and a past member of the USFSA/ISFS, Professional Skaters Association, and Professional Ski Instructors Association.

"Rosie's story is inspiring. In addition, ice skating helped her move forward. How cool is that?!"

-Jo Ann Schneider Farris, US Figure Skating Double Gold Medalist, Silver medalist US National Figure Skating Championships in ice dancing and online magazine "About.com's" 10 year Figure Skating Expert. Author of "MY SKATING LIFE: FIFTY PLUS YEARS OF SKATING." Jo Ann taught her three children to skate and all three attained US Figure Skating Gold Medalists' status.

My Parents' Orphans

The Rosie George Finocchi Story

GOD'S HEALING FOR OUR ORPHAN HEARTS

Rosie George Finocchi

Trilogy Christian Publishers A Wholly Owned Subsidiary of Trinity Broadcasting Network 2442 Michelle Drive Tustin, CA 92780

For information about special discounts for bulk purchases, please contact Trilogy Christian Publishing.

Manufactured in the United States of America

10 9 8 7 6 5 4 3 2 1

Library of Congress Cataloging-in-Publication Data is available.

ISBN 978-1-64088-189-1 (Paperback)
ISBN 978-1-64088-190-7 (ebook)

Dedication

This book is dedicated first to my deceased loving parents, George and Margie Finocchi, (48 and 43) who loved us—their five children—dearly, fiercely, and with a great love;
and
secondly, to my four younger siblings: my oldest younger brother, Daniel Paul, my middle younger brother Peter Joseph, my youngest younger brother Curtis John Michael, and my youngest sibling, my only sister, Lisa Robin Michelle.

We survived the unimaginable and continue to carry on our parents' love for each other, and of family, through our parents' traditions and teachings.

I am proud of each one of you and proud to be your big sister.

If I had this to do all over again, I would not hesitate for a moment as Daniel Paul, Peter Joseph, Curtis John Michael, and Lisa Robin Michelle have always been loved and cherished and have always made my life worth living.

Being confident of this, that He who began a good work in you will carry it on to completion until the day of Christ Jesus.
Phillipians 1:6

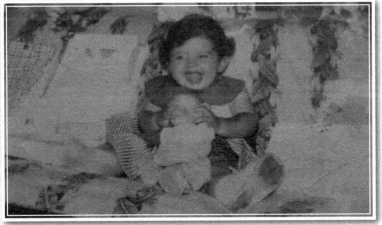

Me, 6 months old, 1953, Buffalo, New York

See, I have placed before you an open door that no one can shut.
Revelation 3:8

Contents

Foreword

Me, center with Teri and Tom Phipps who I met in 1972, I was 19 years old and I had been orphaned 10 days. Now, 45 years later. Long Beach, California

I met Rose for the first time in February 1973, when the man I had just begun dating asked me out on a second date and I didn't have a babysitter.

He asked, if he brought a sitter that worked in our Sunday school nursery, if I would go. So he brought his thirteen-year-old daughter over to be there also, since I didn't know the girl and I did know his daughter.

That began a forty-five-year relationship, not only as a mentor and friend to her—but she also became like a daughter to us.

As the story unfolded, she and her four siblings had become orphaned by the deaths of her mother to cancer and her father to a heart attack. They had been living in Buffalo, New York, when all this transpired. At that point, she and her three younger brothers were to come and live with an uncle in Northern California, and the five-year-old daughter was to stay in New York with an aunt and uncle while they got settled.

That began the story you are about to read.

We are so proud of the woman she has become out of this adversity. She has kept the vow she made to her father to take care of all of them, oftentimes to her disadvantage.

To them she became mother, father, daughter, sister, and friend—a heavy load for a girl of nineteen.

I think you will agree with me that she is an exceptional human being, worthy of our Lord's adage, "Well done, good and faithful servant."

Teri Phipps, writer and author

Dear Rose,

We are so proud of you! I have known Rose since 1972 when she came to Calvary Chapel. I helped run the Children's Ministry and Rose went to work with us to help with the younger children. She became a friend and we adopted her as part of our family and became Mom and Pop. She arrived here homeless and an orphan – and Jesus Christ took her in as His Daughter and she has lived her life in a way that I know Jesus is proud of her. Through this book she will help other folks who have fallen on bad times realize all they need is Jesus and the body of Christ if they will receive His love and guidance of the Holy Spirit He will lead them through life's trials with honor, love, joy and peace.

Love Pops
"Man of God"
Tom Phipps

Left to right back: Brother David, Mom, Dad,
Front row, brother Peter, Me, and brother
Daniel. Kenmore, New York, Easter 1958

Preface

"When your mother and father
forsake you, then I will gather
you up" (Psalm 27:10).

We were the quintessential small-town all-American family with loving parents; I was the oldest of five children. We loved small-town parades, picnics, my mom's deviled eggs, and fireworks. Dad was an Eagle Boy Scout leader, and Mom was a Brownie Troop leader. We were the joyful, happy, traditional family on your Hallmark greeting cards; the kind of family Normal Rockwell used as models for his American Family paintings.

* * *

And suddenly one morning, without even the smallest warning—just like in the movies when there's a horrible, screeching, ripping sound and everything freezes, and the picture you see on the screen literally rips into two jagged pieces—our wonderful, happy, secure life...just ended. *Poof!* Completely, permanently, and forever gone!

I was 13 years old and fatherless.

When I was 19, I added being motherless.

My four younger siblings and I were orphans.

It was 1972 and I was 19, and they were 16, 14, 10 &
5 years of age.

What happened to my family?

* * *

In years to come—years in which I was abandoned
and homeless, struggling with my ninth-grade education to
reclaim my baby sister and to provide for my four younger
siblings—I would have to remember really, really hard to
convince myself that there had once been a time when I did
have such a happy, loving family and such a wonderful life.

But horror does that to your memory. Horror doesn't
care. I've learned that too.

* * *

More importantly, I've also learned that I serve a God
who deeply loves my family; God loved us when we were
the quintessential, small-town all-American family, and God
kept loving us during and after the horror came and tried to
destroy our family. Yet we survived.

But God is a lot like that, I've learned.

When God heals our orphan hearts.

You can learn that too.

This is my story.

This is Your Invitation to Be Healed

*"Come to me, all you who are
weary and burdened, and I will
give you rest" (Matthew 11:28).*

"Don't worry, Daddy, I will." Five simple, simple words. Yet, for me, they quickly became life-changing, destiny-forever-altering words. I spoke them without a second thought on that cold, snowy, wintry, blustery, typical Buffalo morning of April 20, 1967. I spoke them with the simplistic assurance of a confident thirteen-year-old that I was, who up until that moment had not know anything other than a smug, daddy's-girl-in-the-midst-of-six-brothers existence. How was I to know that my white-picket-fence world was imploding—shattering that very moment—as my father, at forty-seven, was dying before my eyes; that my world as I knew it was to forever become nothing but fond memories of happier times? How could I?

"Don't worry, Daddy, I will." Just five simple, everyday words, I spoke them as a thirteen-year-old daughter to her beloved father, unaware that I was witnessing my father's last seconds of life, engulfed in life-ending pain. Speaking those words in the quiet, early morning hours of April 20, 1967, my sole intent was to reassure my father, who was in so much pain. I alone heard the agonizing question my father had desperately uttered: "Oh, God, who will take care of my family?" My response, "Don't worry, Daddy, I will," would haunt and shape my soon-to-be orphan's existence as Mom, at forty-three, would die five years later.

Decades later, I realized my daddy's question was not even directed at or asked of *me!* Yet, because my daddy was in such pain, although I knew I couldn't ease his pain, I hoped to help ease his obvious mental pain and anguish that morning as he suffered in front of me.

And so, with that simple phrase, "Don't worry, Daddy, I will," my life was forever changed; I was instantly transformed from a fun, laughing teenager to a serious, somber one. Not by anyone else's charge, but by my relentless striving—whether consciously or subconsciously—needing to keep my eager, heartfelt promise made to my dying father in 1967. I was the tender age of thirteen, and my mother was six months pregnant with my fourth younger sibling. I was *still determined* to keep my promise when, five years later in 1972, my mother died of breast cancer. Now, I had witnessed my beloved remaining parent's agonizing fight for life, and I sadly realized I and my four younger siblings were orphans. Their ages were sixteen, fourteen, ten and five. I was nineteen; a teenager. This was hell. *Where* was God?

My orphan's heart was hopeless; adrift in a world where nothing was stable. Different became *my* normal; I felt destined for a minimal, survivalist existence. Yet, in the midst of sad circumstances and seemingly insurmountable odds, I still clung to one very simple phrase which continued to be the beacon lighting my path. "Don't worry, Daddy, I will," was my personal measuring stick of my value and worth, constantly measuring—internally and externally—how well I was keeping my promise to my father. Measuring me even when I wasn't aware of its impact—which was actually *most* of the time.

For decades after being orphaned I simply pressed on. It was all I had ever known: press on and find a way to function and care for my parents' orphans. Had there *ever* been joy?

When I was orphaned and homeless, strangers took me in. God provided a second family who loved me as their daughter. Yet, I struggled raising my siblings. I was so angry and so sad.

My orphan's journey included my ninth-grade education, homelessness, being denied welfare, and obesity. At nineteen years of age I relentlessly fought the California legal system, succeeding in becoming my three younger siblings' legal guardian, rescuing them from separate foster homes. At the time of my mother's death I lost my sister, age five—without a good-bye—to relatives, later fighting unsuccessfully to regain her, waiting until she was returned seven years later, and I then became *her* legal guardian.

As happens so often with grief and unrelenting trauma, I believed the untrue thought "Nobody really cares." I know now that was not true. But grief, coupled with unrealistic expectations, produces a less than emotionally healthy person, and I had unwittingly become that person. My unresolved grief made itself at home and bled into every single area of my life. And that grief kept on bleeding, and distorting, and doing me and others harm. Still, I clung to God's promises of restoration with such hope: *I hope my life can change; I hope I can change.* Hope that was grounded in God's love, as I remembered long-ago memories where I had once known great love, joy, and freedom.

My enduring emotional pain, coupled with hope, led me to *Celebrate Recovery* in 2010. In 2011, both hurting and hoping—forty-four years after my father died and thirty-nine years after we were orphaned—my life came full circle when I returned home to Buffalo and visited our family's homes, where we had lived and where my parents had died. Soon, I was again kneeling in the bleak rain by my father's grave where weeping, I gave my parents' orphans *back to my parents*. I laid my child's promise and burden down, telling my daddy, "I've been keeping a promise you never asked me to make. I've been keeping a promise to you that you may not have even known I made. But I'm done now; I give all your children back to you. I get to have my own life." I was forever freed of keeping my promise to my daddy; freed of my journey that started as a teenager, carrying a burden that was never meant to be carried by me.

God's healing for my orphan's heart includes: the honor of serving in *Celebrate Recovery*; overcoming my ninth-grade education and, at age sixty-four when most retire, receiving my Masters of Theology and Ministry Graduate Degree from Fuller Theological Seminary; and careers as an American Bar Association senior trial paralegal, a stockbroker/licensed financial advisor, and a chaplain and pastor. I even found joy again as an Adult United States Figure Skating competitor, winning the first USFS Adult Figure Skating National Showcase! I joyously won over one hundred competitions and hold the most USFS Adult National titles ever by an Adult!

We can have an orphan's heart even with living parents, because of grief and overwhelming traumas we've experienced that were far beyond our control. I was a lonely, sad thirteen-year-old; I was carried through those hard, early years by God's mercy and grace. I was very angry at God, yet

God healed my heart. God can heal your heart. You can also change.

My siblings and I endured and survived the unimaginable. If you have endured the unimaginable, traveled your own journey of grief and hurts that are so difficult to understand and heal from, I understand. Pain is painful, regardless of its source. *We* are the *different* people, unanchored, longing for homes we never had; yet there *is* hope for us, hope for our orphan's hearts. What God's love did for me—giving wholeness and healing to understand, endure, survive, and now thrive in the unimaginable—I promise God will do for you. God loves us so. I'm *not* special. God waits to heal. Trust that you are good and trust that you are valued.

If you have lived unexpected grief, if you are an encourager of orphans' hearts, I *know* God heals our hearts and restores joy. Be encouraged. This is your invitation to heal *your* orphan heart, to find *your* lost joy again. Walk the path with me to wholeness and joy unspeakable, finding and trusting in the hope of God that I found. Trust in yourself and trust in God. Only joy lies ahead. I promise. I finally laid down my twin burdens of grief and anger; lay your grief and anger down too. God will give you safety, purpose, and joy.

Let my story be your story too.

Trust God to heal your orphan heart as God healed mine. I hope you will. There's so very much life to be joyfully lived.

God can and will heal your orphan heart.

Because I've gratefully learned that God loves us and waits to heal our orphan hearts.

Prologue

*"You will know the truth, and the truth
will set you free"- Jesus (John 8:32).*

*"Know the truth about yourself
to be set free." - Joyce Meyer*
Joyce Meyer Ministries

I want to invite you to join me on my journey of God's healing of my orphan heart.

You may be an orphan, or you may not. You may have two living parents, yet life's circumstances may have conspired to leave you feeling abandoned, alone, and very different from others.

If so, then you also possess an orphan heart. Paul Young, author of *The Shack* says, "An orphan is always waiting for someone more qualified to take what they want away from them. We are each uniquely wounded, we are each uniquely hurt, and we don't even know the prisons we are in. Yet with God, we are each uniquely healed."

As I have pondered my individual journey: a picture perfect childhood, ended by me watching my father die, then learning my mother was ill with cancer and our family facing a four-year battle for her life that would, sadly, end with her death in 1972—a death which orphaned me and my four younger siblings, catapulting us into the further destructive dividing of our already decimated family when our baby sister was forcibly taken from us—I continue to marvel at the moment by moment, day after day, month after month and finally, year after year way in which God has relentlessly, ceaselessly, uncompromisingly, deeply cared for me in the gentlest and most tender of ways.

I marvel at how God has met me at what were obviously deeply painful, personally bewildering times, times when I needed to make crucial decisions—decisions that would forever alter my life.

A favorite show of mine is NBC's *This Is Us*. I enjoy this show because I relate so much to the family's early, unexpected death of the loving father, when the three children are still barely teenagers. I relate to the character Randall as he expresses, "I was defined by my early circumstances, even when I wasn't aware I was being defined by them."

That is me: defined by my circumstances, even when I was not aware I was being defined by them. When I have not understood the *why* of my parents' deaths, or losing my sister for years, or the incredible hard work of physically providing for my younger siblings (seventeen, fifteen, and ten years of age), I have always had the benefit of the comforting knowledge of my two twin deeply-carried beliefs.

First, just as when I was a small little girl, dancing and twirling before my delighted earthly father, so I know that our heavenly Father takes that same level of delight and love in me and for me.

And second, knowing how special and important we are to God—just because God chooses to love us—I always knew, deep, deep down in my heart, that as long as God was directing me and helping me, there was absolutely nothing I could not accomplish.

Bible teacher Joyce Meyer says, "God's heart is so much to heal people, if I can help someone else say, 'If God can heal you, maybe God can heal me,' I will tell my story."

I shared Joyce's description of herself when she said, "I was deeply ashamed of who I believed I was: the damaged, hurting child who grew into the woman who could take care of others, but not myself."

To those of us with an orphan heart: whatever the reason is that you picked up this book—if you're thinking, *I cannot keep living my life the way I have been living*—the healing for that reason is right here; please join God on your journey to heal your orphan heart.

I don't know the exact date I was healed; I don't know in which *Celebrate Recovery* Step Study my healing happened; I only know that I was so broken, and now I have been healed of my orphan heart—and you will be healed of your orphan heart too.

Finally, Pastor Alan Jackson said, "My victories can be testimony to others of the power of God in ways more real than anything else." That is why I decided to tell my story; to demonstrate God's power in my life to heal and to restore our hearts to us.

Stay.

Join me on my journey, as I tell my story of God healing my orphan heart as only God can. My Pastor at Cottonwood Church is Pastor Bayless Conley, and he teaches: "God is a miracle-working God who can radically impact your life if you will call out to Him with a sincere heart."

I invite you to please stay and read my story; you've tried everything else. You'll never regret it. I never did, and neither will you as you begin your own journey of healing your orphan heart. It will be the best journey you ever take:

the journey back to yourself, to find yourself again and to find the joy you once had within yourself again.

God promises to restore what the horror took and replaced with your orphan heart.

You deserve to be joyful again, and you deserve to have your orphan heart healed.

Because God, I've gratefully learned, loves and desires to heal our orphan hearts.

"The restoration of God is unlike any other restoration."
Johnny Taylor,
Flowing Oil Ministries.

Chapter 1

"Watch Me Dance, Daddy, Please!"

Me: 5 years old, Dance recital,
Kenmore, New York, 1959

ROSIE GEORGE FINOCCHI

"As arrows are in the hand of a mighty man; so are children of the youth" (Psalm 127:4).

"Watch me dance, Mommy and Daddy!"

My sweet mother and father smiled indulgently at me, their five-year-old daughter, their only girl amongst five rambunctious boys. I was wearing my favorite pink tutu, pink tights, and little black cloth children's ballet slippers. My head was a mass of Mom's deliberate curls, and my smile was huge. I was the picture of the happy, indulged child.

My name is Rosie, and I wasn't always different; I wasn't always one of my parents' orphans. In fact, I was born in Buffalo, New York, into a very happy, normal, idyllic, life-in-the-suburbs family existence. Ours was the quintessential all-American family.

As a child, I lived a perfect Hallmark card, white-picket-fence life. My dad, George, was Superman—or so I thought—and my mom, Margie, was a perfect stay-at-home mom, baking apple pies and doting on her children. My mom was the youngest of thirteen children and had never lived on her own. My father had been married once before he married my mom. Daddy already had three sons: Joseph Jr., Johnny, and David, who were all quite young when he married my mom. I never knew my older "brothers" had a different mom, as she wasn't present in their lives. In quick succession I was joined by two younger brothers, each of whom I thought was great fun, and each of whom I adored. After my father's three sons, I had been the first and only girl. Now we were five boys and one girl—me!

We are an Italian family, and I was the only *girl*! Not just "a" girl, but *the only girl*! The absolute apple of my daddy's

34

eye; I *knew* it and I *absolutely loved* it and took full advantage of it, as my brothers will tell you to this day.

I spent my early years in what I called my "Happy House in Buffalo." My dad had built my "Happy House." I thought *everybody's* dad just built houses. Our street was called Thurston and it resembled a Norman Rockwell, picturesque 1950s all-American neighborhood. My "Happy House" was a simple single story, three bedroom, one bathroom, 750 square foot home. My dad and mom proudly placed a penny in the wet concrete in the basement, telling our family we'd always have a place to look at to be reminded that they loved us and had built a home for us.

I had my own room in our three bedroom, one bath home, as the East Coast in the 1950s was very different from the West Coast, and boys and girls didn't sleep in the same room. My dad had spent hours for several weekends in his basement workshop with me by his side, refinishing and spraying a used bed and turning it into a pretty white bed with robin's-egg-blue speckles on it for me. I was absolutely delighted with my new bed and mesmerized at my daddy's talent to make old things new again. I had a lovely, frilly, lace bedspread and drapes for my bedroom, with a pretty dresser to match my bed, *plus* I had the bedroom all to myself.

In contrast, my five brothers were all crammed in together in the remaining bedroom, with a set of bunk beds against each wall!

Although my room was definitely bigger, my brothers and I spent endless hours laughing, giggling, and playing in *their* cramped and over-crowded bedroom.

Our family was completed by a sweet collie puppy Dad brought home that we named King.

My dad and mom completely doted on their family. On Christmas Eve we had a real live Santa Claus come to our house, and all us kids would take turns sitting on Santa Claus' lap and excitedly telling him what presents we wanted. After Santa Claus left our home my mom would help us bake fresh cookies for Santa when he returned later that night, after we were asleep.

Every winter, my dad made an ice rink in our backyard. Ice rinks are primarily seasonal in Buffalo, and so outdoor ice skating was an inexpensive and very fun pastime for our entire family. My oldest big brother, Joseph, says I put on my very first pair of ice skates when I was only two! I have absolutely no memory of ever "learning" to ice skate; to me, ice skating is as easy and taken for granted as walking is for you!

When our backyard wasn't frozen in the winter with our homemade ice rink, I had my own swing set. The swing set wasn't really just mine, but no one else in our family shared my incredible love of movement. At an early age, I discovered that the weirder the position was in which I could propel myself through the air, the more I liked it! I soon discovered that flipping myself upside down while swinging was almost as much fun as ice skating, even though I'd occasionally flip myself right out of the swing!

My dad was a contractor, and my dad also built our family our own private, large sandbox in our backyard, so *my* backyard was immensely popular with all the children in our neighborhood. I was never without an abundance of friends to play with on those few occasions when my brothers weren't available.

As a contractor, my dad not only built my childhood "Happy Home," he also built the playground down the street as part of the neighborhood's development; so in my child's mind, the playground down the street was also *my* playground. The playground was only about five houses down the street from our home, and it wasn't unusual for me to spend the whole day on the swings and slides and teeter-totters.

The world was mine!

My birthday parties were full of cousins, family, and friends. I have a picture of me with my birthday party hat on, standing on a chair with a smile, saying, "Yes! It is *my* birthday!" Celebrating my birthday is still one of my favorite times of the year. Our home was filled with celebrations on holidays and lots of family dinners with relatives.

My mother didn't work outside our home. My favorite times were when my mom would let me help her make her homemade apple pies and my dad would let me hang out in his basement workshop with him, where he always seemed to be tinkering with some project.

We didn't have much money, but an early memory of mine is being banned from our basement and my dad's workshop one winter, without any reason. This made absolutely no sense to me, yet our basement remained off-limits all winter, spring, and summer. No explanation at all was given to me. One evening, Mom asked me to get my dad for dinner; she'd forgotten my restriction. I raced downstairs, and coming down the basement stairs I observed my dad bent over some upside-down, old, junky, rusty, broken bicycle, tinkering away like he was always doing. He shooed me back upstairs and I forgot about it, but my strange, unexplained basement banishment continued through the rest of the winter, and through the spring; I still couldn't go downstairs.

My birthday came in August, and my dad proudly wheeled out a brand-new, shiny bicycle! Years later, Mom confirmed that Dad had spent the entire winter, spring, and summer turning that junky, broken, rusty old bicycle I had momentarily glimpsed in his basement workshop into my brand-new, shiny one. I spent hours riding back and forth in front of our home. That was my dad and my mom. It really was a wonderful life. I continued to take dance lessons and was the happiest little girl.

My dad was a Boy Scout leader and all my brothers were Boy Scouts, enjoying fun adventures and the annual Soap Box Derby. I was a Brownie, then a Girl Scout, happily earning badges and selling Girl Scout cookies every year.

In second grade, I was in the school play. I had a new, pretty, frilly dress, white frilly socks, and shiny black shoes. My mother again deliberately curled my dark, thick hair into long shiny curls, and I was allowed to wear my mommy's bright red lipstick! I was in *heaven!*

I absolutely *loved* our small, picturesque, white clapboard neighborhood church that actually had a steeple. Our church was only a few blocks away, nestled on a street with a canopy of trees—another picturesque location. Our church had about seventy-five faithful people. Everybody knew everybody's name and family history, and the pastor and his family were regular guests at our home for dinner. I remember learning all the Bible stories and eagerly dressing each Sunday morning, excited to see my friends at church again.

Every Sunday we attended church as a family, which meant each Sunday I dressed in my prettiest dresses. I looked forward all week to wearing my extra-special ruffled little dresses, lacy socks, and black shiny dress shoes. I thought church was fabulous, and I *loved* it!

Easter was even better, for I got to wear real Easter bonnets and I added pretty white lacy gloves for Easter! My brothers wore matching bow ties and jackets and had their own hats just like my dad!

Our church's favorite song, sung every single week, was "Onward Christian Soldiers." It sounds like a marching song, and the pianist always started the chorus with a loud, resounding pounding "Da- to- Da- Ta Daah!" Then the whole church sang at the top of our lungs, "Onward Christian soldiers, marching off to war!" This was our little rally song. Every single Sunday, year after year. I loved this song and loved our church. I belonged and felt so completely surrounded on every side by loving people in everything I did.

I really had such a wonderful, wonderful life.

But I didn't know the horror that was soon to come. How could I?

Even if I had known, there would have been absolutely nothing I or my loving family could have done to stop the horror from streaming towards our happy, laughing, quaint, all-American family.

But horror is a lot like that, I've learned.

Chapter 2

Nobody Knows Like the Rosebush Knows

Me, 7 years old, School play, 1960, Kenmore, New York

MY PARENTS' ORPHANS

*"Let your roots grow down into
him and let your lives be built
on him" (Colossians 2:7)*

"I'm going to be a rosebud in the school play!"

I could not have been more excited! I was now in second grade and was thoroughly enjoying school, my family, and church. My second grade teacher had announced that we would be putting on a school play, and I was chosen to be a rosebud on a rosebush. I would recite a little poem about a rosebud when my turn came. I practiced my small poem over and over, determined to not appear nervous and to make my parents proud of me.

Being a rosebud was a big deal in my family, or so everybody made me think!

When the day of my school play came, my mother curled my long, thick, dark hair, and again I got to wear a dress with even more pretty ruffles and wide pink ribbons around my waist. I felt like a princess! My dad took off from work, and I could see both of my parents in the school auditorium, glowing and smiling their approval.

As I waited my turn, I was not at all nervous. When my big moment came, I walked to the spot our teacher had marked during our rehearsals and looked out at more people in one place than I had ever seen in my life.

Taking a deep breath, I clearly and carefully recited my now new favorite poem:

*"Nobody knows like the rosebush knows
how good mud feels between the toes."*

I listened to the applause and was so pleased I had not messed up my part—and even happier that, as I could see by my parents' big smiles, they were proud of me too.

Our happy life continued, only now Mom and Dad added making homemade glazed sugar donuts in a big frying pan to our family night. Mom made the gooey dough, and all us kids helped Mom punch out the circle-sized donuts with stainless steel circles and watched Dad quickly and carefully place them into the bubbling hot oil. Fascinated, every week we all excitedly crowded around the stove, despite Mom's ever-present warnings to watch out for the sputtering hot oil. The donuts virtually exploded as they went into the hot oil, and that was the fun part we always waited for, laughing anew each time it happened as if we hadn't seen that occur the previous time. As they were quickly browning, Dad flipped them over, and just as quickly the hot, still bubbling donuts were placed on plates where we kids took over with our job of dusting the fluffy donuts with powdered sugar. We were soon rewarded for our completed work with a glass of cold milk to go with the still-warm donuts, and our family night ended around our family dining room table with everybody talking and laughing and slowly getting more sugar on us than ended up on the donuts.

Our family continued playing winter sports, which for me meant ice skating every moment I could get somebody to take me. At home, my dad began to make very elaborate model airplanes. The planes he made had intricate blueprints and the wooden pieces were fragile and slim, and he had a special table where he assembled the planes, and we weren't allowed to touch it. The wingspan was more than three feet wide, and the plane body was more than three feet long. My dad's model airplanes always started exactly the same way: with an intricate blueprint full of intersecting thin lines and intersecting angles. These blueprints were also covered in numbers indicating measurements of 1/16 of an inch. Next to the blueprints were stacks of incredibly fragile, slender sticks of balsa wood. My dad traced on the balsa wood the images of a plane part, and then carefully carved the wood into the traced shapes he had drawn on the soft wood. Then the slim balsa wood frames were glued together and then painstakingly covered in delicate, see-through rice paper in exact detail to match the blueprints; the rice paper was held in place with shiny straight pins. Hour after hour, while my mom took care of the dinner and my younger brothers, I sat and quietly observed my dad working on his fragile planes.

I alone of all us children was always so fascinated to sit quietly by my father's side and simply watch him, for hours on end, ever so slowly and delicately assemble his model airplanes. He was so careful, detailed, and extraordinarily focused. He seemed to be in another world, in which as long as he followed his directions, he was assured of a perfect completed model airplane.

Daddy rarely made a mistake in assembling his model planes and if he did, Daddy just quietly redid his mistake, retracing his previous steps until he achieved his desired perfection. And always the result was the same: a perfectly constructed model airplane of such strength and beauty. We always celebrated my dad's finished model airplane, no matter how many months each plane might have taken to finish.

It quickly became apparent that I was quite happy to spend long, endless hours of what appeared to others as boring, intricate, talk-free quiet time with my father. I didn't really care at all—I liked just being in my father's presence, and the goals, and the steady, focused concentration which often entailed stretching our tedious crafts over several weeks.

The quieter and more focused our mutual projects were, the better I liked them.

Once my dad and mom realized how I enjoyed crafts and long hours of detailed, focused work, they bought me every conceivable craft. I remember I especially liked the paint-by-number oil painting sets that came with two similar pictures to each set. I liked these sets because my dad and I would each take a picture, and after carefully consulting the numbers on the paintings and coordinating them with the small, individually numbered paint containers, we'd scrutinize which oil paint colors went where on the painting canvases and carefully lay out our plans to paint only in areas that didn't touch each other—thus allowing maximum time together. Once the selected areas were painted by each of us on our individual painting, we'd set the unfinished painting aside to dry and repeat the process each day until our paintings were done. We didn't talk a lot, just enjoyed being in each other's presence, accomplishing a project step by step.

Again, I just thought everybody's dad spent hours painting with them.

Perhaps it was watching my dad painstakingly and slowly build his extremely detailed models—regardless of how incrementally small his progress was—hour after hour, day after day, taking weeks to complete his complicated model airplanes, coupled with our hours together slowly completing the tiny little areas of paint that became beautiful oil paintings, that caused there to begin to build within me the patience needed to stick to a project—no matter how long my project might take, no matter how difficult my endeavor might be, always keeping focused on the goal, keeping the end in sight, always keeping my eyes on the desired prize, concentrating on each individual step.

Early on, as a young child, I had a bedrock belief that even if I was progressing only one percent with each step, each one percent brought me that much closer to my goals. My personal math was quite childish, quite simple, yet surprisingly effective. Each step yielded one percent and sooner or later, *as long as I didn't quit and nobody moved my goal,* each one percent step when added together, no matter how long it took me, meant I could—and more importantly, *would*—achieve my goal. I didn't care one bit if it took me ten times longer than anyone else to master the skill to achieve my goals, I quickly learned that as long as I just did not *quit,* I definitely could not be stopped from achieving my goals and purposes.

This reasoning of mine occasionally got me into trouble, as I'd often simply weigh what I *wanted* against what I *knew* the inevitable consequences might be of my pursuing an activity that might be frowned on, or not allowed by my parents.

I was told that I was a very well-behaved child, the kind of child who obeyed their parents and didn't get into much trouble. However, I was also told that once I determined I wanted to do something, nothing stopped me from obtaining my goal.

I have vivid memories of taking deliberate actions after determining that my goals were worth the consequences. Our neighborhood had a great community center several blocks away. I had learned to swim there when I was five years old and really liked the community center. I was eager to go back there and remembered you just turned right and went for a long way, and then I always recognized the big, square building where the pool was visible. I didn't ask my mom if I could go there alone, as I already knew I wasn't allowed to go that far on my tricycle. I knew I'd get in trouble for going so far away but decided my punishment would be worth it. So, I talked my very reluctant little girlfriend into making the journey with me. After getting our fill of seeing people swimming that afternoon, we pedaled back to our street to find both of our parents extremely worried and—once our safety was assured—very, very angry.

The next time we spoke, I asked her what her punishment was and she said she hadn't been punished because she explained that I had "talked her into going!" That sure didn't seem fair to me, but I was still glad I had gone—though I never went alone again.

Being in such a happy family, we continued to thrive in school, in sports, and in our home life. Without realizing the tremendous amount of nurturing I was so fortunate to be receiving, my child's mind only knew that as I grew in my early childhood years, I was surrounded by incredible love, joy, and kindness, with doting parents and protective, fun-loving brothers everywhere. I became extremely confident, quietly believing I would never fail at anything I attempted. The result was that I feared nothing and was intimidated by no one. I seemed to excel at everything I tried, even as a young child.

Little did I know or realize that my twin life skills of detailed patience and laser beam focus which I was learning from both my parents in these early childhood years would serve me very well once the ever-closer horror arrived and dismantled my parents' sweet, loving, precious family in a matter of horrific seconds.

But determination, detailed patience, and laser beam focus—coupled with an indomitable belief in God and oneself—is a lot like that, I've learned.

Chapter 3

◀◀———◦———▶▶

California, Here We Come

Mom and Dad Wedding Day, 1953, Buffalo, New York

ROSIE GEORGE FINOCCHI

"Now lift up your eyes and look from the place where you are, northward and southward and eastward and westward" (Genesis 13:14).

"Why aren't my mom and dad home?"

One day in the fall, while I was in second grade, I arrived home to find neither of my parents was home. This was very, very odd. Arrangements had been made for a babysitter, and we were told Mom and Dad had gone to the local hospital emergency room earlier in the day. Since our adventurous family was familiar with a large assortment of injuries necessitating constant medical attention, I really didn't pay much attention to the announcement.

Later, when a hospital bed appeared in our family dining room I was puzzled, as only a few days earlier we'd powdered and enjoyed the hot, homemade, sugared donuts we made as a family. Being only eight years old, I lacked any true understanding of what had happened.

The reality of what I had not yet been told was that my father, not yet forty years old, had been rushed to the emergency room as he was having a heart attack. Even if I had been told the truth about my father's condition, I wouldn't have been able to grasp the seriousness of his health crisis, nor the impact this sudden brush with death would bring.

I only understood that my daddy had been sick and now needed a lot of rest. With his hospital bed in our dining room he was home all day long, and I could spend as much time with him as I wanted to. I had little understanding of how much in my charmed life had instantly changed.

As my dad got healthier and stronger, at some point my parents made the decision to move our family to California. My mom had family in both Northern California, just outside of San Francisco, and in Southern California, just outside of Los Angeles.

So, we packed up in the standard station wagon and made the cross-country road trip from Buffalo, New York to California in 1961, driving across the United States on the old Route 66 in search of a healthier new life for my dad. My dad was now forty years old and my mom was thirty years old.

We arrived first in the San Francisco area and met and stayed with my mom's brother and his family. My uncle helped my dad to look for work, but when my father was unable to find work in the San Francisco area, my parents decided to travel to Southern California in search of work, as my mom's brother's family lived there. We again packed ourselves into our family car, and this time we drove from Northern California to Los Angeles, California, along beautiful, wide roadways with widely varying landscapes. We traveled through the center of the state, alternating with wide open highways allowing us to travel on the very edge of the incredible Pacific Ocean.

Coming from the snowy, crowded neighborhoods in Buffalo, New York, we were all amazed at California's wide open, majestic mountains, coupled with clear skies and crystal blue, foaming waves crashing on the pristine sandy shore as far as our eyes could see in both directions, on the beaches that stretched for miles and miles as we drove on the Pacific Coast Highway on our way to our hoped-for new life in Los Angeles.

We were particularly impressed with California's miles of orange and almond tree groves, vineyards, and strawberry fields. The highways in northern and central California were often just long, lonely stretches of very rural countryside, with only an occasional house in the midst of mile after mile of neatly arranged, meticulously cared-for, perfectly-cut square fields of produce.

My mom had long had a special love for dark, plump, purple seeded grapes. Knowing this, as we were passing a vineyard, my dad chose a random spot in the middle of the rows and rows of grapevines visible from the two-lane highway, pulled over to the dusty side of the highway, and stopped. When Dad stopped our car, we were able to see field workers dotting the neatly planted rows of grapevines. They seemed to be everywhere. The men were wearing large brimmed straw hats. All the men were quickly and methodically in various stages of bending, cutting, and harvesting huge clusters of dark, plump, purple grapes. It looked like a choreographed dance of movement: bend, grab a huge cluster, cut, stand, and place the huge cut grape clusters in the harvesting containers. We all watched silently, mesmerized by the methodical methods of these field workers.

My dad walked up one to of the field workers cutting the huge grape clusters off the gigantic tangled vines and began to speak to him. We couldn't hear their conversation, but repeatedly my dad would turn and gesture to our car as he and the field worker talked, with the field worker repeatedly nodding his head every time my dad turned and gestured at our family sitting in our car several feet away.

After several minutes of their animated conversation, and with a big smile, the field worker handed my dad one of the largest of the freshly cut, plump, deep purple clusters of grapes. My dad received the huge cluster of grapes with an equally big smile, and they exchanged an enthusiastic handshake under the blazing California sun. The field worker went back to his grape harvesting, and my dad walked back to our car—holding high his trophy cluster of grapes—and came around to the passenger side where my mom was seated.

My mom's face completely lit up as my dad, with an equally huge grin, presented the grapes to my mom with a laugh and one last gesture back to the field worker. Mom quickly pulled a couple of grapes off their stems and popped them in her mouth, eyes closed, smiling as she savored the flavor. The cluster of grapes was passed around the back seat. My brothers and I instantly agreed that those were the biggest and tastiest grapes we had ever eaten.

The field worker's gift of the gigantic grapes allowed my family to enjoy quite an incredible welcome to our new home state of California.

We settled in Lomita, California, where the homes were built for the year-round sunshine. A typical suburban tract of homes, it was full of kids our age, good schools, safe streets, and lots of fun things for our family to enjoy.

My wonderful life continued—still my daddy's girl, secure and happy; life was delightful. I was adventurous and determined. I continued as a Girl Scout and proudly added badge after badge to my green sash, while my brothers continued in the Cub and Boy Scouts. My brother David was a Wise Man in the church Christmas play and I thought he looked so grown-up.

I was also a very industrious and creative child. When it became apparent that there were only so many potholders and other homemade craft projects of mine that our small kitchen could hold, I was allowed to go door-to-door in our neighborhood, first taking orders for my handmade $.25 potholders and then delivering them and collecting my money. I saved enough money from my potholder project to buy my mom a cuckoo clock, which she proudly hung on our living room wall for all to see and listen to!

Our family continued to grow with the birth of my youngest brother, Curtis John Michael, whom we call

Michael. Michael was the classically handsome little Italian boy with a head of riotous dark curls and big, smiling brown eyes. Michael is so proud of the fact that although we all consider ourselves Californians, Michael is the only native Californian in our family.

Michael's birth added so much additional joy to our already happy family.

We quickly adapted to living without snow, enjoying the free Southern California miles and miles of pristine, white sandy beaches—beaches where we could build a campfire right at the ocean's edge and roast marshmallows and cook hotdogs and hamburgers. With the San Bernardino Mountains so close, we often took tents up to the mountains, quickly set up our tents, and then enjoyed dusk-to-dawn hours of exploring the hiking trails and jumping off the cliff ledges into the clean, clear, rushing steams tumbling by below us.

We fished in those clean mountain lakes, my parents preparing our prize catches for our evening meals which we enjoyed at the outside picnic table. We played horseshoes in the evenings, and our family's campsite resounded with laughter and jokes about who would claim the title of our family's best horseshoe player of the day.

I thoroughly enjoyed being the only girl and always felt I enjoyed the best of both worlds, as one of the advantages of hanging out with all my brothers was that I had my own baseball mitt for games of catch and quickly learned to throw a football in a perfect spiral pass. My brothers were my perfect guardian angels, always making sure my adventurous, fearless heart didn't get me either injured or into trouble with my parents.

My brothers and I especially loved it when Dad took us to the stock car Figure Eight Demolition Derby, where the cars drive backwards in a figure eight and of course end up smashing into each other.

My very favorite part of living in Southern California, as my family quickly discovered—and as strange as it sounds, as Southern California is best known for its sandy beaches and surfers—was the local *indoor* ice skating rink just a few miles from our home. I still loved ice skating, and now I was no longer restricted by the weather. I could ice skate as often as my parents gave in to me begging to be taken there.

The indoor ice rink had a large pipe organ in a glass room overlooking the ice, but my favorite part was the large circular fireplace pit with circular benches around the entire fireplace so I could stay warm while changing my skates. I had only ice skated in the cold, windy, snow-blowing-around-me, seasonal outdoor ice rinks, so I loved the concept of an *indoor* ice rink where number one, I didn't need to be bundled up with so many clothes I could barely move, and number two, I could skate all day long and all year long.

The ice rink quickly became my personal babysitter. I loved being there and never got tired of ice skating. It was my special joy.

I would get dropped outside at the ice rink early on Saturday mornings, and one of my parents would come back about six hours later and pick me up. Though not yet ten years old—and because this was the late 1950s—I could be safely left at the neighborhood ice rink all day on weekends and after school. My only instruction was to never, ever go outside the building, as my parents would always come inside the ice rink to pick me up.

I never wanted to leave the ice rink, so I happily spent the whole day ice skating, just as happy as could be.

I especially liked when my dad would drop me off at the ice rink, because he would park our car and come inside and lace my skates up. Then my daddy would sit on the rough wooden benches and watch me skate for a while before he left, always smiling and waving at me each time I came around the oval ice rink and caught his eye as he stood waving to me from the stands.

As much as I loved my daddy lacing up my ice skates and watching me skate, I never had the heart to tell him that he *always* laced my skates way too tight; so, once my dad had left the ice rink and was safely back in our family car, I'd race off the ice and with great relief untie my ice skates, so my feet would stop being numb from my dad's strong hands tying my skates too tightly.

On many occasions our whole family went ice skating, but I was the only one in our family who couldn't get enough of being on the ice. Everyone else loved the sunshine and lack of cold weather, but I was in my own little heaven every time I got to ice skate. There was something about being on the ice—I felt like I was flying, and when I heard music I could skate to the rhythm of the music and just skate for hours and hours, as happy and content as could be.

Our large family didn't have any extra money and I wasn't able to take any lessons at all—not even an occasional group lesson—so I was content just watching the other more advanced skaters as I experimented and figured out some basic skating skills. I was very determined to get better, as I enjoyed challenging myself so much. I was thrilled when I found myself improving, no matter how slowly or how small the improvements on the ice were.

Again, my determined mindset that I was born with which was first apparent as a small child in New York doing tedious craft projects—believing, no matter how small, that progress is progress—came into play in my childhood years of ice skating, and I remained focused and quite happy learning new ice skating skills, no matter how long it took.

Although ice skaters share the ice with other ice skaters, true ice skating champions know and understand that ice skating skills are accomplished by repeated, solitary practice of the delicate balancing for the edges needed to improve those skating skills. I spent innumerable hours on the ice—surrounded by other ice skaters, yet completely immersed in my solitary world of figuring out how to get my body to be still yet powerfully balanced, to accomplish the skilled elements I wanted so badly to learn.

As I always skated in a public ice skating session, I soon discovered a new treat the ice rink offered. There were special times when the ice rink would occasionally rope off the end of the rink and offer a free introductory group lesson to all the public session ice skaters. I would race to the roped-off end of the ice rink as others gathered there after the announcement.

I would eagerly try to get as close as I could to the front of the group to be able to hear and see what the ice skating instructors were explaining and demonstrating.

Although there were easily more than fifty people crammed into the little roped-off area at the end of the ice rink, and these free group lessons weren't tailored to me or to my limited abilities, they did prove to be very valuable to me as I received just enough expert instruction—coupled with my fearless and curious determination to learn to ice skate faster, as I so wanted to learn to spin around—that I did eventually learn how to do the very simple jumps, crossovers, and basic beginning spins.

Over the course of a few weeks of experimenting with the incredibly fun pursuit of spinning, I discovered that speed coupled with a quick, sharp turn from front to back would result in a slow, weak spin. I was so enchanted with spinning, something I saw all the advanced skaters doing, that I doggedly kept trying. I fell over onto my left arm and left elbow so many times in my attempts to master spinning that my left arm became so purple and so swollen, I ended up at the Torrance Hospital emergency room with a diagnosis of extreme bruising, much to my relief, and not a broken arm from repeated falls.

But even my emergency room doctor's admonition to not try spinning for a month didn't keep me off the ice, as I just loved the flowing, flying feeling ice skating always gave me.

But my love of fast, flying movement wasn't just restricted to ice skating.

Nope.

Soon, I wanted to be the very antithesis of the delicate, feminine, well-mannered and quiet-spoken ice skater, demure in every way.

I had seen a brand-new entertainment sport on our small black and white TV.

That new entertainment sport was called Roller Derby.

I was ten years old, and I loved it!

But Roller Derby will do that to a ten-year-old who loves skating fast, I've learned.

Chapter 4

Roller Derby Queen

*"Train up a child in the way they should
go and when they are old they will not
depart from it" (Proverbs 22:6).*

"I want to be a Roller Derby Queen, please!"

The year was 1961, and a new entertainment sport involving skating arrived by way of our family's small black and white television. Roller Derby!

To my parents' great consternation, my love of freedom of movement and skating caused me to fall in love with the Roller Derby!

Yes! The rough-and-tumble, tough-talking, rowdy skaters, and the opponent-smacking, free-wheeling and action-packed Roller Derby!

When I wasn't practicing figure skating in the cold ice rink, I dreamed of being one of the Los Angeles Thunderbirds Roller Derby skaters, as every Sunday night our local TV station broadcast the incredible, fast-skated, action-packed Roller Derby directly into our home. My eager little ten-year-old eyes were glued to the TV, dreaming of joining them one day.

The LA Thunderbirds' announcer was Chick Hern. Each week, I listened excitedly as Chick announced each Roller Derby skater's name and offered all the details of their roller skating career. The excitement built, and then matches started, with Chick describing in detail every turn of the roller skate wheels—and my idols that wore them—as they competed against other Roller Derby teams.

Now, I did know that I had been raised to be a lady, so I didn't want to be one of the rough-and-tumble, trash-talking, furniture-throwing Roller Derby skaters. As I watched each week, I learned that each team always had one skater who was lady-like and skated really fast, and *that* Roller Derby skater did all the scoring and never got into any fights.

That's the Roller Derby skater I planned to be. The lady-like one who skated fast.

My poor parents; they had one frilly, lacy, curly-haired little girl, and I dreamed of being the good, lady-like skater in the Roller Derby!

My street had a gentle hill to it, and while everyone else in my neighborhood had discovered skateboarding, I was thrilled at Christmas to open a big, heavy box with a big red ribbon; to my squeals of delight, I discovered the red, white, and blue box cover with a picture of roller skates on it, and the official announcement on the box that I was now the proud owner of pretty white roller skates with silver wheels that were the "Official Roller Derby Roller Skates."

And they were all mine!

Since it was rarely practical for me to be at the ice rink on weekdays, now, with my own roller skates, when I wasn't at the ice rink I'd come barreling down the hill on the side-walk, tucked as tightly as I could be and going as fast as I could, dodging imaginary roller derby skaters on the way down, and *always* scoring the winning points in the last few seconds at the bottom of the hill.

I'd dramatically finish my downhill run with my hands first on my hips and then raised in the air, signaling my triumphant win for my team!

Occasionally, as I liked fast skating the very best, if I was rolling downhill faster than I could control I'd just run onto the grass with my roller skates—which I'm sure my parents and the neighbors loved!

So, I spent happy months roller skating up and down the neighborhood hill, lost in my imaginary world, dreaming of someday having my own Roller Derby jersey with my name on it and with Chick Hern announcing *my* name!

I knew nothing of the true rough-and-tumble world of Roller Derby as a business. I would never have believed anyone if they'd had the audacity to tell me that the "grudge matches" and "close games" were actually staged, even though my hometown team, the LA Thunderbirds, ALWAYS won every game in a nail-biting finale.

My parents were very wise in indulging my love of Roller Derby, so much so that my dad bought two tickets and took me to the old Shrine Auditorium in downtown Los Angeles to see a <u>live</u> LA Thunderbirds game. I practically floated to the car! I had never been to any professional sports venue!

Walking in, I could see the blazing TV lights above the large oval track where soon, my Roller Derby idols the Los Angeles Thunderbirds would roar into action, and I'd see and hear Chick Hern in person.

I was so thoroughly thrilled to be there.

I knew I was the luckiest girl in the world, with the very best parents.

So, imagine my surprise as my joy quickly turned to dismay and then disgust when we found our seats, and instead of a gleaming sports venue, I discovered that the Shrine Auditorium inside was very old—and in my mind, very dirty—and filled with the smells of alcohol and gas station bathrooms. I wasn't even sure I wanted to sit in the seats, which I thought looked grimy, with large wads of gum stuck on the backs of the seats in front of us.

My dad and I sat in the crowd with many other regular, well-mannered people sitting around us, but I was so horrified to also be sitting in a crowd where the drunk, swearing people—including drunk, swearing _women_—seemed to easily outnumber the quiet, polite spectators.

There were so many drunk, unruly spectators—including the woman sitting next to my daddy, who was even throwing food at the raised oval track while screaming obscenities at the top of her voice after she'd take a drink from her beer bottle!

This certainly wasn't what I'd expected.

This Roller Derby was dirty and grimy. This Roller Derby didn't look like fun anymore.

My dad and I drove home in silence.

My up-close-and-personal encounter with the less-than-glamorous, real world of Roller Derby was all it took for me to quickly decide I'd be just fine enjoying my LA Thunderbirds Roller Derby team from the safety of my Sunday night living room, and I turned my full attention to ice skating.

Back at the ice rink, I noticed that the other young girls practicing spinning and jumping wore pretty, one-piece, colorful, short dresses with pleated skirts that made wavy patterns in the colorful skirt fabric.

I knew there wasn't any money to pay for one of those colorful, expensive dresses with the pleated, wavy skirts. I was quite happy being dropped off at the ice rink, where I could spend my day continuing to diligently practice the moves I saw others doing.

As a surprise, my parents saved for a long time and bought me a pretty, blue, short ice skating skirt with the special waving, spinning pleats in it!

Again, their surprise skating gift to me was met with squeals of delight!

Now, when I did finally learn to do a short, slow spin, I was rewarded with my pretty, blue, pleated skirt gracefully waving in a pretty pattern around my waist. Seeing that pretty waving pattern every time I did a little spin really encouraged me to practice spinning even more. Soon another pretty, short skirt with the wavy, spinning pleats in it was another gift from my parents. This one was a pretty mint green, and I would carefully iron each pleat individually into its pretty pattern in excited anticipation of my reward later that day, as my new ice skating skirt made waves. Practicing so much helped my spins to get longer and stronger, and I would excitedly count the little circles my blade made when I spun on the ice.

I just couldn't imagine a happier life than the one I was living.

My wonderful life in Southern California continued.

My brothers went to Boy Scouts.

My dad had no heart attacks.

Mom baked apple pies and curled my long dark hair.

But the horror continued to edge closer with each passing happy day.

Unknown and unabated.

Hour by hour, the horror inching ever closer, ever bolder.

And had we known of the horror to come, there was absolutely no way to slow it down nor any way to stop it.

But horror is like that, I've learned.

Chapter 5

Painting Houses in California, Buffalo: Home Again, and New York City

"Me, 8 years old, bike my Dad refurbished."

"Love always protects, always trusts,
always hopes, always perseveres"
(1 Corinthians 13:7).

"I really like helping you paint houses, Daddy!"

My dad worked as a welder when we lived in Southern California. He would work the 3:00 p.m. to 11:00 p.m. shift, and he also painted houses to earn extra money. I often helped Dad paint the low, easy to reach areas, so we spent time painting homes together.

It was during my early years in Southern California, that my mother went to work to help with the expenses of our growing family. An extended family member, a teenager only a few years older than me, was my babysitter. Sadly, he took the opportunity to sexually molest me when he was my babysitter. I only remember feeling very frightened, very sad and very confused and fearing my father would kill him, I never told anyone what had occurred with my babysitter. The extended family member soon moved to another state and I soon discovered that as awful as the event had made me feel, I felt very safe knowing my father was around, even the times that he was at work, my sense of safety continued knowing he would be home and that my father always had my best interests at heart. My world was safe once more because my father was in it.

When I was eleven my father's only brother, Carmen, flew out to Southern California and convinced my parents to return to Buffalo, to enable my father to work with my Uncle Carmen in his new business of early fire detection for homes and businesses.

Our family moved back home again to Buffalo, New York, where my Uncle Carmen's new business allowed my dad to wear a suit and tie and to work at an office during the day. My dad would go on evening appointments to various families' homes, demonstrating how dangerous home fires were and selling the early fire alarms.

My brothers and I would help my dad prepare his large presentation book with the flip pages showing how a fire quickly progresses, and we were often rewarded by being allowed to go along with my dad to his evening appointments to homes in the Buffalo suburban areas.

We enjoyed the long rides where we each had Dad all to ourselves, and when we arrived at his appointment we played with the family's kids while our dad did his presentation.

On weekends my dad would travel to the cities of Niagara Falls, Rochester, and Syracuse, where his additional offices were located. Each office was about an hour's drive from our home. Once again, my brothers and I would often be rewarded by being allowed to accompany my dad on these short road trips. We had such fun on those road trips.

A special treat at the end of each road trip was an ice cream sundae at Watson's Ice Cream Parlor on Saturday afternoon.

When our family first returned to Buffalo, we rented an apartment for about a year. However, because the fire detection system my dad sold proved to be so successful, within a year my parents had saved enough money to buy a beautiful, four bedroom, two bathroom house on a quiet, tree-lined street.

Our new home was so big; we'd never before had a garage, four bedrooms, and a dining room and two bathrooms. I felt so rich!

Our new home had a gigantic, fenced backyard where we could pitch our tent and make-believe we were camping, a huge covered patio in the front of our home, and a very large front yard, which quickly became our personal playground as our family played games of horseshoes and croquet.

My dad, as was his custom, quickly made flower beds around the border of our new home, both in our front yard and our backyard. There were flowers on all four sides of our backyard.

My dad then dug up the side yard and turned that area into another flower garden. Everywhere you looked, my dad had turned the brown ground into colorful, full gardens with a variety of flowers.

My dad's favorite flowers were petunias and gladiolas, and these colorful flowers were soon in full bloom giving a fresh, wonderful bloom of color to our front yard, our side yard, and our backyard.

We all took turns watering the gardens, and I always enjoyed the peaceful time when I would stand in the warm evening sun, watching the rainbows the sprinkling water made arching gracefully over my dad's well-tended flower beds.

In the winter time our large yards allowed us plenty of snow, and we rolled up giant snowmen and made arms out of twigs and dressed them in our extra clothes.

There was a community center not far from our home, and it offered the dual pleasures of swimming in the spring and summertime, and ice skating in the fall and wintertime.

Although I wasn't happy that I'd lost the use of our year-long indoor rink when we left Southern California, I really liked the idea that this community rink was within walking distance from my home and only cost twenty-five cents—meaning I was able to continue enjoying ice skating and spent many beautiful, chilly winter evenings gliding in the moonlight, marveling at this new way to enjoy my fun sport.

Our home was often filled with cousins, aunts, and uncles, celebrating the holidays and all of our family's birthdays in-between. Even if there wasn't a special reason, our home was perfect for big family gatherings, and my parents enjoyed entertaining our relatives and friends as much as us kids liked having them around to play with.

In February of 1967 I was thirteen years old, and my dad took just me to New York City for a few days of vacation. I had become aware that my dad always carried a small white envelope in his shirt pocket. There were tiny white nitroglycerin pills inside the white envelope. Although I had never seen my father take one of his "heart pills," I knew they were important.

Before we left for New York, my father carefully instructed me that if he had chest pain or fell down, I was to put his nitroglycerin tablets under his tongue and immediately find a policeman.

We took a train to New York City and when we arrived, I was fascinated by the subways, Times Square, and Wall Street. I'd never seen the kinds of advertising and activity I saw in Times Square.

We had such a great time there. We visited the Statute of Liberty, the Empire State Building, and Rockefeller Center. The Rockettes had always been a favorite staple of the Macy's Thanksgiving Day Parade, so to see the building and the marquee lit up with their name on it was quite a thrill.

It didn't bother me at all that my dad and I didn't go to any of the live Broadway shows; I enjoyed walking around—with my dad all to myself—so much and seeing all the sights.

Early in the morning, on our second day in New York City, my dad and I took the Staten Island Ferry to Ellis Island to see the Statue of Liberty up close. Although I'd seen it from a distance, I was amazed at how large it was.

The Statue of Liberty was attached to a building that served as a platform, allowing the statue to rise high above the waters of New York Harbor. The platform had elevators, but the inside of the statue contained a very long, very circular, very narrow, winding twenty story staircase that started at the base of the Statue of Liberty and wound around and around inside the statue until the stairway opened up—thirteen stories later—leaving tourists high above New York Harbor in the Statue of Liberty's crown, which sat upon the magnificent structure's head.

The stairway inside the Statute of Liberty is very difficult, consisting of 354 steps, which is like climbing twenty stories; they recommend you don't make the climb unless you're in good shape. Even though my dad wasn't in good shape, he still tried to make the climb with me.

Neither of us had a way to know that the circular stairway inside the Statue of Liberty was so restricted and narrow, it could only accommodate one person at a time. We were instructed at the start of our climb up the 354 steps and twenty stories to the crown that the "right of way" belonged to the person coming down the staircase. Metal benches were strategically placed every two stories to anyone needing a rest.

I felt bad for my dad, as he was unable to handle the extreme twenty-story climb and waited for me on a lower level bench, breathing quite heavily, while I completed the climb to the crown.

My climb was rewarded with a tiny, cramped area in the crown where the crown windows are greenish with algae; but still, the view was spectacular and well worth the long climb.

Every morning while we were in New York my dad took me to a restaurant in Times Square and we ordered the same breakfast: blueberry pancakes. My dad and I were the only ones who loved blueberries, so we smiled at each other as we indulged in our special pancakes. I especially liked our breakfasts together, as the restaurant had huge windows, and my dad and I talked about the different people and unusual sights of Times Square. We took as long as we wanted for breakfast, unlike our hurried breakfasts at home during the week before he rushed off to work.

My favorite place of all was the United Nations building, with all the flags of all the countries placed in a long row, flying in the breeze.

As we toured the United Nations, we were allowed to go into the large General Assembly rooms as the United Nations' delegates were not in session.

Our tour guide pointed out the headphones available next to each seat, explaining that each country's delegate had their own private interpreter, so each country's representative heard the United Nations' session in their native language. This was the first time I was really aware of other nations with different languages and cultures. I'd only been aware that Mexico was different and that Spanish was spoken by its citizens.

While trying to take in all the United Nations offered, I looked at the neatly dressed tour guides, and each country's interpreters' equipment and headphones resting next to the delegates' chairs, and I was thinking how much fun it'd be to be an interpreter. Soon we returned to Buffalo and resumed our usual routine.

Back home, Dad and I watched TV in our basement, and I traveled to his sales appointments with him.

Dad was ever the home builder and started to finish our basement. Soon walls appeared, and we could hear my dad hammering away in the basement each night and on weekends. Prior to the basement's completion, Dad put a large straw archery target at the far end of the basement and produced a complete set of a bow and arrows. This was a simple bow, and we all quickly became proficient at shooting the arrows pretty close to dead center. We all enjoyed target practice with the steel-tipped arrows so much that we pretty much wore out the center of the target, and soon our arrows could be heard hitting the back cement wall before they fell to the ground. We kept practicing, taking turns shooting the arrows, and Dad didn't seem to mind that the steel-tipped arrows got flatter and flatter.

We went to the fireman's picnic and rode the rides and ate our mom's special deviled eggs at the picnic, playing horseshoes and tossing a football around.

My youngest brother Curtis John Michael and I remember going to the lake with my dad, and my dad, who had been a lifeguard, swimming with Curtis John Michael's arms around his neck. He also remembers that our dad built a huge six foot by nine foot miniature railroad display in our basement, and we all spent hours with my dad adding new pieces and running the trains.

He also remembers that my dad would cut all three of my brothers' hair in the basement.

I'm glad my youngest brother has some good memories of his dad, even if there aren't very many.

I've always wished that all my siblings had more memories of our parents.

But the horror to come would make certain that there were no more loving memories with my father for my mother, my siblings, and me.

But horror is a lot like that, I've learned.

Chapter 6

The Horror of the Night

Me, 5 years old, before the horror arrived.

ROSIE GEORGE FINOCCHI

*"You will not fear the terror that
comes at night" (Psalm 91: 5).*

For each of us, there are questions that we will never know the answers to.

I ask: why is it that sometimes our brains function, conveniently and mercifully, to completely suppress our most unthinkable and unimaginable traumas? We've all heard of traumas where accident victims have absolutely no memory of a horrific accident, or crime victims that wake up in the hospital with no memory other than seeing a person approaching or walking into an area where we now know that a vicious attack took place.

Why is it that our brains, so meticulously and intricately wired, seem to randomly select which horrific and terrifying memories to erase from our minds—thereby keeping the horrors forever hidden from our conscious thoughts; thereby sparing the person who witnessed the unimaginable from the need to overcome the tragedy?

Yet other times that same amazing brain of ours, with uncaring cruelty, burns devastating memories of traumas witnessed and lived so deeply and indelibly into our brains that the memory seems to leave us frozen in time, where daily we relive the horror of that frightening, life-forever-altering moment that yielded such tragic results.

Sadly for me, my brain did the latter, searing the quiet, snowy morning of Thursday, April 20, 1967, forever in my consciousness—like an old broken clock with the time frozen on its face, forever marking the moment when time stopped and time stood still; when horror reigned, with reckless disregard for neither time nor person.

April 20, 1967 – The morning when I awoke as a happy, loved, secure, just-thirteen-years-old teenager, my daddy's girl, and I ended that day ripped open and stunned by grief—feeling forever changed, feeling forever unsafe, and feeling forever different—as before night fell, I was fatherless forever.

Although I didn't hear it or know it when I kissed and hugged my parents goodnight and then went to bed on the normal, quiet, snowy evening of April 19, 1967, the horror that had targeted my family—and had been stalking and lurking unseen and unknown in the shadows for years—would start to show its deadly face during the early hours of the morning of April 20, 1967, while I slept peacefully in my bed, grounded in the serene security that I was part of a thriving, happy family. I was confident that I was deeply loved by my parents—who not only adored each other, but lived to give us, their children, a wonderful life.

My parents and I played the bus game every school day morning: if I missed my bus, I could ride to school with my dad as he passed by my school on his way to work; so, *I missed my bus every day.*

When I awoke on that fateful morning of April 20, 1967, the day appeared just like any other normal morning. Stretching in my pretty white bed, warm and cozy under my fluffy, lacy quilts, I was thirteen years old and eagerly anticipating another ride with my dad to school after I "missed" my bus.

I didn't know that the horror had arrived.

I didn't know that the horror had made itself at home in our family's home while my brothers and I slept so peacefully.

I didn't know the horror that was waiting for me on the other side of my bedroom door when I opened it that snowy, quiet morning.

Much like Jacob in the Bible, who wrestles with an angel through the night, the horror had been engaged in a tug-of-war with my father, who had been fighting for his life all through the night. And now as the daylight was appearing, the horror patiently and quietly waited for me to enter the living room where my father sat in his black and white recliner chair and where, unbeknownst to me, my father was courageously still fighting for his life.

I desperately joined in my father's efforts, unaware of the true gravity of my father's situation. Despite all my daddy's best efforts the horror would win, and Daddy and our family would lose. Our family would all lose so much; so very, very much.

But I didn't know that when I woke up on that quiet morning of April 20, 1967.

I didn't know how hard my beloved father would fight; I didn't know how much I would fight, and I didn't know how much, how very much we all would lose.

Such is my memory of that peaceful, snowy, early morning that took place on April 20, 1967, when I went to bed in our all-American family dream home and woke in the morning to greet the runaway horror that would strip our family of our beloved father. With his last labored breaths that he would breathe on this earth he was agonizingly pleading for his life, asking God to spare his life, as my father's only concern was for what only and always was his priority: his family.

When I returned to my bed that evening, my Uncle Charlie tightly holding me as I cried myself to sleep, the day's events had completed the effect of forever changing my identity: who I was, what I was, and what I thought my only purpose on earth was.

And so it was in the quiet, unsuspecting, early morning hours of Thursday, April 20, 1967 that the horror—which had been shadowing our family for more than ten years now—stepped out of the shadows and reared its ugly head with full force; a force that would mercilessly shatter my parents' peaceful existence and push and propel me unwillingly on the first step of my journey to become the oldest of my parents' orphans.

I wish you did not have to witness my family's horror.

I wish my family did not have to live out the horror of that quiet, snowy day.

But I was powerless against the horror.

My mother and siblings were powerless against the horror.

We all are powerless against the horror.

But horror is like that, I've learned.

Chapter 7

"Oh, God, Who's Going to Take Care of My Family?"

My Daddy's last words, as he was dying

"Don't Worry Daddy, I Will."

Me, 13 years old, the last words I spoke to my Daddy

*"God sustains the fatherless and
the widow" (Psalm 146:9).*

When I awoke on that fateful morning of April 20, 1967, the dawning day appeared just like any other normal morning. I expected breakfast and a ride to school with my dad. My three younger brothers were still sleeping in their bedrooms down the hall. Both of my parents would already be awake and preparing for the day ahead.

My mom was six months pregnant, and usually when I got up and walked through our living room to our kitchen where we ate breakfast, Dad would be seated at the breakfast table reading his newspaper, and Mom would be preparing his breakfast of eggs and toast. We normally ate at breakfast at different times, as my brothers' school started later in the morning. However, on this morning when I went out into our living room, my father was uncharacteristically sitting in his favorite black and white recliner chair, obviously in great pain, struggling for both breath and words.

I would learn decades later that one of my younger brothers had awakened during the night and had seen my dad, in pain, pacing in the hallway throughout the night as I had been asleep.

In the mornings on school days, my brothers weren't allowed to come out of their rooms until my mom called them, and so they were still in their rooms when I first saw my dad seated in his recliner, having such severe pain and struggling to breathe.

I wasn't aware that my dad was having a heart attack in front of me; I just knew I wanted to give my dad his little white nitroglycerin pills that he'd shown me when we'd visited New York City a few months earlier, but my mom was in charge.

My mom was in the kitchen using the wall phone to summon help. There wasn't any 911 to call for emergency medical help in 1967. My mom was very scared as she dialed the phone.

I was alone in our living room with my dad. As my dad struggled to breathe, each breath growing more and more labored, I heard him cry out, "Oh, God, who's going to take care of my family?"

My dad wasn't even speaking to *me*. I instinctively knew that my dad was afraid he was going to die. Hoping to be reassuring, I patted my dad's familiar, strong hand, looked at his kind face, and said, "Don't worry, Daddy, I will."

Those were the last words I spoke to my father.

Looking up into my dad's pain-contorted face, my heart-felt words of promise, "Don't worry, Daddy, I will," were sincere. I don't know if my father even heard my attempt at an assuring promise. But I knew what I had said, and I meant what I said.

A friend once asked me why I didn't say, "Mom will." Perhaps I already knew that my mom was going to be so grief-stricken she wouldn't be okay: intensely grieving for my father the rest of her life, never again regaining her joyous love of life.

I don't know why I said those words, except that knowing I couldn't ease my dad's physical pain, I thought I could ease his emotional anguish as he suffered in front of me.

After calling, the ambulance and the firemen arrived, and my mother urgently sent me next door to get the nurse that lived there. Although the nurse went back to my house, the next-door neighbors would not allow me to return home.

While I was next door at the neighbors each of my three younger brothers, separately, came into our living room and saw my dad sitting in his recliner in great pain and struggling to breathe. My three younger brothers, ages nine, eight and five, were also not fully comprehending what was happening, yet they tried to speak with our dad; each brother trying, in spite of their tender years, to comfort our dad.

Tragically, my father was still in his recliner chair but unresponsive by the time my youngest brother, Curtis John Michael, five years old, stood in front of him—remembering he thought our Dad's feet were really huge. He remembers looking up into the face of his father whom he, like his older brothers, dearly loved, but he remembers realizing, at the tender age of 5, looking at his father, that our dad had died.

Just a few weeks earlier, our family had enjoyed a fun time before Easter church services as we helped my dad and mom make our family's Easter traditional breakfast of frittatas.

After Easter breakfast, my three younger brothers had dressed in suits, ties, and hats that matched my dad's attire as our family attended Easter Sunday services and posed for our family photos.

I've always felt bad when I remember hearing of each of my brothers' somber memories of seeing our dad suffering, and their mutual efforts—at such undeniably young ages—to attempt to communicate with our dad that are each equally heart-breaking and horrifying. I think, *How does a young son in any way comprehend watching his father, his buddy, his hero, die before his young eyes?*

When the ambulance and the fireman arrived, my middle younger brother Peter, eight years old, was held back in our home's hallway by the firemen, fighting to go into our living room as the firemen placed my father on the carpet and continued frantically trying to save my father's life.

The ambulance took my father the short seven-minute ride to Kenmore Mercy Hospital. My mother rode with the ambulance.

Somehow my three younger brothers all walked to school; I remained at the next-door neighbor's house. Neither my brothers nor I knew that by the time they had reached their school a few short blocks away, our father had been pronounced dead upon arrival at Kenmore Mercy Hospital's emergency room.

As my young brothers walked to school one of them said, "I don't think Dad's going to be alright." I don't know how a young son of nine years of age knows instinctively that his father has died, but my brother did. Both my younger brothers knew, when the school aide came into their separate classrooms about an hour later and handed their teacher a note—while their teacher was still reading the note—that the note was for them; both my father's sons knew the note said that our father had died.

Exactly how do young sons, still children, live with that horror?

I was not allowed to come back home from the next-door neighbors' until much later in the morning, and I returned home to a completely empty home. Our normally joyful home was eerily quiet, and I wandered from room to room trying to sort out what had happened earlier that morning. Unlike my brother, all I knew was that my dad had been taken to the hospital and was in a lot of pain when I last saw him.

But it never occurred to me that I would never see my beloved father alive again. Such an unimaginable thought never entered my mind. I didn't even know any other kids our age that didn't have their dad at home with them. As I wandered alone through our quiet home, I figured like before, in a few days, my dad would come home; then he would again regain his strength and we would go on being our perfect all-American family. My wonderful life would continue—the only life I had ever known.

What I still had not grasped, in spite of all that I had seen that fateful morning, was that the horror that had been stalking my unsuspecting, loving, all-American family for almost a decade had finally arrived—ushered into my life with the sudden ringing of our wall phone which shattered the eerie silence as I wandered through our empty home, waiting for at least my mom to come home from the hospital.

I ran to our kitchen as the wall phone kept ringing. I picked up the slender phone handle and suddenly—just like in the movies when there's a horrible, screeching, ripping sound and everything freezes, and the picture literally rips in two pieces—my wonderful, happy, secure life...just ended. *Poof!* Completely gone!

"Hello?"

"Baby, your Daddy's gone."

It was my mother's youngest brother, Uncle Angelo, calling me from the hospital.

I don't recall the rest of the conversation that morning between my Uncle Angelo and me, or if there even was one. In fact, after hearing those numbing words, I have absolutely no memory of the rest of the day. I don't know when my mom came home from the hospital; I don't know how and when my three younger brothers came home.

All I do remember—vividly—is not being able to stop crying; so much so that when I finally went to bed another of my uncles, Uncle Charlie, held me in his arms until I cried myself to sleep—a scene that was repeated for many, many nights to come.

As I cried myself to sleep that night of Thursday, April 20, 1967, on the night that was the first of what would be weeks of crying myself to sleep, little did I know that the very last words that I ever spoke to my beloved father—my words spoken to reassure my dying father, "Don't worry, Daddy, I will,"—would start my life's journey of grief and sadness, and my family co-dependency of enabling and trying to rescue my family. I did everything I could to keep my heartfelt promise to my dying father, until 2010 when I came to *Celebrate Recovery*.

It was at *Celebrate Recovery* that I came to realize I was trying to keep a promise I had made to my dying father that no one—not my mother, not my brothers or my sister, not even my father—had *ever asked me* to make or to keep.

But I didn't know that on the cold evenings of April 1967. All I knew for certain, each night as I cried myself to sleep, was that I was now fatherless forever. My father was forever gone from me on this earth. I was thirteen years old.

Each morning as I awoke, I was jolted afresh into the reality of my father's death. How do my words even begin to adequately convey the overwhelmingly numbing, terrifying feeling that everything I knew my world to be was now irrevocably, completely gone?

My sense of security, gone!

My sense of competency and safety, shattered!

My mother became quite alarmed as for days I continued to cry all day long, and then for hours at night until exhausted. Then—with an alarmingly swollen face and eyes—I finally fell asleep, only to awaken in the morning and realize that my father's death hadn't been a dream; then I'd immediately start crying again.

I wasn't able to return to school. After several days, someone produced black and purple capsules and told me that they would help me sleep, and that I would start to feel better. I took them as I was told, and a week after my father's death I returned to my eighth grade classes.

From my first days back at my school, the sidelong glances and whispered stares of my classmates made me acutely aware that a shift of some type had occurred, and that I was now quite different from my classmates. As I walked into our school's cafeteria and saw all my classmates lined up and waiting against the wall, I felt weirdly disconnected from them—like a fog separated us, and I would never again be the same as they were.

I was unaware of exactly how word had spread so quickly. Now, instead of the old smiles and joyful teenage banter between classes, I sadly discovered that I moved in a weirdly familiar, yet irreparably changed and damaged identity at school—forever different from my classmates, for I was now "that girl whose father just died." I was now looked at sideways with eyes of pity and fear by classmates and teachers alike, because if *my* father could die, then so could *theirs*.

In my little picket-fence, perfect world, I did not know anyone who didn't have a living, married, mother and father at home. Certainly, those existed, but this was the 1960s in a quiet little suburb, and my friends and I didn't know of any other fatherless kids but me. I stood out alone and my presence screamed, "Beware, this could happen to you; your father or husband could also die."

I quickly sensed that no one wanted to be close to me, because to be my friend was to accept that bad things happened to young families and daddies died; and you still had to come to school, even though your father had died, and pretend to be normal.

I continued to finish eighth grade although my grades disappeared overnight, just like my father had. My mother and I seemed distant; I had always been Daddy's girl, and my grief was deep and private. I don't recall speaking to anyone in any deep or meaningful way. My mom did try to get me help. She made me an appointment with a counselor. The counselor sat behind his large desk in a big, bright office. It reminded me of the principal's office at school.

I don't remember going to more than the initial visit with the counselor, so it may well have been due to my refusal, or my discomfort to speak my innermost feelings to a stranger. It may have been the money the appointments cost; but I doubt that, as my mom took me initially and obviously wanted to help me in my grief and pain. I did think, although I didn't tell her, that my mom was very brave to admit that I obviously wasn't doing well—my mom did see that—as well as to recognize her inability to reach and help me, possibly due to my still being so shocked.

I appreciated my mom trying to get help for me, but I was far too deeply traumatized—not just by my father's death, but from *witnessing* it—and was too deeply frozen within myself to have been able to accept or even want the help being offered to me.

The only thing I felt was an absence of any true feelings, other than the feelings of total numbness and complete emptiness. I couldn't describe to anyone that what was left in the gaping hole of what had been my secure, happy world was now a thin, filmy, slippery transparency of what my life used to be.

A famous ride at the original Disneyland in California was the Haunted House. You sat in a roller coaster car on tracks as it wound through the dimly lit, cavernous Disney haunted house, being repeatedly scared by pop-up, unexpected ghosts and goblins. What was fascinating and scary was that in this ride, long before today's world of technology, Disneyland made use of "holograms." A hologram is a very life-like light image made with a laser light beam, projected in a manner so that the images of people, animals, and objects, although transparent, appear real and to have depth rather than appearing flat and still.

Similarly—overnight—my happy, wonderful life had been turned into a hologram: flat and fake, so that while appearing lifelike, the reality was that I was now lacking any meaningful substance for myself. I felt as hollow and fake as the Disneyland holograms.

I was as lost as I could possibly be, and so very sad. People offered help, but I just didn't know how to move forward and out of my grief. I remember looking at the caring people and feeling like I was looking at faces I cared nothing for or about. Nothing would bring my father back or erase what I had seen and what our final words had been.

Nothing anybody could say or do could change that.

Sad and grieving for so many reasons, I withdrew deeper into myself, continuing to find my only comfort in food and silence. My chubbiness at age thirteen became more than seventy-five pounds over a normal, healthy weight.

Waking each morning forced me to keep going, even though all I felt was numb, strange and very, very different from everybody else—at the crucial time of my life when all a normal thirteen-year-old wants is to be exactly like everybody else. I sadly resigned myself to my fate: that no amount of make-up, cool, trendy, fashionable clothes, or the latest hair-style would ever make me fit in again; instead, my plight had spread like wildfire throughout my school, so school became a sad and useless place for me: the girl whose father had died.

Every year the school nurse measured each student's height and our weight. This was done one at a time, in front of the class. We sat on a row of chairs, and each one of us got on the big, metal scale where the lower metal squares dropped with a heavy, metal *clang* into the grooves as the scale registered our weight in fifty-pound increments. The upper metal square slid along a bar with quarter-pound increments that went up to fifty pounds before the lower metal square needed to be moved up another fifty pounds, and the upper square started anew at the one pound end and was slid until the bar was balanced in space, indicating our weight.

I was five feet and one and a half inches tall.

When my turn came to be weighed, the nurse dropped the lower metal square into the one-hundred-pound groove. I silently held my breath and hoped desperately as she slid the upper metal square farther and farther to the right, praying that the scale would balance in mid-air before she reached the fifty-pound mark, which would tell my whole class I weighed more than one hundred fifty pounds.

I discovered that even praying won't make a school scale lie. And it didn't.

So, to my utter mortification and the barely-hid snickers of my classmates, the nurse slid the upper square weight to the end of the fifty-pound indicator, and then reached down and slid the lower metal square into the mortifying one-hundred-fifty-pound groove and slid the upper metal square again, coming to rest at one hundred seventy-three pounds.

I was five feet, one and a half inches tall and weighed one hundred seventy-three pounds. Not good; not so good at all.

My humiliation was complete when my gym class gave us swimming lessons, and one-piece swimsuits were handed out with colors corresponding to our weight. The gym teacher would stand in front of the line of my classmates and me, then loudly call out our color of bathing suit to her assistant after assessing our body size. Red for small; blue for normal; and the despised green for the chubby girls. She took a quick glance at my increasing chubbiness and loudly announced that I was to wear the hated green chubby swimsuit. I would be officially branded as a chubby girl by my hated green swimsuit for the entire time we took swimming classes.

As much as I detested the gym class chubby-girl green swimsuit, as far as having any interest in eating healthier or addressing my grief, I simply didn't care what happened at school—or whether I was there or not. I half-heartedly did homework. Who cared? I sure didn't, and no one seemed to mind or even notice.

There was no guidance, no direction; no talks with a wise relative or friend encouraging me to look at school for the purposes of my own future—to look towards the day when I would have my own life, separate from my family and their individual problems.

In fairness to my relatives and friends, there may well have been some very concerned people trying to get through to me, but I felt so hopelessly sad and different that I was indifferent to everything and everyone—because if you couldn't bring my father and my happy, wonderful life back, I probably didn't hear the help and love you were trying to provide to me.

I was, as it is said, my own worst enemy.

School was awkward, embarrassing, and hard. I stayed friends with another girl named Linda after my father died, but I always felt so awkward at her home. I'd walk in and see her family so happy: her mom busy in the kitchen, and her father usually in his recliner in front of the television in their living room. Perhaps it was Linda's family's happiness and their activities' resemblance to the unbroken family I once had, but I came to spend less and less time at her home, feeling out of place. But again, always saying nothing. Yet I always wished my family was still happy like Linda's family.

My other friend from before my father died was JoAnn Scinta. JoAnn lived at the other end of Woodgate, the long, winding street we both lived on. JoAnn was Italian like me and rode horses, which super impressed me. I never met JoAnn's mother and seldom saw her father, so I felt more comfortable hanging out with her. JoAnn had a large family, and her brothers were my brothers' ages.

JoAnn laughed a lot, and was fun; and best of all, JoAnn still liked me after my father died. She didn't seem to care what anyone said about me; I was her friend.

JoAnn was always a bright, fun spot in my life. JoAnn would remain a friend for years until we lost touch, separated by time and distance.

The numbing month of April 1967 finally over, I muddled through May and finally June, secretly happy when Father's Day, a cruel reminder of my loss, was over. I had stayed out of stores and avoided Father's Day cards.

At the end of June I was finished with eighth grade—still uncommunicative, sober, and gaining weight at an alarming pace. With much sympathy and understanding, my junior high school teachers made the decision to promote me to ninth grade. It didn't matter much to me either way. I did take solace that at least I hadn't disappointed my already distressed and sad mom, now nine months pregnant and due any day. I stayed somber, quiet, and very withdrawn; I was quite the sad loner.

Yet, despite my personal somber existence, one bright spot remained for me and my family. On the day my father died, my mother and father were expecting their fifth child. Our family's bright spot was my mom's pregnancy, which ended on July 13, 1967, when my new baby sister Lisa Robin Michelle was happily and triumphantly born.

On this day of July 13, 1967, for a time, the horror was nowhere to be found and our joyful celebration of Lisa's birth was a much-needed and welcomed relief.

But what I didn't know was that the horror was not done with my family yet.

None of us did. But once again, had we known, there was nothing we could have done to stop the horror that was still to strike a second time—then third time—and then one fourth and final heartless strike would complete the horror's merciless agenda for my once happy family.

It would come a second time, to again strike death into my already devastated family. And then, with relentless cruelty, the horror would strike a third time, when we—our parents' five orphans—surprisingly and helplessly, would be blindsided by the unthinkable and the unimaginable: when my three younger brothers and I would unexpectedly, and without notice, lose our five-year-old baby sister to relatives who were supposed to love us, but instead chose to cause our dwindling family even more pain. And one last cruel blow10 days after we were orphaned when I'd be forcible separated from my brothers, not allowed to tell them the truth; the truth which was that I was being abandoned at 19 to become entirely alone and homeless.

Because, as I was continuing to learn, horror has no mercy.

Yes, none of the future horror was known to us on the happy, wondrous day of July 13, 1967. As sad as my family was from my father's untimely death, my mom was healthy; and along with my mom, my three younger brothers and I eagerly awaited the birth of our new sibling.

We all hoped that just maybe, life could be wonderful again and joy could win.

Even when the horror has no mercy, joy can win.

Because life is wonderful, and joy does win, I've learned.

Chapter 8

My Baby Sister Lisa: the Daughter Our Father Never Knew

Mom, 7 months pregnant & me, 13 years old, One month after Dad's death. 1967, Buffalo, New York

MY PARENTS' ORPHANS

*"Say unto Wisdom, you are
my sister" (Proverbs 7:4).*

"You have a sister, honey." It was July 13, 1967, early evening on a pretty summer's day. And now again, as had happened just three short months earlier, my life was forever changed with five very simple words. But this time, five very simple words changed my life forever for the better, because for my whole life I had been sandwiched between three older brothers and three younger brothers, and I now had a sister! I had my very own perfectly perfect, adorable, lovely, smiling, and cooing baby sister.

Listening to my mom's tired yet obviously pleased voice over the phone, I recalled how a year earlier, when we returned to Buffalo, New York, my parents had achieved one of their dreams and purchased a beautiful four bedroom, two bathroom home in the charming suburb of Tonawanda, situated just outside of Buffalo. This was the first home my parents had owned since we moved from Buffalo to Southern California in 1959, and they had both been so happy and full of plans for their young family of then four children. We had continued to dress in our Sunday school best and took photos on the front lawn of our new pretty home. My idyllic, peaceful, fun life had continued.

In our family's new home, in the fall of 1966, my parents happily announced that they were having another baby. It had been more than five years since my youngest brother Curtis John Michael had been born, so this was a very exciting and joyous time for all of us.

Unexpectedly and sorrowfully, my mom had been six months pregnant on April 20, 1967, when my father had suddenly died.

We were grateful that my mom hadn't lost her baby from the suddenness and the sorrow she experienced, as my mom could not possibly have imagined that she would lose her beloved husband and give birth to their child all in less than a three-month span of time.

Yet it happened, and my mom was a young widow of thirty-seven. Our now fatherless family continued to be pulled down a stream of events that seemed to be picking up speed with every passing day, with me leaving the perfect, idyllic life I had known with my dad further and further behind. I continued to become more and more withdrawn and confused, yet more determined than ever to keep my final words of promise to my dying father—although I felt powerless to really affect any changes in what had quickly become our bleak reality of overwhelming sadness and tough changes, which we tried to but could not control.

But now there was a bright spot in our family.

On that pretty, warm summer's day of July 13, 1967, I came in from playing outside and called for my mom as usual. I went through the house and found my mom sitting on the edge of my parents' bed, clutching my deceased father's wind-up alarm clock.

Mom said she was having labor pains and was timing the length of time between them. Mom went to the hospital, and later that evening I got a phone call and one of my relatives told me I now had a baby sister. This was great news. I was one month shy of my fourteenth birthday and had only known brothers—now, *finally*! I had a sister of my very own. I was very excited!

My mom named her new daughter, my newborn sister, Lisa Robin Michelle. That name was so very different from all our Italian relatives' names, and later I would find out why.

In an odd twist, the hospital where my mom delivered her new baby was the same hospital where my dad had been taken when he died.

Perhaps my mom wanted a happier memory of that hospital; my mom often told the story of how at the hospital, the nurses had called her as-yet-unnamed baby girl "Mona Lisa," as my mom's new baby had been the only dark-haired baby girl in the nursery in recent days. My mom liked the name so much it became my newborn sister's name, plus my sister has a fun story to tell of being named after the famous artist Leonardo da Vinci's masterpiece painting, the *Mona Lisa*. Being that the famous artist Leonardo da Vinci was also Italian, we all agreed the name was fitting as well as fun.

Soon enough, Mom brought my baby sister Lisa home. She was adorable and pink and soft, and immediately I shifted all the grief and uncertainty I felt in the unexpected and bewildering loss of my dad away to focus on my new baby sister Lisa. All my questions and loneliness were now willingly ignored and swallowed up and replaced by caring for Lisa. What almost-fourteen-year-old isn't totally and completely intrigued and delighted by being allowed to play with a new baby? It seems to be part of a teenage girl's DNA.

My mom was more than happy to allow me to take over as much care of Lisa as I could. I would get up for Lisa's nighttime feedings and deeply enjoyed bottle-feeding, dressing, bathing, and changing her. I would sit in the same black and white recliner where my father had passed away and hold Lisa as I would rock her and sing her church songs, hymns, and lullabies for hours on end—continuing long after Lisa had fallen asleep and I could have carefully laid her down to sleep in her crib.

I found it very, very comforting to be able to hold, cuddle, kiss, and lavish as much physical love and sweet words as

I could on my baby sister Lisa, knowing that Lisa was the last, living, breathing part of my father. My mom never restricted the large amount of time I spent with my sister.

I didn't realize it then, but perhaps my mom allowed me to help with my sister so much because she intuitively knew how deeply I needed something that resembled a purpose and joy.

With my mom having quite a lot to do—already caring for five children by herself, and still deeply grieving our father's death less than three months earlier—I gladly stepped up and stepped in as my baby sister's additional caregiver, eager to have a purpose, eager to have a meaning, and eager to add an entirely new joy in my life to somehow compensate for the overwhelming and gaping hole in my heart and my life, a hole that had once been filled with my love for my dad—and more importantly, my dad's love for me.

I was too young to have understood then, but I realize now—and still can't fathom—how difficult it must have been for my mom to complete her pregnancy without my dad's presence to guide her, steady her, and love her. How hard it must have been for my mom to continue to prepare to give birth to a new life when she was still so obviously grieving and missing her husband and his always steady guidance and love, while continuing to take on my father's responsibilities for our home and family.

Summer passed, and so did my fourteenth birthday. When fall came I returned to junior high, now in the ninth grade. I had continued to gain weight and in the few short months since my dad's death had progressed from chubby to obese. Still only five feet, one and a half inches, I now weighed almost one hundred eighty-five pounds and remained deeply embarrassed, yet unwilling to actively do anything constructive or meaningful to achieve any weight loss.

My school grades continued their downward slide, and I cared for very little of anything concerning school. School seemed to do little for me other than to hold a mirror to my deepest fears, insecurities, and beliefs about myself, my values, my purposes, and my worth.

School continually showed me that I was glaringly different, as it had quickly become a mass of people my age who were hugely different from me in so many ways. *They* were everything I wanted to be and could not be, because I just did not have any more fun or love for life left in me. I was just different and could not figure out how to be fun and light-hearted again, even if I had wanted to be—which I really did not want to be. I was jealous of them and all that *they* did with such ease.

All I ever saw, detached from a distance, was: *they* laughed, *they* joked, and *they* had fun, while I was somber and quiet. *They* all seemed to have a loving mom and dad and were a happy family, while I had none of these things. *They* all seemed to know what I already knew—what I had felt that very first day when I had returned to school and walked into the school cafeteria and felt a strange feeling; a feeling I was to come to deeply recognize and know at every major turn of my life—I was DIFFERENT.

I had learned on my first day back at school that I was now forever different from ever other student in that school cafeteria line; I was now different from every other person in the school; and as far as I was concerned, I was now different from every other person in the world; and nothing would ever change that.

Different, marked, and scarred for life. I felt that even in the midst of my family I was still alone in the world, and the world as I knew it now was unsafe and very sad for me.

Little did I know how much worse my world could become.

But again, the horror knew, and patiently waited to strike again.

Because horror is a lot like that, I've sadly learned.

Chapter 9

The Home I'll Never Know

"And I will fasten him as a nail in a sure
place; and he shall be for a glorious throne
to his father's house" (Isaiah 22:23).

For reasons I will never know, my mother declined to pay our home's mortgage, and the day came when she began to receive bank foreclosure notices. I have pondered that perhaps my mom didn't want to see her dying husband on the floor, with the firemen's heart monitor wires draped across his chest; perhaps my mother didn't want to walk through the living room on the rug where he died. I had seen my father's bank payment booklet, and I knew that our monthly mortgage was only $124. I never knew why my mom didn't pay our family's home mortgage; I only know that she didn't.

The foreclosure notices and instructions continued to arrive at our modest little home. My mom decided at the last moment, when warned of the bank auction, to try and sell our home herself—and that was sadly unsuccessful, bringing my mom more emotional pain. It was sad because a ruthless realtor, trying to obtain our home's listing, had heartlessly mailed my mom a flyer with a cartoon of a giant sign over a little home which read, "WARNING! For Sale By Owner."

My mom was particularly hurt at receiving that flyer in the mail, saying she thought it was cruel of the realtor to have sent it to her when he knew that my mom was selling because her husband had died. As young as I was, I was angry at this unknown realtor and I agreed with my mom: the realtor's behavior was needlessly cruel. Wasn't my mom suffering enough without being tormented by his greed?

All the events surrounding losing our home perplexed me, but as usual, I did not say anything to anyone. Soon, my mom explained to us that our family's dream home on Woodgate was to be sold at a bank auction once the bank's foreclosure process was over. This was the home my parents had excitedly bought with visions of decades of family love to unfold in our future of more cherished family moments, which was now sadly denied to us.

After this news, I found solace sitting on the porch or watering my dad's beautiful flowers in their glorious spring blooms, wishing my father was there to enjoy the flowers he loved so much. It gave me comfort to stand alone, watering my father's flowers, remembering when we planted and gardened together just a short year ago.

With our father's death still so fresh in our minds, we tried to comprehend that our loved family home would be forcibly taken away from us. It was all so overwhelming.

Actually, quite stunning.

A month or so later—a year after my dad had died, in May of 1968—on a cool, cloudy evening, Uncle Charlie stopped by to bring the sad news that our beloved family home had been sold at the bank's auction.

I remember that day so clearly, like it was yesterday. I was standing alone on the covered patio where our family had enjoyed so many barbecues and birthday parties, my dad always in his short-sleeve collared shirt and my mom always in a pretty, colorful summer dress. I never saw my dad in a tee shirt other than in pictures from his youth.

On that day my Uncle Charlie drove up, slowly got out of his car, and stood on the walkway below, in front of my father's beloved rose bushes. It was just him and me. His head stayed down, and he quietly and sadly told me that he had been to the bank foreclosure proceeding, and that my dad's little dream home for his family's future had been sold at the bank's auction.

Inside, I silently felt another heavy brick take shape in the stoic, heavy wall I was unconsciously building around myself that grew taller and thicker—forever separating me from my secure, wonderful, stable, loving childhood. My memory freezes on Uncle Charlie's face, looking as sad and bewildered as I suddenly felt. None of this made any sense. I felt stunned and confused and didn't say much. I remember thinking how very sad my Uncle Charlie looked at having to bring my mom—his baby sister—and our family this news.

In the midst of my sadness at his news, I also thought that it was so very kind of my Uncle Charlie to have taken his time and gone to our family's little home's auction. My Uncle Charlie was always very kind to our family, and I could see it pained him a great deal to walk through this, my mom's new normal life—as a widow with five small children—with her. I knew, even without him saying a word to me, that Uncle Charlie had advised my mom, and things had not gone the way Uncle Charlie had hoped they would.

Soon enough summer came, and although my grades fell to all Cs I finished ninth grade and junior high and was promoted to tenth grade. Those dismal grades, of which I was secretly embarrassed and ashamed, would be last semblance of normalcy for me and my education.

Before my father had died, shortly after my mom and dad had bought and moved into their dream home on Woodgate, my father had celebrated his success at his new job with his brother, my Uncle Carmen, by buying my mother a really pretty red Rambler automobile. My mom really loved that car; it was new and shiny and we all loved it when my mom would drive us places while our dad was still alive. Now, my mom's red Rambler sat in our driveway as yet another reminder of the broken dreams and plans my parents had been so happy to make but had not been able fulfill together.

Summer came soon after my Uncle Charlie's sad news that we had lost our family home, and as soon as school was over, during June of 1968, we packed our family home up and put as many personal belongings into my mom's red Rambler as it could hold and still have room for my mom and her five children.

For the next few days we walked up and down our street on both sides and said our goodbyes to our friends and to our lovely neighborhood, the reality sinking in every day that we were saying goodbye to the home my parents had bought when I was ten years old, during the early days when my parents had so much hope and our family's future had seemed so bright. Goodbye to Fourth of July fireworks at the park and small-town parades on Main Street, when my dad held my youngest brother Curtis John Michael on his shoulders to see the parade.

How could my parents have envisioned our family's future as anything but a bright, happy one for their young family? When they bought our home on Woodgate, our dad was forty-five and our mom was thirty-five, with healthy, happy children. My dad had a great job, and there was no reason to envision anything other than a very bright, happy future stretching out decades ahead for all of us.

How very wrong our plans had been. And now, all that was left were the tearful good-byes of neighbors helplessly watching our personal horror play out in front of them.

On our final day living in our family's home on Woodgate, Uncle Charlie appeared with a U-Haul truck. Our life as we had known it in the little quaint Town of Tonawanda, New York, was carefully packed up into the back of Uncle Charlie's U-Haul truck, and this time with my mom in charge, once again our family set out for Southern California.

If my mom had, at any time after my father's death, shared her plans and thoughts with me regarding the move back to California, I don't recall what my mom said to me and what her reasons were.

All I can do is speculate.

After my father's death, my dad's side of the family had had an icy relationship with my mom—my mom wishing, naturally, that my dad had never, ever listened to Uncle Carmen and come back to Buffalo for work. My father's older sister, my Aunt Mary, was always a shrill, unhappy woman and along with Uncle Carmen, they had voiced their concerns openly that my mom hadn't done enough for my father during his last hours of life.

I know that my mother and my father's brother and siblings loved my dad fiercely, and I've learned, as a chaplain and a person, that deep grief can cause us to say things we wish we had never uttered. I still don't know why my mom left Buffalo, but I've always assumed my mom didn't want to spend her life walking into the living room and reliving the last moments my father had spent, dying in our living room while the firemen worked on him and her children were huddled and scared at the doorway opening. My mom's desire to leave behind forever those visual reminders of those heart-wrenching memories is quite understandable.

I was fourteen and I vividly remember as we drove down the quiet little tree-lined street of the home I loved—that my parents had bought together, filled with dreams of a happy future for all of us—that I cried bitterly, weeping openly, tears increasingly falling down my cheeks unstopped and unashamed. I was leaving my home, my memories of where we had happily lived with my dad, and I didn't want to go. I wanted to stay there where I had lived with my dad. My dad wasn't here any longer, but his essence had remained in every corner of our home.

I felt no sense of excitement or adventure in returning to California, no joy in moving on to a "new beginning" with a hope of a brighter future for me and my family.

As we passed each neighbor's home for the last time on our way out of the housing tract, and as my beloved home grew more distant behind what was left of our family, my weeping increased—for I knew that the last visage of a concrete connection to my beloved father was fading further in the rear window with each turn of the tires on my mother's red Rambler car, which she was so stoically driving out of our neighborhood.

Uncle Charlie was a bedrock of strength, as he had always been, and drove the big U-Haul truck on the more than 3,000-mile trek back to Southern California while my mom drove our family car. The plan my Uncle Charlie and my mom made was that they would drive together, within sight of each other, the entire 3,000 plus miles so that my mom would not be left feeling like she was driving across the country alone, especially with all of us kids in the car.

As good as their plan was, unfortunately, at some point my mom and my Uncle Charlie did get separated. Without any form of communication on the 3,000-mile trip, my mom kept at the driving all alone—handling that long drive, braving the mountains, the elements, and the hot summertime deserts all by herself, while bravely handling us five kids as well. My mom was as tough as they came when it came to doing what she needed to do for her family. Obviously, I wasn't the only one in my family who was determined to take care of my father's children.

I think a great deal of my determination to complete what I start, no matter the cost or how slow my progress, comes from my mother.

After our family arrived in Southern California, we rented a home in Huntington Beach, California and celebrated my sister Lisa's first birthday. We settled into going to school and enjoying the pretty, year-round sunshine.

Our family never again was able to live in a home we owned, and neither have I.

I didn't understand why my mom used to talk to me about how much she wished she could buy a home back in our old neighborhood and live there again. She had the Buffalo newspaper sent to her and would circle the homes in our old neighborhood and call the realtors and inquire about a purchase.

My mom had no income other than my father's limited monthly death benefits, so a home purchase was never possible. I often wondered why we lost our home, but with all my mom's sadness and overwhelming responsibilities I didn't have the heart to bring the subject up, lest she have to relieve her painful memories of my father's death again.

Sometimes our past unwittingly becomes our future, in spite of our best efforts.

For a few very short months the grief of losing my father seemed to be less on my mind, but I remained rather quiet and withdrawn.

My new high school was gigantic, and I knew no one and didn't care to make any friends; my classmates all seemed so silly and immature, when they really were what I wished I was: carefree, happy teenagers whose biggest concerns were surfboards and suntan lotion.

My sweet mom remembered that I liked to ice skate and asked me if I still wanted to go. I answered yes, so she would drive me the thirty-minute drive to the ice rink on Harbor Boulevard: Glacier Falls Ice Rink in Anaheim. The ice rink was across the street from Disneyland, but I never had any desire to go to Disneyland; I just wanted to go ice skating, so mom would drop me off in the mornings and come back for me in the early evenings.

The ice rink had a big glass window in the restaurant that looked out on the ice, and when the public session was over I'd have a bite to eat and watch, fascinated, as the elite skaters would train. It was at Glacier Falls that I first watched and knew of National Champion Dorian Shields, and the woman who would decades later fulfill my lifelong dream of being a real competitive ice skater: Karen Grobba, an incredibly talented choreographer and skater.

My time in the ice rink still held the ability to make the rest of the world stand outside the door, so all that mattered were my awkward spins and simple self-taught beginner jumps.

Yet I still just loved skating so much, and I was so grateful that my mom was so kind to care enough about the only thing besides my family that would bring me a smile that she would make two hour-long drives in the same day, sometimes in heavy traffic. Yet my mom never complained, and she always made sure I got to go ice skating at least once a week. As overweight as I was, close to 200 pounds, I never felt anything but fast and light on the ice, even if in reality I was anything but fast and light.

Surprisingly, I made a few friends with the other teenagers who went ice skating every weekend too. They were my only friends. I had none at school, as my classmates and I shared nothing in common.

For a few short months, life felt the tiniest bit less sad. I felt like I had taken my head out from under the water and could finally take a full breath of fresh, clear air.

But the horror intended for my family had again targeted us, creeping steadily closer without any warning or concern that we were still reeling from losing our father.

But horror is a lot like that, I've learned.

But I also learned that God was using my love of ice skating to plant the seeds of what would become my ultimate safety net when the horror would fully strike—not once, not twice but three times more, completely dismantling our remaining family.

Bible teacher Joyce Meyer always says, "God is working on my behalf every day, even when I don't see it and it doesn't look like it."

I have gratefully learned that Joyce is 100 percent correct.

Because God really is like that when He heals our orphan hearts.

Chapter 10

"I Felt the Lump in My Breast When Your Dad Was Alive"

My mom, California, 1968

*"As a mother comforts her child, so
will I comfort you" (Isaiah 66:13).*

"I felt the lump when Dad was alive." That was all my mom said to me by way of explanation amidst the latest numbing news I had just been given that my mom had breast cancer.

My mom was sitting quietly in our condominium and seemed so stunned and so quiet. She frightened me, as she looked exactly like she had looked in the first few days after my dad had died. I had just come home from attending my tenth grade classes at Huntington Beach High School. My brothers were still at their respective schools and my sister Lisa, still too young for school, was playing in the living room while my mom and I talked. I was still happy to help take care of my little sister when I was home, as Lisa continued to bring me great joy.

Upon hearing my mom's quiet words I immediately felt an incredibly familiar weight and sadness settle over me, as I instinctively knew that this was the horror now targeting my only remaining parent. In doing so, the horror had also once again targeted my family and would again cause much pain, as we were all still so frail and tender-hearted from my father's death.

Why did the horror have to come back again? We were just getting our breath back and feeling like we could possibly survive the swooning tsunami of tragedy that had taken our dad from his family and caused my mom to give up our family home.

We'd been living in Huntington Beach in Southern California for less than a year, and my mom had done a wonderful job of creating the home we had once had when our dad was alive. My mom made certain to carry on all our holiday traditions and to give each of us as much personal time and attention as she could.

When my father had died, my mom had told Daniel, the oldest of my younger brothers that he was now the head of the house, and he proudly and lovingly stepped into my dad's shoes and duties as well as any ten-year-old son could have, given his young age. Daniel was a constant comfort to my mom, and he took over our joyful Easter traditional Sicilian breakfast of cooking the frittata in the special deep round pan, as that honor was reserved for the oldest male in the Italian household. My brother did an excellent job of getting none of the ingredients to stick to the bottom and succeeded in skillfully flipping the delicate and fragile, semi-cooked frittata to the second pan, as if he'd been doing this feat his whole life.

I was so proud of my brother Daniel and happy for him; he'd done such a great job cooking. Our dad would've been so proud too.

The frittata my brother cooked was absolutely perfect and quite delicious, as good as any our dad had made. My mom had also continued our family's Thanksgiving tradition of giant turkeys with her special meat dressing, which we all loved. We even still had the big Christmas tree with gifts piled high underneath the tree, though I don't know how my mom managed to buy so many gifts—but she was quite amazing.

As much as Mom could manage it, she did all she could to not wallow in her own sadness and to provide fun times, even taking us camping; which meant she had to do most of the traditional "guy" duties herself—although again, Daniel and Peter, the two older of my younger brothers were huge helps. She joined a group of family campers and we enjoyed camping with other families. It wasn't the same as when my dad was alive, but it was the next best thing, and we enjoyed family fun together camping again.

We all had nice bicycles, and I had the extra joy of my mom making sure I still had my ice skates. My mom would always make sure she found a way for me to go ice skating at least once a week, even though it still meant two round trips of at least an hour apiece; but my mom was always sacrificing for her family. When possible, we spent weekends at the beach enjoying the sun and sand and swimming, and my brothers learned to body surf.

My mom also heard of an organization called Big Brothers, which would match a fatherless boy with a male volunteer who would come and visit every couple of weeks and serve as a male role model to the fatherless boy the man was matched with.

All the volunteers were carefully screened and had criminal background checks done by the agency, so my mom felt very safe allowing my three younger brothers to each have their own individual Big Brother. Each of my brothers' Big Brothers proved to be an excellent match and took my brothers to various events such as fishing, or just hanging out at our home, or running errands together—ways in which my brothers could spend the quality, private time which was so vitally important to my brothers.

My mom was always very thankful for the positive effect the three Big Brothers had on my brothers' lives, and my brothers still talk fondly now of the fun times their three Big Brothers enjoyed with them.

Money was very scarce, as Mom only had my dad's small monthly death benefit as her resources. My dad had been in the midst of trying to secure life insurance at the time of his death, and the application was not yet completed.

My mom was frugal and an excellent cook, so we never realized at that time how carefully my mom budgeted her resources. My mom was masterful at making our meals nutritious with coupons and bargain food buys. We had everything we wanted and needed for school and after-school activities, so we thought we were just fine.

Our home was sparsely furnished, but we all had beds and proper clothes and enjoyed our family as much as we were able to, given our dad's untimely death.

How my mom managed it all on her own, I really don't know—but she just kept going, raising us the way she and our dad had always done.

I don't recall why my mother went to the doctor; it may have been for a regular routine visit. She didn't appear sick. Suddenly, and without any warning, my mom went into the hospital and when she came home, she was quite visibly shaken. My mom looked even sadder than she often had since my dad had died, and I could not imagine what had happened that made her look so sad and upset.

"When I went to the hospital, the doctors found out I have breast cancer." My mom quietly spoke these words to only me and was again very quiet. This was 1968 and Betty Ford had not yet made breast cancer a public conversation, so I knew very little about it. I didn't know enough about breast cancer to even be frightened. I don't think I even really associated cancer with a death sentence, as I had not ever known anyone who had cancer—and I didn't know anybody who even knew somebody else that had any cancer. I only knew that breast cancer, or any cancer for that matter, was bad and scary. I didn't know what would happen next, to my mom or to our family.

I didn't understand what my mom was trying to explain to me, but as I listened my mom explained that they had removed her breast and had also taken what are called lymph nodes, and they would test her lymph nodes to see if the cancer had spread. I didn't understand what was even meant by "her cancer had spread," but I was soon to learn the language of spreading cancer, lymph nodes, radiation therapy, and chemotherapy.

In 1968, breast cancer treatments were nowhere as advanced as cancer treatments are today. Many of the treatments were kind of done as a "hit or miss" approach; they were just hoping that by bombarding a cancer patient's system, the desired outcome of cancer remission would be achieved.

Once again, my life became a very serious, task orientated one and I and my younger siblings were all thrust into the role of trying to help my mother and her medical team save her life. Daniel, the oldest of my younger brothers and

I took turns driving my mom to her cancer appointments, although neither of us was old enough to drive.

With the suddenness and seriousness of my mom's unexpected cancer diagnosis, I began to take my last words promising my father to "take care of his family" very, very seriously.

With lightning speed, we were now suddenly juggling our mom's doctors, cancer consultations, treatment options, radiation, and chemotherapies, and their adverse effects on my mom—all while trying to maintain some show of normalcy regarding education and family life for our already beleaguered family.

I took my promise to my father even more seriously than ever. We all banded together with our only mutual goal: to save my mother's life. No matter what it took.

It didn't take very long for this recipe to take its toll on all of us. We tried very hard to maintain a semblance of normalcy, but every day, normalcy was slipping further and further away despite our best efforts to keep it close at hand.

Looking back, we were all so touchingly young— including my mom, just thirty-nine years old. We were all so touchingly naïve, believing we could weather this latest horror. We would stick together; we were *our* family, and we would prevail.

There is a certain beauty in youthful naiveté: the beauty of believing we are young and therefore we can bend destiny to *our* will, not knowing yet that we don't possess that power and never will. None of us knew that no matter how much we believed together in solidarity as a family, and how much we wanted it to, our family's reality would prove to be nothing at all like our hopes.

How could any of my family have known that my mother's cancer diagnosis was just a foreshadowing of the new horrors still to come?

There was no way to know—and it was better that our family did not.

That way, we still believed we were invincible.

It was 1969, and I was fifteen years old.

It was 1969, and my mom was thirty-eight years old, a widow raising five children completely alone with extremely meager funds.

But the horror didn't care.

It never does. But God does.

God cares about our horrors when He heals our orphan hearts.

Chapter 11

"Two Scoops of Mashed Potatoes and Gravy, Please"

Me, Huntington Beach High School
cafeteria, California, 1968

*"But Jesus said to them, 'I
have food to eat that you know
nothing about'" (John 4:32).*

"Two scoops of mashed potatoes and gravy, please." I always
asked so very quietly, and always so very politely. And no
one ever suspected that I was so sad and so very lonely. I
missed my dad and our home and my happy, wonderful life
so much. And now, knowing that my mom had breast cancer only served to deepen my sadness and to strengthen my
resolve to keep the promise I had made to my dad as he was
dying in front of me.

The year was 1969, and I was now a fifteen-year-old
teenager in the tenth grade at Huntington Beach High School,
a quaint little seaside town known mainly for surfing, in sunny

Southern California. Most would think I was living every teen-ager's dream, as the Beach Boys kept singing "California Girls," and I drove past the sunny beaches and surfers on a daily basis. Instead, at fifteen years old, I was a quiet, withdrawn, friend-less, seventy-five-pounds-overweight teenager, standing at the school cafeteria counter where every day a nice, hair-netted, grandmotherly woman sweetly asked what I wanted for lunch that day. My polite, quiet answer never varied.

"Two scoops of mashed potatoes and gravy, please."

I always felt the twin feelings of joy and utter despair as I asked, ever so politely, "Two scoops of mashed potatoes and gravy, please." But what I didn't understand or realize was that I was suffering from the deep wounds of grief that I carried—and if I *had* understood, I didn't know what in my sad little world to *do* with those feelings. So, every school day, I stood sadly alone and quietly and politely repeated my cafeteria mantra, "Two scoops of mashed potatoes and gravy, please," as if even the tiniest routine could ease my sadness and help the constant instability I felt.

I would carefully take my plastic tray with my treasure and find my way to my seat in the cafeteria, where I would sit alone. Surrounded by the noise of happy, chattering teen-agers, I never sat with a friend; I didn't have any, and I don't recall anyone ever reaching out to me in friendship. I don't think it ever occurred to me to reach out and initiate being friends with any of my classmates; so, burrowing deeper into my private world of grief and stunned silence at school and at home, I just survived and functioned, always feeling so weird and oddly different. I never knew what to do, or who to have a conversation with, to change how sad and alone and scared I now felt with my mom's new cancer diagnosis.

So, my routine never varied, nor did my sadness as I would look down at my two scoops of mashed potatoes and gravy and realize anew how sad I was every school day, quietly eating two scoops of mashed potatoes alone at my high school lunch table. One day in particular—after realizing that another dance would come and go without me even hoping I could attend—as I looked at the big, gooey, gravy-covered potatoes, I felt such an overwhelming sadness. I felt such a sense of how extremely different and lonely I felt. Even sadder, I didn't have a clue how to change my circumstances, and I certainly didn't have a clue how to change myself.

I only knew that I continued to live as a stranger in my strange circumstances, still feeling exactly as I had that very first day when I returned to my junior high school after I had witnessed my father die. Then, I had stood alone in my junior high cafeteria and looked at every one of my fellow students lining the wall, with the consuming sadness that came with my dawning realization that I was completely and instantly different. The underlying feeling was, "I am different. I am alone. None of this is real. Someday I will live in my *real* life again, and this isn't it."

From the day my father died, I can honestly say I never felt safe and secure in any sense of the word, as if I already instinctively knew my life was getting sadder and infinitely harder with each passing day.

All I had—on that first day back to junior high school and now on these, my high school days—was sadness and food.

Sadness and food; my new twin best friends.

For the few short months that I attended tenth grade, I was either very late or missed my classes altogether for numerous reasons. My mom had been diagnosed with aggressive breast cancer; and combined with her continued grieving of my father's death, much of the responsibility for home care and my siblings—especially the two youngest ones—fell to me. I can't honestly say I didn't like that responsibility; it did give me a sense of purpose and joy, as I deeply loved my siblings and my mom.

As my mom's treatments escalated, my brother and I needed to drive her to the doctors' appointments, chemotherapy, and radiation appointments, and no one else was available. My brother and I drove my mom, missing school in order to get our mom her life-saving treatments.

I look back on the few months of my very short-lived high school years at Huntington Beach High School with a strange, detached indifference—like I'm looking at those years through a long, hollow tube; like I'm looking at someone else, not really at me.

I feel like that because I felt like I was attending high school while living in a long, hollow tube inside of myself, unable to connect or enjoy any of the normal high school fun and events.

My dear friend Bob Leonard, who lives in Pennsylvania and shares my love of all things concerning my favorite football team, the Pittsburgh Steelers, has shared with me that when his mom died while he was in high school, he also felt so different and also remembers himself as feeling "hollow," in spite of familiar surroundings.

Sorrowfully, it is true that only those of us who have known the early death of our parent(s) truly understand how wretched and painful the experience is—leaving us feeling hollowed out and different from friends who have not undergone the same trauma.

A few vivid memories stand out of my few short months of tenth grade at Huntington Beach High School.

I took a sewing class as an elective, and one of my classmates was making a suit for her fiancé. Each day I watched her working on her fiancé's suit, laughing and planning for their future. And each day as I watched her, I felt like she lived in another world—a world where you got to be happy and make plans for your future. Whereas my world was "two scoops of mashed potatoes and gravy, please," eaten alone and solemnly in the high school cafeteria day after day—hopelessly frozen in the day my father had died in front of me, and now terrifyingly alone and worrying that my mom was next to die.

I sat in my English class every morning and listened to the day's announcements, broadcast over the big speaker mounted over the large green chalkboards. Each day the announcements were similar: upcoming dances, football and basketball games. Some fun school events were free. Every day over the large wall speaker, the announcer would excitedly encourage us attend the many fun school activities we would undoubtedly enjoy. Every day, as the announcer made his announcements, I'd listen to all my classmates around me commenting and laughing about going to the events, knowing I'd never go to any of them.

Things were so hard at home that I never even told my mom about the events.

One time, during school hours, instead of class we were taken to the large gymnasium for a pep rally for the basketball team. Intuitively, I knew that I wasn't a part of any of the raucous, joyful fun going on around me. I sat alone and somberly watched the pretty, happy, perky cheerleaders going through their cheers as the school's basketball team was introduced, and everybody cheered. I felt as disconnected from everything I was watching and hearing as I had the very first day I had returned back to junior high the week after my father had died. I no longer fit in with these "young, fun, laughing people." I wasn't a young person anymore. I was a worried, sad adult in a teenager's body, without any teenager thoughts. Not ever.

I never, ever attended a high school dance, or a high school football, baseball or basketball game. I never attended a high school prom.

Soon after the pep rally, I was unable to attend school as my mom was admitted to the hospital and Lisa, three years old, couldn't stay home alone while I went to class. When I was able to go back to school, as a neighbor or another brother stayed with Lisa, I explained at the attendance window that I was unable to get a note, as my mom was still in the hospital and I wasn't old enough to visit her. I was told that if I didn't return the next day with a note from my mom explaining my absence, I'd be suspended. With my mom still in the hospital, I returned to school the next day and I was promptly suspended.

When this same reason for unexcused absences was repeated numerous times over a few short months, I was expelled and sent to Wintersburg Continuation High School—which also lasted only a very short time, as I couldn't even attend those adjusted classes with any sense of regularity.

Simultaneous to my assignment to Continuation or Alternative High School, the social workers assigned to my mom's case came to our home and very matter-of-factly told my mother and me that we had two choices. The social workers said that I could voluntarily drop out of school now that I was sixteen years old. Sixteen years old, we were told, was the legal age a student could drop out of school in California in 1969 without any consequences from the authorities.

Then the social workers informed my mom and me that my other choice was that if I chose to remain in school—even in the Wintersburg Continuation Alternative High School— they, the social workers, would begin to file and process the necessary paperwork for my four younger siblings to be made wards of the state of California. The social workers planned to sign, under penalty of perjury, that my mother's advancing cancer left her far too medically incapacitated to effectively handle the remaining four younger children while I was in school, thus posing an immediate danger to the safety and welfare of my four younger siblings.

Although alarmed, I agreed—as since my father's death, I really didn't even have a clue what school was for, or why I was being forced to go.

No one ever spoke to me of what *I* wanted to be when I grew up. No one ever spoke to me of what *my* future might hold. It had never, ever occurred to me that the day would come when I would have my own life, making choices to benefit myself first, with a plan and goal to fashion a happy life for myself.

I was much too frozen looking backwards to even turn around and look forward beyond the grief and pain of my everyday life. Death's horror seemed to now be dropping its shadow of death ever so slowly—yet deliberately and deadly—over my beloved mother's young life.

Instead, from the day I entered tenth grade, my aimless, unmonitored class attendance and lack of completed home-work and projects had earned me an "F" in every single class, with the exception of my English class.

The only class I even cared about, with what little capac-ity I had left for caring about school, was my English class. I'd always enjoyed writing; it had always come very easily for me. I found great comfort in sitting quietly, pen in hand, and writing the thoughts that came to me. I received a "D" in that class, and I was strangely proud of myself that I had not failed my English class as I had failed every other class. I also felt that my English teacher was sympathetic towards my family situation, so in some small way, I felt that I had not disappointed him by not failing his class—and hoped he had somehow known that my "D" grade was not an indicator of me not liking English, nor of his skill as my English teacher. I simply did not have it in me to try or even care. We were trying to save our mother's life, and English papers just didn't factor into that goal.

I always loved to read and write and liked my English class and teacher. Although my completed assignments and attendance were sporadic at best, his class was always a bright spot in my school day when I did attend—though I never told him or anyone else how much I enjoyed his class. I didn't really talk much to anyone, any place, other than when I would go ice skating. Perhaps the early sexual abuse I had survived had left me thinking that talking only made things worse or stirred up trouble. The ice rink had always been my safe, private world, so those friends were safe in a special way. I talked to them, but not to anyone at my high school or about my high school.

My tenth grade English teacher was a kind, handsome man, who taught with enthusiasm and who genuinely liked his students. Becoming concerned, my kind English teacher met with me privately, explaining that he was bewildered at my sporadic attendance and lack of homework completions—as when I did complete assignments, they were very good.

After I explained my home situation, he expressed his sympathy for my family's plight. He said that he thought I was gifted in English and had decided, kindly, to give me a grade of "D." He also said that he was giving me an opportunity to improve my grade before the semester was over.

When my mid-term report card arrived, I remember experiencing the twin feelings of incredible sadness at seeing almost straight "Fs" on my report card, yet a feeling of elation that I had not failed English, as English was always my easiest subject.

I never had a chance to improve my English grade or to live up to my English teacher's belief in me. I had wanted so much to not disappoint him, as it had been years since any-one had seemed to believe in me enough to tell me that I was good at *anything*. I never told my English teacher I felt bad that I had let his belief in me go unfulfilled, as I was expelled from high school because I couldn't bring an excused absence note from my again-hospitalized mother. I wish I had not left school without telling him how much I had enjoyed simply being in his class, listening to him teach, and knowing there was one person who believed in me.

But as I said, I had developed the habit, after my dad died, of never telling anybody anything about myself, as I believed nobody cared anything about me other than my ability to keep my family together and keep my siblings out of foster care.

Although the social workers insisted I drop out of school, I saw this latest unwelcome change as nothing more than another sad milestone in my life. I became an official tenth-grade-dropout the day I left my high school campus for the last time in 1969.

I added my new title of dropout to my fatherless title.

I was now a tenth-grade-dropout, fatherless teenager.

Because horror is a lot like that, I've learned.

I would not return to my Huntington Beach High School campus until twenty-one years later in 1989—when as an orphan, now 36 years old, I needed to find out how to get a GED so that I could begin the long, arduous, and deeply satisfying journey of reclaiming and enjoying my own life.

Because God helps us reclaim and enjoy our lives, when God heals our orphan hearts.

Chapter 12

Standing in the Gap (Or Trying To)

"I sought for a man among them who would...stand in the gap" (Ezekiel 22:30).

Of course there was a gap!

How in the world did I, as a thirteen-year-old, on the day after my father died, even begin to believe and think that I could keep my promise to my dying father and stand in the gap which his sudden and completely unexpected and demoralizing death had brought about?

In so many ways, how absurdly unrealistic—and yet very much exactly what I, a very typical thirteen-year-old, believed *I could control.*

I don't recall an exact moment when my life radically shifted from the wonderment and fun of childhood to what became my daily world of sadness and somber responsibilities. It seemed like from the very moment I heard my Uncle Angelo's voice on the phone telling me that my father had died, I never again felt the same carefree, joyful, child-like security and freedom I had felt when my dad was alive.

Now, here in Southern California with my mom's new cancer diagnosis, so much information seemed to be drowning me. I don't know whether it was the normal increasing appetites of five growing children, or that my mom's cancer treatments were so understandably exhausting—leaving my mom without the strength to be as creative with home cooked meals—but our already limited resources suddenly didn't seem to go as far as previously; soon we had to move, as my mom had not been able to keep up with our rent payments.

My youngest brother John Michael remembers that I sewed he and I matching pants from colorful fabric and then I saved my babysitting money and took him to Disneyland in an attempt to give a normal, fun day.

Real estate in Southern California had also started to rapidly increase in value, which also drove up rental property rates. We seemed to be caught in the middle: we needed enough room for my mom and us five children, yet our income from my dad's monthly death benefit did not have any way to grow along with the children's normal, increasing physical growth and our family's normal, increasing monetary needs.

We began frequently moving from one nice home to the next nice home, as my mom wanted us to live in nice neighborhoods with good schools, yet we didn't have the resources for those expensive neighborhoods. So, we would move into a nice home, pay for a few months until my mom got behind, and then during the sixty-to-ninety-day formal eviction process my mom would not pay the current landlord any rent. This sixty-to-ninety-day formal eviction process gave my mom a window of time in which to save her monthly income from my deceased father's death benefit, and this saved money is what my mom would use to pay the new landlord for our next nice home, in a nice neighbor-hood, with good schools.

Fortunately, this was in the 1970s, before there were credit reporting bureaus and eviction records. My mom was doing the very best she could, often moving us within the same school district so that schools did not need to be changed. She was trying so hard to raise her family, but I look back and think how very sad all of these uncontrollable events were for her. My brother Peter, who is the younger middle brother, has told me that my mom told him she cried for my father every single night.

When Peter told me this a few years ago, I remember thinking, *How very sad for Peter to hear our mom say this to him, and how sad for my mom to tell this truth to him.* There was so much sadness surrounding our family.

My mother also told me on several occasions that she would frequently dream of my father, and her dreams were always exactly the same. My mom would see my dad, and she always said the very same thing in each dream she had: "Oh, George, you're back; now everything will be okay again."

Even though I didn't understand all my mother was having to endure, I did know that she was very sad, grieving for my father, and feeling very overwhelmed at figuring out how to provide for all of us and maintain a nice home—all things she had always done with my father.

I was doing the usual babysitting for neighborhood families, and I made about $3 a night. I discovered there was a car wash on the main highway near the beach, and I was told that if I showed up really early, before 7:00 a.m., I could get hired. The best part was that the car wash manager didn't check identification to make sure we were old enough to work—which I wasn't.

I showed up at the car wash the next Saturday and was hired for the day. I vacuumed cars all day long for $1 an hour. At the end of the day, I had earned $8 and I was elated.

Back at our home, there was a small convalescent hospital at the end of our block. I spoke to the administration and they hired me as a nurses' aide on the afternoon shift and the 3:00 p.m. – 11:00 p.m. shift, and on weekends I would work from 7:00 a.m. – 3:00 p.m. I was able to work those hours because in the evenings, my two brothers—the oldest of the younger ones was thirteen, and Peter was eleven—were able to help my mom with Curtis John Michael and Lisa so I could be gone working.

The extra money I made was given to my mom to help us with our family's expenses. I saw many sad things in the convalescent hospital—including patient deaths—that confused me, but I didn't have anybody to talk to about the older people becoming so frail, and how they didn't seem to get good medical care. I didn't want to worry my mom by talking to her about my job, so I always told her I liked working in the convalescent home a lot and was happy there.

I saw death there in the convalescent home in ways I wish I'd never, ever seen, much less with the innocent eyes of a sixteen-year-old.

I had saved a $100 bill from my job and always kept it in my wallet, as I was happier to know that I had $100 than I was to be able to go and spend $100. I was so proud of having made and saved this $100 without any plans or intent to buy anything special. I would take my $100 bill out of my wallet when I was alone, and I would look at it and feel so happy and proud, knowing I had been able to make and save $100 all on my own.

Soon, it became apparent that my mom's breast cancer did not seem to be responding to her cancer treatments the way her doctors had hoped. Again, my mom made the decision to return back home to Buffalo, New York, as the world-famous, state-of-the-art Roswell Park Cancer Institute was conveniently located in Buffalo. Moving back to Buffalo would afford my mom the opportunity to be treated at Roswell Park Cancer Institute, as well as to be surrounded by the loving family and support that we all needed.

We packed up our family's red Rambler that my dad had bought my mom before he died, and with nothing more than what we could fit in the car, my mom again drove the entire 3,000-mile cross-country trip all alone with her five children in the car.

Arriving back in Buffalo, we were all very glad that my mom would be able to be treated at Roswell Park Cancer Institute—what we hoped and prayed would be the final treatments that would bring my mom into complete remission and healing, allowing her to return to enjoying her formerly healthier lifestyle.

My mom was weak from our long trip, and having very little money, we stayed with friends from our former church. Our relatives and friends from church tried to figure out how to provide a home and food for my mom and our family of five children.

One day, about a week after our arrival, the couple from church asked to speak to me alone. They didn't waste any words. The wife looked at me and said, "Your mother told us you have a $100 bill in your wallet, and of course you're going to give it to us so that we are able to use your money to help find a home for *your* family."

I was so stunned and so surprised. The words "of course you're going to give it to us," were very strongly emphasized, as were the words "to help your family." First, I wondered why my mom wasn't with them when this demand was made of me. Second, once again—just like being told I had no choice but to drop out of school—people that were in charge were telling me, not asking me, what was expected of me for the good of my family.

I felt deflated and stupid, realizing that there was not any way I would ever be able to do anything for just me; all I could ever do, and what was continually expected of me, was to keep my promise to my father to take care of our family.

Clearly, I had absolutely no choice in the matter. Without a word, I took my $100 bill out of my wallet and silently handed it over to this couple, thinking how foolish it had been of me to think that I could actually work for money and then be allowed to have something for myself.

Soon, we were living in a nice townhouse in a suburb of Buffalo with nice schools my brothers could attend. My sister, Lisa, was still too young to be attending school, so I stayed home with my sister every day, driving my mom to all her doctor's appointments and treatments at Roswell Park Cancer Institute.

I was able to find a job during the day babysitting, and I would take my younger sister with me. It was a long drive on winding country roads to a small town on the outskirts of Buffalo—often with icy, snowy roads in the winter—but I was simply continuing to do exactly what I had done since my father had died: everything I could do to help our family. No matter what it took, we were going to find a way to stay together.

Our home didn't have a garage, and with the freezing Buffalo winter temperatures, as soon as I got home—always in the dark—from babysitting, I would open the hood of the car and put several blankets over the engine in an effort to keep the engine from freezing overnight in the sub-zero temperatures. I needed our car to start in the morning, because I needed to go to work. Our family income was far too fragile for me to miss even one hour of work.

Again, Daniel, the oldest of my younger brothers was a big help in assisting with our younger brothers, and he still continued to be a big comfort and help to my mom, doing many things around our house that my dad would have been doing.

My brothers were all able to join the local Pop Warner football teams, as they met directly across the street. It was really fun to see all three of my brothers doing normal childhood things, and they all really enjoyed practicing with their teammates. Their games were a highlight of my family's weekend.

On Sundays we again dressed in our best clothes, and once again we attended the little church with the white steeple that we had attended since we were very young, when our dad was still alive. I didn't have the pretty dresses, hats, and gloves I had loved as a little girl, but I did find it comforting at our church that these people had known my dad, and would often talk to me about him in a kind and loving way.

After we had lived in Buffalo for several months my cousin Janice, an educator, spoke with my mom and found a place that allowed me to attend a type of night school each week. I don't remember if the classes were for a standard high school diploma or for a GED. I would go to classes in a downtown building. I wasn't anxious attending, so much as I felt a deep sense of both wonderment at being at a regular school and being given an opportunity to have a high school education, and also trepidation—since my dad died, we had moved so much it had been impossible for me to take any action to carry out any plans for myself and my future.

Wonderfully, my mom's cancer went into complete remission, and that seemed to awaken in my mother her persistent desire to go back and live in Southern California. The cost of living has always been substantially higher in Southern California, so perhaps my mom took this financial fact into account and had planned to find a part-time job she could do once we returned, as Mom was now in full and complete cancer remission.

With plans to return to Southern California as soon as my mother could arrange it, my attempt at education with my cousin Janice came to an abrupt end. I have always been so deeply, deeply grateful to my cousin Janice that she cared about me and tried so hard to help me find a way to finish my own education. At the time Janice arranged for me to attend nighttime classes, I had only experienced a lack of concern regarding my own separate future plans. I felt like no one ever regarded me as a teenager who should have had some type of adult life guidance. I didn't feel like I was ever evaluated in any way apart from my mom's sickness, and my ability to fill in and care for four younger siblings.

Although my two younger brothers were closer in age to me and didn't require as much physical care and supervision, there still was the legal necessity for them to be in school—which left me as the only person who could legally stay home and assist my mom without bringing unwanted attention and scrutiny from Buffalo Child Protective Services.

I never knew and never allowed myself any room to think about whether I even had a future beyond the dire need of my family's fragile situation. I was never cognizant of being able to, in any type of meaningful or future-focused manner, look towards the day when I would have my own life, separate from my family and their individual problems. I was never able to see beyond all that was needed to care for my sick mom and help with my younger siblings.

But therein lay the inherent problem: there simply wasn't anyone else to do what I could do by staying out of school.

Wasn't that exactly what the social workers had told me?

"Drop out of school, or else we will split up your family into separate foster homes."

Hadn't the social workers made it abundantly clear that these family responsibilities were mine—because the alternative was to have my family split up and my siblings taken away and placed in foster homes?

I was intently driven by my determination to keep my promise to my father, and keeping that promise also meant making sure our family did not get split up into foster homes.

There weren't going to be *any* foster homes for my brothers and sister; *that* was *not* going to happen, if I could help it.

I lived in a type of make-believe world where I believed I could fight, and my mother would stay alive and become healthy again by way of my sheer determination.

Looking back, I don't recall discussing my fears and my determination with anyone, not any relatives nor even my siblings. I may have; but no conversations are found in my memory.

I was to learn later that during the years between my father's and mother's deaths, I was in classic denial—one of the many stages of grief. I was still actively grieving my father's death, and I had added to that grief the denial of the horror of my mother's cancer diagnosis.

If it was possible to will my mother to stay alive, I was going to be the one who would do that. I was certainly strong-willed.

With my mom's breast cancer in full remission, my mom made arrangements for me to fly back to Southern California by myself, where my assignment was to find a home for my mom to come out to when she once again drove back to Southern California.

I was now seventeen years old.

In California by myself, I stayed with a woman I had helped with babysitting, and I did manage to find a nice home for our family to move into. Payment was arranged, and I was given the keys.

Just like my father had taught me to do, I was able to paint the inside of the home before my mom arrived, as I wanted our home to feel new and inviting.

On the other side of the country my brothers again finished their school year in Buffalo, and again my mom packed everything in our family's red Rambler. Now, for the third time since my father's death three years earlier, my mom again made the 3,000-mile cross-country car trip, driving the entire 3,000 miles herself and attending to my four younger siblings while she drove back to California.

Upon her arrival in Southern California, my mom came to the home that I had found, rented, and painted for our family, and we settled again into what our family hoped and prayed would be the start of a return to stability and happiness.

Unfortunately, during the year we had spent in Buffalo the cost of living in Southern California had increased, and my mom quickly found herself with far too little money left at the end of each month, when my father's death benefit checks had already been spent. My brothers were eating like normal young men, my sister was no longer a toddler, and I had continued to steadily gain weight—now weighing 200 pounds and still only five feet, one and a half inches tall.

I learned how to make more sophisticated clothes and charged a neighbor to make her some homemade, custom dresses. I was also able to pick up as many babysitting and other jobs as I could, but no amount of little odd jobs that I could find as a teenager made much of a dent in the monthly, growing, gaping hole of monetary need in our family.

When the oldest of my younger brothers was sixteen he got a part-time job after school, and that helped to take some of the pressure off. I do believe that even under the very best of circumstances, sheltering, feeding, and clothing a family of six people is expensive by anyone's measure. But my mom worked as hard as she could to continue to give us as normal a life as we could hope for.

For a very short time, we enjoyed going to the beach again and even had some camping and family day adventures.

San Diego was 240 miles round trip, and one Saturday my mom loaded us in the car and we spent the day enjoying San Diego. Our family had always been fascinated by Sea World, and we were also able to see Shamu the Killer Whale and the other water exhibits and to enjoy the other attractions.

Some sadder memories exist even from when my mom was in remission. One afternoon when just my mom and I were home and Lisa, now three years old, was sleeping, my mom invited me into the downstairs bathroom, took off her underclothes, and showed me the very long, dark red scar that was left where her cancerous breast had been removed. I had not asked to see her scar, and so I am not sure what motivated my mom to show her cancer mastectomy scar to me. The scar was very jagged, like from an old-fashioned can opener—not one, smooth, thin continuous line; this one seemed to go up and down and back and forth across my mom's chest wall and up into her armpit all at the seem time. The incision line itself was close to a quarter inch thick, and as I looked at the dark red scar the thought came that it seemed to be angry or protesting this unnatural treatment that had happened to my mom. My mom explained that she had had an operation called a complete or radical mastectomy, which means the surgical removal of all or part of the breast and, in my mom's case, the associated lymph nodes and muscles.

Once again, I felt such overwhelming sadness for my mom. My mom was so sweet and so young—at thirty-nine, how do you cope with all of this death and loss? The surgery was in 1969, and there was not yet the automatically performed breast implant at the time of the cancerous breast's removal. My mom would wear a regular bra, and she had a soft, flesh-colored "boobie" (as we called it) that would fill out the bra cup where her breast was gone. I really had not thought much of the small reddish line I could sometimes see peeking past the neckline of her dresses.

My youngest brother, Curtis John Michael, who was seven years old at the time of my mom's surgery, remembers our mom holding him on her lap and rocking him and whistling. My mom loved rocking chairs and whistling.

My mom often had strangers come up to her and compliment her on her whistling abilities. Curtis John Michael also inherited our mom's ability to whistle brilliantly; I pretend it's my mom whistling whenever I hear him whistling, and I am comforted and smile.

Curtis John Michael also has a much sadder memory of my mom—again holding him on her lap, and again rocking him and whistling. Only in this memory my mom's dress had shifted a bit to the side, and Curtis John Michael remembers seeing the deep, red surgery scar on our mom's chest, but not really comprehending at that tender age what it actually was—or what the deep, red cancer scar represented.

After she showed me her scar, I would observe my mom doing exercises like walking her arm on the surgical side of her chest up the wall, and she explained that was because the surgery had limited the range of motion of that arm. She also had a small red rubber ball that she would squeeze to help with the damage her mastectomy had done to the nerves and movement in her arm and hand.

Continuing to feel the crunch of not having enough money, my mom creatively maintained us living in good neighborhoods with good schools and we sadly continued our earlier pattern of renting a nice home in a nice neighborhood with good schools for my three younger brothers and then, very predictably, after a few months the landlord would start the eviction process. Soon we would find ourselves repeating the pattern of moving again to another new home, in a nice neighborhood, with good schools. I lost count of how many times we repeated this pattern.

The folded, court-seal stamped eviction notice stapled to the front wooden door frame of our home was a familiar sight to me when I would come home from running errands with my family.

My mother discovered the new, planned concept community of Lake Forest in south Orange County, California, which was about thirty miles south of where we were living. In retrospect this move seems odd, as south Orange County and the newer communities of El Toro and Mission Viejo were even more expensive than the ones we had been living in.

Once again we made the move to yet another new home, in a nice neighborhood, with good schools. It was here in this new neighborhood that our family was to meet and make friends with families and their children who went to school with my brothers, and who remain friends with our family still today. The families we met were respectful, fun, traditional families with a mom, dad, and children my brothers' and sister's ages. We enjoyed the new families and the usual mix of school and after-school fun activities. The interesting thing about the town we lived in was that it was so isolated from the next larger cities, more than thirty minutes away, that in many ways our town had a small-town atmosphere. There was only one high school and a couple of restaurants, and there was even a curfew for the high school kids—and the local Orange County Sheriff's Department was quite diligent in enforcing the curfew.

My brothers engaged in school sports, and I was very proud of them. I was still able to go ice skating and made a few friends at the ice rink who would come and visit me at my home, and I was able to visit them at theirs. Our family was starting to have fun again.

And then the unthinkable happened, again. The horror that had once again been patiently waiting reared its head with full force and determination to once again try to destroy my family.

Horror loves to destroy, because its nature is to lie, cheat, steal, and destroy.

Horror is a lot like that, I've learned.

But I've also learned that God's nature is to heal what the horror lies about, cheats, steals, and destroys.

Because God is like that, I've learned, when God heals our orphan hearts.

Chapter 13

＊ ⊹ ＊

More Sadness as Mom's Cancer Returns

"You number my wanderings;
Put my tears into Your
bottle" (Psalm 56:8).

There are certain memories that are so deeply burned into my mind—memories that are burned into it ironically and sadly with such brilliance, because the brilliant light comes from the incredible sadness and significance attached to them.

Such is the memory of the moment when I learned that my mom's cancer had returned—that singular moment, so bewildering, so staggeringly sad, so incomprehensibly life-changing. I vividly recall being stunned at the very core of everything that was *me*, everything that had once known normalcy, happiness, and joy.

It was about three years after my mom's initial cancer diagnosis, and almost two years after she had been declared cancer-free and in remission by Roswell Park Cancer Institute.

I had taken my mom to her regular doctor's appointment and had been waiting in the waiting room. My mom and her doctor had been talking privately in the doctor's office; not in one of the patient rooms.

I was called into the doctor's office and I will never, ever forget seeing my mom slumped sideways, sitting in the chair in front of the doctor's desk. My mom's head was down, and she had one hand covering her face. My mom didn't even look up when I entered the doctor's office. As I stood in the doorway I took in my mom sitting there, so alone and so sad, and I could just feel that something horrible was in that room. Then the doctor quietly and solemnly said, "Your mom's cancer has come back."

I kept standing in the doorway; I still didn't sit down. I couldn't take my eyes off my mom. Still my mom did not react; she just sat there, frozen in the horror's grip, trying to comprehend and take in what this tragic news now meant for her life, and the consequences of this news for the lives of us, my mom's and our deceased father's five children.

HOW could this be happening again? I don't think I even grasped that the doctor's words were effectively pronouncing a death sentence on my mom; rather, I just stood there wishing I could protect my mom, wishing my mom didn't have to face yet another shattering, exhausting, monstrous obstacle. Was it asking too much for my mom to be able to have a reprieve from all the horrors and griefs she had already suffered at her young age of forty-one? Why couldn't MY mom just be happy and enjoy her family?

These were not questions to which I had answers, nor would I ever. I only knew with a sudden certainty that as bad as things were for my mom and for our already fragmented family, things were about to get much, much worse.

As I robotically walked, numbed, through the next demoralizing, incomprehensible year and the tragic events still to come, it seemed like each new layer of sadness that was added to my heart went deeper and did even more damage to my already wounded, fatherless heart than the previous sadness had. In some ways these new horrors and experiences, and the sadness they brought to me, were much more capable of hurting me easily—because I already felt fragile and incomplete and incapable, and I simply couldn't defend myself in any way or soften these cruel blows that never stopped attacking me.

Somehow and from someplace, since my father had died, I had come to believe that I SHOULD be able to make a difference; I SHOULD be able to change our family's destiny; I SHOULD be able to make it all right again—like my mom's dreams of my father that she always wished would happen. Had we not ALL suffered enough by watching our father die in front of our eyes?

Yet, as emotionally fragile and brittle as I felt, with the realization of how crucial and life-threatening each new piece of my mom's medical news was to our family, I felt even more strongly that my father would be deeply and sadly disappointed in me because I wasn't doing a very good job of taking care of his family—as I had promised my dying father I would.

As much of a failure as I thought I was, as much as I continued to believe myself to be failing in my self-assigned role of family savior—because I had been shown by the doctor's announcement of the cancer's return that I was, in fact, totally incapable of helping my mom save her life—I clung more closely to my inner belief that I COULD still make a difference, and that I still could do SOMETHING to save my mother's life.

In spite of my ever-worsening and crushing fears that my mom would die, and despite falling deeper and deeper into despair and feeling more helpless and ill-equipped and overwhelmed than I ever had, it never occurred to me to seek out anyone to talk to, not even my brothers.

I was around a lot of people every day, but I felt completely alone in my sad, fatherless, and very likely soon-to-be motherless world.

When I would go to bed, the totality of what my family was facing would loom in the darkness, waiting for our home to be quiet while I waited for the rest of my family to be asleep. Once it was safe, and I knew I wouldn't bother or wake anyone, I would silently cry bitterly in my bed, tears running down the sides of my face, questions whirling in my mind, as I kept whispering out loud, "I don't want my mom to die too." "I don't want to be all alone." "Please don't let my mom die too."

I don't recall having anyone to talk to beyond the obligatory, "How are you doing?" to which I would reply, "Fine." There was nothing "fine" about watching my mom slowly dying after my father had died. I don't recall one single coping action, other than eating more food and feeling even sadder than I had in the moments preceding this, the latest sadness.

I was now completely consumed with helping my mom in every way I could and silently trying to beat back the horror of the steady march of her possible death; which, if it did occur, would strand all five of my father's and mother's children as orphans.

I was now seventeen years old. But the horror didn't care how old or how young any of us were. The horror didn't care that my mom was forty-one; it didn't care that I was seventeen. It didn't care that my siblings were fourteen, eleven, nine, and four years old.

Horror thrives on being cruel.

Horror is a lot like that, I've learned.

But God loves and is tender-hearted to those of us whom the horror has tried to destroy.

Because God is like that, I've learned, when God heals our orphan hearts.

Chapter 14

"Mom, Peter's Sister Rosie Has a Mom Face and She's Only Fifteen"

Sherry Hauck McLaughlin,
14, to her mom, California, 1971

"Is your daddy still alive? He is?
Oh, that's nice." -Our Mom

"Mom, Peter's sister Rosie has a mom face and she's only fifteen years old."

That's what my friend, Sherry Hauck Mclaughlin, told me she had told her own mom after coming to our home and meeting our family in 1971.

That visit occurred after my mom's devastating news that her cancer had returned for a second, usually terminal time. In the early 1970s, knowing that this news usually preceded the doctor's inability to get a patient's cancer under control which would allow the patent to go back into remission, we continued to live in the small, sleepy little master-planned town of El Toro in Southern California.

My mom's health was rapidly declining, and yet our family's financial needs were continuing to grow as all of us children were continuing normal growth patterns.

With money so very scarce, we continued our desperate pattern of renting, falling behind in the rent, then saving the current landlord's rent money while he carried out our eviction process, and then moving close by into another nice house, in a good neighborhood, with good schools for my brothers.

Living in El Toro with my mom so sick, it never would have occurred to me to go and hang out with a teenaged girlfriend; my job was to help with cooking, and the kids, and all the things that needed to be done in our family's home.

Sherry Hauck Mclaughlin, who has been one of my friends since the days when my mom was still alive in 1971, remembers those days as very hard for my family. She recalls how she first met my middle brother Peter and then expected that she had a new girlfriend in me.

As Sherry tells the story, "I was outside hanging out in front of my home, and my mom was inside. Peter came up on his bicycle and asked me if he could borrow some bread, because he wanted to make some toast for his little brother and sister. I was quite alarmed." Sherry recalls, "I took Peter inside to meet my mom, who was immediately equally alarmed. My mom asked Peter where he lived and if his parents were home. Peter said that his dad had died, and that his mom was home but she was really, really sick, and that his big sister, Rose, took care of him. After we talked to him for a long time to make sure he was alright and his family was alright, Peter left our house with a loaf of bread, some eggs, and a half gallon of milk my mom gave him from our refrigerator."

As El Toro was such a same, quaint little town in the 1970s, Sherry soon saw Peter again in the neighborhood and they became friends. Sherry also remembers that the very first time she came to our family's home she was excited to find out that Peter had a sister, me, who was around her age; I was fifteen years old.

As Sherry again tells of her memory of visiting our home, "I came to your home with Peter and I was all excited to meet you because you were a teenager like me, and I was expecting you to be all bubbly and excited and say, 'Hi, let's go in my room and I'll show you my new shorts that I bought.' But instead, when I walked in you were in the kitchen with all the younger kids around you. I was so surprised, because even though you were a teenager, you had a mom face and that wasn't what I had expected. I saw your mom face and thought, *Rosie should have a teenager's face,* and instead you had a mom face. And you never left the kids, and the younger kids were all around you, and Lisa had lots of curls. You never left the kitchen, and you and I never did anything fun and never even talked for more than a little bit when I visited your home. Your mom looked really, really sick, and you just stayed in the kitchen and kept taking care of the younger kids, even though I was hoping we could hang out.

"Because Peter had told my mom and me that your mom was really, really sick, I wasn't surprised when I met your mother and she was very, very quiet and looked very frail. Your mom was very nice to me. When your mom realized that it had been my mother who had given Peter the food he had brought back home on the day we met him on his bicycle, she said, 'Thank you.' Then your mom looked at me and said, 'Is your daddy still alive?' When I told your mother that my daddy was still alive, your mother just said very quietly, 'He is? Oh, that's nice.'"

In talking to Sherry about her memories, this story of my mom asking if Sherry's daddy was still alive was a story I had not previously heard. It was painful to hear that my mom's question, upon meeting Sherry, was to inquire whether or not Sherry's dad was alive. My mom's response of thinking it was "nice" that Sherry's dad was still alive showed me that my mom was no doubt comparing Sherry's traditional home life with our fatherless home. This quiet acknowledgement of my mom to Sherry made me wish again—even now, fifty years after these events—that my mom had not been so acutely aware of how different our family was from the other families in our neighborhood.

I've always wished I could have made life easier for my mom. I never could, but I always hoped and wished I could.

Many of the young people attending El Toro High School with my brothers are still friends with me today, and I am both very grateful to know them and also so proud of the wonderful people they have each become, and the families they themselves have raised.

Several of those now adult friends have shared their memories of my mom and our family with me. Even though they last saw my mom in the very early 1970s, they clearly remember my mom and our family—as well as also clearly recalling certain events that burned both fun and sad memories into our friends' young minds at the time my mom was still alive.

My friend Bob Strausheim, today of Berkshire Hathaway California Properties, still lives and works in Southern California in the area where my family knew him when I was sixteen years old. I am grateful that I have known Bob for all these years, as he offers me great perspective on my life journey since he has known my whole family except for my dad. Bob remembers my mom as "being very quiet and not saying very much." Bob recalls me taking care of my family rather than going to high school and doing the more normal, traditional activities one would expect a teenage girl to be doing.

Bob also remembers my ice skating friend who would visit me at our home. Surprisingly, my friend Bob remembers me as "being very bubbly," probably because Bob is a wonderful, kind man and he always made me laugh with his fun stories and typical teenage behaviors and antics. Also, I did find that I had fun when my ice skating friends were around, as they shared my love of ice skating.

Many visits included my ice skating friends joining with my friend Bob, and others, to hang out. Bob especially liked certain R & B songs and artists, and he could and would do absolutely perfect imitations of their hit records—including their falsetto voices—and that would always make me laugh so much. My favorite song Bob performed was Al Green's "I'm So Tired of Being Alone" which he sang perfectly, always adding in special fancy choreography including hand movements. It still makes me laugh to this day, thinking of Bob singing and dancing to Motown and other hit R & B songs.

Some of the only fun, laughing times I experienced after my mom's cancer returned were my friend Bob and my ice skating friends making me laugh when we were all together, listening to music. I've always been grateful that Bob provided me some light moments during those somber years.

One universal comment from all of my brothers' high school friends is that my family, and often just my brothers, were often over at their homes eating.

Pat Kelly, who met our family when he and my middle brother Peter were both fourteen, often laughs and laughs when telling me, "Rosie, I think Peter tried to come over to our house as often as he could, because Peter just loved my mom's spaghetti. Peter was always really polite, and he would eat plate after plate. Peter always said it was so good."

My middle younger brother Peter is notoriously famous for loving really good spaghetti and always remembers our Aunt Connie's and my cousin's really good spaghetti too. Given Peter's proclivity for loving good spaghetti, I always tease Pat and say, "Did Peter leave any spaghetti for anybody else?" And Pat assures me that Peter was always very polite and did not eat it all.

Peter has a very kind and tender heart, so I laugh and enjoy stories of him with his teenage friends at their homes.

Another friend, Julie Moffatt Meszaros, met our family when she and Peter were both thirteen. Julie's family appeared to be one of the well-off families in our new neighborhood because they lived in the wooded Lake Forest homes, and our standard tract homes seemed so small in comparison. Julie's family was very friendly, fun, and very kind. I've always enjoyed Julie's mom, Doris Moffatt, and so did my mom.

While my mom was still able to drive a little bit, since Julie's family lived quite close Julie remembers my mom coming over for dinner a lot—and also my brothers, especially Peter, coming to their home for breakfast.

Soon enough, the days after learning the news that my mom's cancer had returned became steadily very sad. My mom questioned so many things around her, and we would sit at our kitchen table and she would talk to me about her ever-increasing list of concerns.

It seemed like my mom had to take more and more medicines, and some were similar to the medications she had taken at Roswell Park Cancer Institute in Buffalo, New York, where her cancer had gone into remission. My mom questioned whether the California medicine was as potent, as the Buffalo medicine had a large amount of blue flecks of color on the white tablets. When my mom compared her current Orange County Medical Center medication of the same name, she laid both tablets on our kitchen table and worriedly and correctly pointed out that the California tablets had noticeably much fewer flecks of blue in them. My mom wondered, if the blue flecks were the "active, cancer-killing ingredients, then doesn't the absence of the blue flecks mean these California medications aren't as strong to kill my cancer?"

How do I begin to answer a question like that? There was no good or right answer. I gave my mom the only answer I knew to give—I told her I simply did not know which pills were better at killing her cancer. But I secretly suspected that a California county medical center that possessed very limited state budget funding, and whose primary purpose was to treat the county's large number of uninsured patients—including the cancer patients—that other doctors and private hospitals refused, *just might* have less potent drugs than a world-renowned, state-of-the-art cancer treatment facility like Roswell Park Cancer Institute in Buffalo that had funding and grants, and where my mom's cancer had gone into complete remission.

I went to bed that night deeply disturbed at my mom's worsening physical condition and growing more alarmed at how each day seemed to find our family struggling even harder to just have the most basic of necessities, including enough food on our table. Most alarming of all, as I pondered all my fears—always keeping them strictly to myself—was my belief that I was disappointing my mom and my siblings, in that I couldn't figure out how to do anything at all that seemed to help. I was eighteen years old.

I was eighteen years old, and I had never felt more alone or more scared than when I thought about what would happen to my mom as she got sicker. What would happen to us five children if she continued to get so sick that she actually died?

Some thoughts were just too horrible, so I continued to concentrate more on finding some way—no matter how improbable or seemingly impossible—of making a difference in the outcome of my mom's cancer.

Why couldn't I make a difference? Shouldn't I be able to make a difference?

What I didn't know was that the horror still to come was only getting started. When it reached full force, the horror would snap our family like a twig in a ferocious ice storm.

Horror is a lot like that, I've learned.

But I've also learned that what the horror means for evil, God means for our good.

Because God is a lot like that, I know, when God heals our orphan hearts.

Chapter 15

◄◄━━━━━◆━━━━━►►

"Will You Please Take My Children After I Die?"

Our Mom to a neighbor, Sept 1972

*"A father to the fatherless, a
defender of widows, is God in his
holy dwelling" (Psalm 68:5).*

"Your mom asked my dad, 'Will you please take my four children after I die?'"

That's what our family's childhood friend Julie Moffatt Meszaros said to me when we spoke in 2018, forty-six years after Julie had overheard the conversation between my mom and her dad—a conversation I had never known had ever taken place; a conversation that told me how, in 1972, my mom had realized her illness was terminal and her untimely death was imminent.

I was so stunned and saddened upon hearing of this conversation of my mom's. Saddened—as my mom had not ever spoken to me about realizing that her death was approaching, and this relayed conversation showed me that my beleaguered mother had looked the horror in its raging face and faced her own death with the same raw courage with which she had faced everything since her husband, father to us five children, had unexpectedly died; and stunned—as I did not think it was possible for new, fresh wounds to still come from my parents' deaths, yet it was. My mom had five children; I was the oldest child of five, yet my mother had asked only for care to be given to four of her children.

Julie had insisted on telling me her memories of my mom and our family over the phone and not in a text or email, and now I understood why. I had not been included in my mother's heartbreaking request to Julie's dad on that day in 1972, just a few months prior to my mom's death. Julie and her mom, Doris Moffatt, had been our family's friends since Julie was thirteen, and we all lived in the small town of El Toro in Southern California in the early 1970s.

Julie said, "It was 1972 and your mom came over to my house, and that's what I heard your mom ask my dad, Rosie—if my dad could please take her four children after she died. I'm sorry your mom did not include you in her question to my dad."

The events leading up to this conversation had been deeply troubling and harrowing for my mom. In our home, living in El Toro in 1971, it had become a familiar scene: my mom and me, sitting at the kitchen table talking while my baby sister played with her toys nearby and my brothers were in school. This time we carefully went over our family's meager income and budget, acknowledging what we both already knew: that there simply wasn't enough money to cover our expenses, even with my part-time jobs added into our budget. Food was limited at our home, and all meals were planned in advance to stretch every dollar; nothing was ever wasted that was bought or cooked. No one ever complained, but managing our limited budget was getting more and more difficult as we all kept getting older. Teenage boys are not known as light eaters.

After my mom and I discussed our dismal balance sheet, my mom made a very brave and courageous decision: she decided to get a part-time job, deciding it would work out better for me to watch my baby sister during the day. She would work at the local McDonald's for a few hours each day, a few days a week.

The first few days, my mom came home from her McDonald's job very discouraged and dismayed. My mom said she worked mostly with teenagers, and the El Toro McDonald's location manager expected everybody to work very fast on the food preparation assembly lines for their numerous products. My mom said she was surprised at how much trouble she was having keeping up with the pace of the assembly line of food preparation. McDonald's had refined the assembly line for food preparation, and every step of preparation was done at a different food station. There were very clear, specific procedures that needed to be followed to ensure the uniformity of the food products that McDonald's was famous for. My mom said she was also, surprisingly, having trouble remembering the exact order of some of the ingredients.

My mom (who had not told McDonald's about her cancer diagnosis) and I discussed that part of her difficulties might be her new cancer treatments, which understandably would make her tired—and this tiredness might be why she wasn't able to work the assembly line food preparation as fast as they wanted her to work. We also discussed the possibility that my mom's new cancer medications might be having an adverse and unexpected effect on her memory. My mom was so worried that she might not be able to keep her new, much-needed job, as her job literally meant keeping food on our family's table. I assured my mom she would get the hang of the job and would do much better. My mom seemed comforted.

My mom and I didn't discuss the obvious—that it was quite possible she was tired and not moving quickly because the cancer itself was slowing her down as it was spreading and taking a toll on her physically. Then, furthermore, I knew the very real possibility existed that my mom was having trouble remembering the exact order of the food preparation ingredients, and various never-changing order of the hamburger condiments, because her cancer's progression had spread to her brain and was now affecting her memory.

I told no one of my private fears that day, and I never did; I never had talked to anyone about my mounting fears for my mom, so I didn't see the wisdom of starting now. Even if I had wanted to discuss my fears that my mom was declining, there wasn't anybody that I could think of to talk to. I wasn't in school, and my home responsibilities left no time for me to do anything besides stay at home and help my mom by driving her to various cancer-treatment-related appointments and errands. The oldest of my younger brothers also helped with driving my mom and with the younger kids.

So that night, I went to bed—as I was to start doing with increasing frequency—feeling so awful that my mom had to contend with such demoralizing job conditions, where she was not afforded any dignity or indulgences. I knew that my mom had told neither the hiring department nor her young boss at Mc Donald's that she had cancer; they just saw a forty-one-year-old mom who should be able to keep up. It was all so sad, and like all the sad things I kept observing in my mom's heath decline, I never could do anything at all to change things for my mom. I couldn't do anything at all to shield my mom from these continuous hurts and disappointments.

The third day of my mom working at McDonald's proved to be her last day of working there. I still remember her coming home so clearly. My mom was really sad and very embarrassed. When I asked what had happened and why she was so upset, my mom quietly—and with tears welling up in her eyes—said she had been fired, because she had not prepared the large metal tray of McDonald's hamburgers properly. My mom elaborated on what had happened and told me she was supposed to put ketchup, mustard, pickle, and then tomato, in that exact order, on each one of the trademark McDonald's hamburgers. They were arranged in rows on the large trays that came down the McDonald's food preparation assembly line, before the large metal tray containing the rows of hamburgers was passed onto its next assembly line station, on its way to the waiting customers.

Somehow, my mom said, she had gotten mixed up, and had put more of some of the condiments on the burgers, and had not put the condiments on in the exact order, but still had managed to put all the right condiments on the hamburgers. The young manager had seen her mistake and had fired my mom, berating and belittling her in front of the mainly teenage crew. I hated how rude and cruel that El Toro McDonald's young manager was to her, when my mom was obviously trying so hard to do her best.

My mom kept asking me, "If I got all the items on all on the hamburgers, what did it matter if I did ketchup/mustard/pickles/tomatoes or mustard/ketchup/pickles/tomatoes? I kept telling my manager I got everything on the hamburger. I need this job."

Even more upsetting to my mom—always thinking of her children and how hard it was to feed us—was that the young McDonald's manager had been so enraged at my mom's mistake in not having the condiments in the exact order that he made a huge, loud, very belittling and embarrassing announcement to everyone in front of my already embarrassed mom. Because of my mother's "huge mistake," he had "no choice but to throw the entire tray of the out-of-order-condiment hamburgers straight into the large plastic garbage pails" right in front of my mother and the other food preparation McDonald's workers. My mom, knowing that there were at least twenty-four perfectly good hamburgers on her "mistake" metal tray, said that she didn't care how bad she looked in front of the whole young crew—so she had begged the young McDonald's manager, "Can I please, please, PLEASE take the hamburgers home to my five young children rather than have them wasted and thrown into the trash?"

Obviously relishing and taking great pleasure in continuing to humiliate my mom, the immature, cruel young manager had then made an even bigger scene, berating my mother about her mistake. Then the young manager took great pleasure in making sure my mom saw him make a very dramatic scene of sliding every single one of the "wrong order of condiments" hamburgers into the trash pail while my mom watched in anguish, knowing both that she had lost her job and that all that precious food had been wasted to punish her in front of others.

Perhaps McDonald's policy forbade employees from taking home "mistake food," but I'm certain it was not McDonald's policy for the young manager to so brutally embarrass and humiliate my mom in front of the other workers.

My mom kept asking me, "Since I was already fired, and he had already embarrassed me, why did he have to throw all the perfectly good hamburgers away? Why couldn't he let me bring them home so we could have had them to eat for a few days? Why did he have to be so heartless? They were perfectly good hamburgers, and he just threw them all away in the trash. Why would he do that, when we could have eaten them?"

Over and over I kept softly telling my anguished mom, "I really wish I knew why that young McDonald's manager seemed to enjoy embarrassing you and being so deliberately cruel. Don't worry, Mom, we'll find a way to feed everybody; we always do. You're doing a good job, Mom; he was not a good manager, and things will work out to be okay for our family. We'll be fine—we all still have each other, and that's all that really matters."

I would go to bed again that night, like I was doing on many nights, hating what my mom was enduring in her determined fight to take care of our family. I can't imagine how hard the emotions and frustrations felt to my mom. How hard for my mom—to be a mother and feel you can't provide enough food for your children. But my mom kept fighting for us, doing everything she could to look out for our future. I would not learn just how desperate my mom was to take care of her family's future until September of 2018, when I spoke to our dear friend Julie Moffatt Meszaros to collect memories for this book.

When I asked to speak to Julie about her memories of my family, I had said she could just email them to me; but curiously, and insistently, Julie kept saying she clearly remembered when my mother had come to talk to her father and said she wanted to tell me about their conversation over the phone rather than to put it in an email. Julie's dad's name was Bob.

Julie asked me several times, "So Rosie, you don't know about the conversation your mom had with my dad when she came over to our house to talk to him?" I answered no, and assumed that my mom had asked Julie's dad, Bob, for a loan, as our budget was so stretched and money was so tight.

When I spoke with Julie, I immediately understood why, and I appreciated Julie's sensitivity to my own feelings— even at this point in my life, forty-six years after my mother died. I understood and appreciated why Julie had been so protective of me in telling me as close to "in-person" as she could about the summer of 1972 conversation between my mom and her dad.

I'll let Julie tell my mom's story: "Your mom came over to our house and asked to speak with my dad. I could overhear their conversation because of how open our home was. Your mom said, 'Bob, would you please take my four younger children when I die? I know you would take good care of them.' My dad said, 'I feel so bad for you and know you're in a very hard place, but I have my own four children and it would be very, very difficult. As much as this is hard, I can't take your children. I'm so sorry.'"

Listening to Julie tell me of my mom's previously unknown, desperate, brave, unselfish, conversation, I needed a moment to catch my breath for several reasons.

First, I had never known until that evening of September 7, 2018, that this conversation had *ever* taken place between Julie's dad and my mom in the summer of 1972.

Second, I had never known that my mom was so acutely cognizant of the closeness of *her* impending death that she was *actively* trying to find a home for her children *after* her death. How incredibly, heartbreakingly tragic for my mom to have driven to Julie's home and made this anguished request of Julie's dad.

What was equally painful for me to hear from Julie was her saying that my mom was looking to find a home where a family would take care of her "*four* children." I sat stunned—I knew my mom had five children; *I* was her oldest child of five. Yes, I was then eighteen, and eighteen was legal age in California, but what was my mom thinking? I wasn't away at university somewhere. I wasn't engaged to be married soon. I wasn't even dating anyone at all. My thoughts continued to tumble back to that summer of 1972 as Julie continued speaking over the phone. I was remembering that I didn't have any close friends—no girlfriends' families where my mom could have been thinking or hoping they would take me in after she died.

As painful as this memory was to hear, to have Julie now confirm to me that my mother had unequivocally known and believed herself to be facing her own imminent death—and the agony of knowing that my mom had continued relentlessly trying to take care of her children by finding them a home of her choice after her death was staggering in that moment—I was also, equally, so deeply stung hearing that my mom had only been concerned with finding a home for "my four younger children."

A month earlier, prior to this conversation, I had spoken with my Buffalo relatives in an effort to bring more clarity to the weeks following my mother's death, and had been told that my parents' relatives had also *not included me* in *their* discussions of what would happen to us five children now that we were my parents' orphans.

In New York State, where my mom and us five children lived at the time of my mom's death, twenty-one was the legal age; I was only nineteen when I was orphaned, so it had still been painful to learn, forty-six years later, that my relatives who were making the decisions about us had not given any thought to my well-being or future. Not all of my older cousins were included in the conversations. Many have said they had no idea talks were in progress. The relatives who can answer those questions as to why I was excluded have died.

As my older cousin had said, "Rosie, honey, I don't know why, but all I know is that whenever meetings were held about what was going to happen to you kids, you were *never included.*"

But this was worse—much, much worse; to learn that my mother herself had not sought a home for me in view of her knowledge of her heartrending, expected death and the undoubtedly catastrophic effect it would have on her five children, as we would become our parents' orphans, without any money or plans in place for our future.

In the deepest place of my heart, where I had relentlessly pursued being healed of so much of my orphan's pain, I had always resisted believing that I had never been my mother's priority. I did not really want to believe that I had not held a position of priority in my mother's life. I resisting believing that I had not been seen as her daughter who should have someone to love me, someone to protect me, and someone to parent me and care about what would happen to me. I resisted believing those facts about the relationship between my mom and me, as I did not want to feel unimportant to the person who I believed should have cared the most about me.

I had wanted—and most importantly, *needed*—to believe that about my mom in my own pressing, incapacitating pain, frozen in my own grief; frozen in my own incapacity to process so much tragedy unfolding in a few short years before my eyes. I had fashioned a set of beliefs portraying my mom and me as not just being close; but I believed I had fashioned a needed set of beliefs showing my mom as not believing me to be important.

I had always thought that in the years following my mother's death, mired in the sadness and overwhelming responsibilities of my four younger siblings, I had manufactured for myself a story of being unimportant to my mom so I could more easily feel sorry for myself as the victim; that I had manufactured my beliefs about my mom and myself so I could have an easy, understandable excuse to not take responsibility for my own actions.

But now, sitting in my quiet, peaceful home, I sat frozen in my fifty-year-old memories as my trusted friend Julie confirmed what I had always known in the deepest, darkest, most scared and sacred part of my heart. It hadn't been a twisted set of circumstances, and my own poor attitude, and a lack of loving communication with my mom that had contributed to this stunning knowledge. I needed to sit with the news, however it stung, that in those last few fleeting months of my mom's ebbing life my feelings from fifty years ago had not betrayed me; the glaring truth, the jarring truth was that I really had not been included as one of my mom's children, and my personal future really had *not* been a consideration of my mom's when she sought a home for her "four younger children" as she bravely faced her death. Julie now was confirming that I had not, at the time I became an orphan and in the years following that monumental event, conveniently manufactured a set of false beliefs that I made up to feel like more of a helpless orphan.

If my mom had ever discussed with me her attempts at finding homes, or her desire to find homes, or her thoughts of what I might do or become, I sure would have remembered *that* conversation.

I had always known, but doggedly and determinedly denied, what I was now hearing from Julie: the truth of my place in our family after my father died.

I take full responsibility for my rude, headstrong, belligerent teenage behaviors that brought this fact to life and probably caused everyone to think that instead of the grieving, heartbroken, orphaned teenager I became upon my mother's death, that I'd be—*somehow, miraculously*—just fine. Maybe it was because I never told anyone how bewildered and horrified and hurt I was by watching both my parents die that they thought I wasn't hurting to my very core and grieving with every breath?

So, these puzzling facts will be laid to rest as another mystery to which I will never know the answer: the mystery of *exactly what* my mom and our relatives thought I was going to do at nineteen, with a ninth grade education, single, and all alone.

This latest news really stung; in a way, I thought the forty-seven passing years since my mom's death had kept me from being hurt. But I was very wrong; wounded places, even those with thick scars, still hurt if you poke them just right.

In the summer of 1972, in my mom's efforts to find a home for her children, she had sought a home for only four of her children. My mom had sought a home for my four younger siblings; I just had not mattered. It had not been important to find a loving, decent home for me, because I was not important.

As I sat in my home, letting this news settle around me, I reminded myself that when I started *Celebrate Recovery* and I learned the need to forgive all involved with my pain, I had promised myself and God that there would never be anything new that I could or would find out—about my family, and their deaths, and my siblings, and my subsequent years—that would push me backwards to those dark places of anger, pain and resentment.

Remembering that promise to myself and to God—my promise made to ensure my own continued healthy, happy, thriving life—I thought through all the facts that I had just heard and learned, including a moment to think about what I did not know until now.

I knew, logically, that my mom may have very well had plans to talk to me about what and where I wanted to go and what I wanted to do—IF her request to Julie's dad, Bob, had been accepted. Perhaps my mom had another family in mind to talk to about me IF her offer to Julie's dad had been accepted.

So, now, upon hearing this brand-new story that occurred 46 years ago, I made a conscious choice to not go backwards, not to go back to those places of feeling sorry for myself which had the potential to make me stuck and morose again. I refused to go back to that soggy, stuck world of "what ifs" and "would've, could've, should've." Instead, I chose to love and appreciate my mom's lion's heart, which enabled her to, with her final breaths, adamantly seek a home for her younger, more defenseless children; to seek a home so her four younger children would not have to run the risk of being split up.

I was proud of my mom's fierce, courageous love for her children—literally using her last dying strength and breath to find a home, so she could die knowing that her and her beloved deceased husband's children were safe and in a good home. I was saddened at the grief my mom must've carried alone when Julie's dad had said he wanted to, but just couldn't, help my mom with her request.

I sat the rest of that evening in my home in Southern California, thinking of my mom and what a sad, sad, tragic last few years my mom endured; years of grief and sadness no mother should have to endure. I was always sad that I wasn't older and couldn't have done more to help her in her tragic last days.

Now, I won't lie to you—to find out the news that I had been left out of my mom's attempt to find a home for my four siblings still really hurt; it really hurt a lot that night. But God already knew about that hurt of being left out of plans for others long before I did, and God had that hurt covered long before I needed that hurt covered.

Because God is a lot like that, I've learned, when God heals our orphan hearts.

My Mom Margie Ann, 22 years old.

My dad building my childhood
"Happy home", Kenmore, New York, 1954

Me & younger brother Peter, Kenmore, New York 1957

Mom's Orange County Register "Get
Well" cards, California 1971

My mobile home trailer while going to school,
food stamps and food banks, 2005, California

My Orange County Food Stamp Card
while in school, California

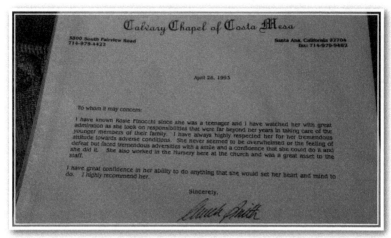

Pastor Chuck Smith, 21 years Letter of
Recommendation, Calvary Chapel, 1993

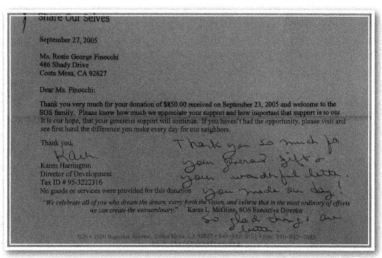

Share Our Selves Food Bank "Thank you" letter, 2005

2017 Master's Degree of Theology and Ministry
Graduation from Fuller Theological Seminary
with Tom Phipps - "Poppa" Since 1972. Met Tom
when 19 years old, 15 days after being orphaned

Me, Speaking at *Celebrate Recovery*, 2018, designed by
St. John's Lutheran Church of Orange Media Team

Me, 19, Legal Guardian to left to right, brothers
Peter 14, John Michael, 10 and Daniel 17. We'd
lost our parents and our sister Lisa, 5, but we were
together again forever. California, June 1973

Younger brothers Peter, John Michael,
me & Daniel, 2017

My baby sister Lisa, 4 years old, 1971,
1 year before taken from us

My baby sister Lisa & I, together again forever, 2018

Chapter 16

"You Will Not Put My Children in Foster Care"

My mom, six weeks before she died. California, 1972

*"Greater love has no man than he lay his
life down for another" (John 15:13).*

I have always felt that if my mother had not died when she did, and in the manner and circumstances that she did, I would not have ever been introduced to Calvary Chapel of Costa Mesa and been given the precious opportunity to rededicate my life back to God—a decision which has made all the difference in the world to me.

I have always felt and known that my mother would have done absolutely anything she possibly could have done for my father and for our family; her love for us was so great.

The memories of my mother's last days are memories of deep sadness, and heart-breaking remembrances of incident after incident of my mom trying desperately to keep our family together and to stretch our limited income from my dad's meager monthly death benefit while she courageously battled her deadly, ever-consuming, weakening, life-draining disease.

Although we liked living in El Toro in south Orange County, California, it was definitely a more expensive place to live. As my mom's health continued its decline the need to move again caught up with us, and we moved once again.

Our last home in California that my mother lived in, before we returned back home to Buffalo in 1972, was in the beachside community of Huntington Beach, California—a town of surfers and miles of pristine white beaches, waves foaming white as they crashed on the beach. The homes were standard middle-class America: neat and tidy, with good schools.

My mom often took us to the beach before she got sick, but now she was restricted to the house, except when we took her to Orange County Medical Center for her cancer treatments.

Daniel, the oldest of my younger brothers and I shared the driving duties to the medical center. Daniel, was very, very good to our mom, and they were quite close, perhaps because she had told him, "You are now the head of the family, since your dad is gone." He was very, very good with our mom and the younger children too. Daniel had always been able to be a great comfort to our mom, and he continued to be one now. My mom would to talk to him a lot about why she felt certain areas were good areas to raise her family, as this was always of great comfort, priority, and importance to our mom.

The long drives to my mom's cancer treatment were always very, very somber drives, as my mother had grown increasingly weak and even walking was very, very difficult for her. Mom would take a few steps hanging onto the countertops, or if we were outside, she would hold onto the car. It was agonizingly slow, and quite painful now, for my mom to get in and out of the car. Every bump in the road brought more pain.

I was to find out later that my mom's breast cancer had aggressively spread to her bones, and bone cancer is such an extremely painful, debilitating cancer.

And so we drove to the medical center and went to the department with the ominous "Radiation Therapy" sign over its equally ominous steel doors. We all knew the kind and sympathetic nurses' and medical assistants' names. They would smile their brightest smiles and sweetly ask how our family was doing. We always smiled brightly and said "fine," and "wonderful," because we knew that if the nurses really knew how scarce our food was, how barely-hanging-on our lifestyle was, then they would be required to report our family to Child Protective Services—and our family had been united in one simple cause since our father died: "It's us against them, and we stay together no matter what it takes."

City of Hope, in Duarte, California, which is also in Southern California, is a state-of-the-art, world-renowned cancer center offering patients cutting-edge new cancer treatments and technology to combat their cancers. City of Hope patients are offered extensive, excellent courses of treatment, often at no cost to the patients themselves. However, a patient must be referred to City of Hope by their personal physician, and after a thorough review of the referred patient's medical records, testing, and latest results, the referred patient must be *accepted* for treatment at the City of Hope hospital.

One day during the summer of 1972, at the Orange County Medical Center which was my mother's normal treatment center, I saw the nurse with my mom and my mom was given a letter. After reading the letter, I saw my mom talking very animatedly with her nurses and her doctors—gesturing, and seeming to plead with them about something I wasn't a party to hearing. The doctor took the letter, placed it in an envelope, and handed the letter back to my mom, who then very quietly went and had her normal radiation treatment.

We drove home in silence, my mother obviously very much lost in thought. Once we arrived home and the other kids were not around, my mom called to me to join her where she was sitting at the dining room table. As I sat at the table I could see that there was a formal letter on the table in front of my mom. My mom's eyes were full of tears as she handed me the letter I had seen earlier in the day at her doctor's treatment department.

Quietly, my mom explained to me that she and her doctors at her normal treatment hospital had referred my mom to the City of Hope for more advanced and aggressive treatment. My mom told me to read the letter, as it was the response from the City of Hope to the doctors' referral of my mom to them. As I silently read the letter from the City of Hope my heart was breaking, knowing that my mother had also had to read this letter.

The City of Hope letter, addressed to my mom's doctors, thanked them for their referral of my mother to the City of Hope. The letter went on to say that it was with deep regret that they were informing my mom's doctors that the City of Hope was not able to take my mother as a patient at this time.

Before I could read any further, tears started to spill down her cheeks as she silently pointed to the next paragraph and quietly said, "Look, Rose Mary, look at *why* the City of Hope said they can't accept me." I looked at the place in the City of Hope's letter where my mother pointed. Tears were still falling from my mom's eyes; I saw why the letter was so upsetting. "We further regret to inform you that we are not able to accept Mrs. Margie Finocchi at this time *given the advanced state of her cancer, as we do not feel our treatment would be of benefit to her.*"

I looked up, my own eyes now full of tears, and silently met my mother's eyes, seeing only fear and sadness. Strangely, seeing the written words of "advanced state of cancer" still didn't register with me to mean that my mother would unquestionably and undoubtedly die. All I comprehended at that moment was that I just knew this was bad, very, very bad, and very, very sad for my mom and for our whole family. My mom and I talked a little while longer, each assuring the other that our family would be okay, and then dinner was made.

There was no further mention to me of either the City of Hope's letter or of its meaning, and not of its consequences.

I still don't know if any of my mom's doctors at the Orange County Medical Center, prior to the arrival of the letter from the City of Hope, had ever had a serious discussion with my mom informing her that her cancer was in an "advanced stage," and what that meant long-term as to the consequences for our family.

Looking back, I can't even fathom how my mom simply stood all this bad news coming at her. In the 1970s, with only regular telephone service, the cheapest times to call back east (eastern time zone was three hours later) were between 11 p.m. at night and before 7 a.m. in the morning. I would wake up several mornings and hear my mom talking to her older sister, my Aunt Connie, but I do not know what those conversations were about—as my mom was always frightened that if people knew how sick she was and how much our family struggled financially, we would be taken away and sent to foster homes. So it's entirely possible that my mom did not tell anyone of her diagnosis of advanced cancer. I know I didn't. I still didn't have anyone to tell or to talk to about my mother's cancer.

Even if I did, I still was not at all cognizant, at that point in the cruel progression of my mother's cancer, that her "advanced cancer" diagnosis meant that the horror was looming once again to eventually strike with certain death now a second time—to take our remaining parent, making us orphans. I had not ever known anyone who had died from cancer. I just thought it meant my mom would be sick forever. My mom would go into the hospital and always come home once she was stronger, so my mom being sick wasn't a death sentence to me.

Perhaps I didn't make the journey of connecting the dots of her "advanced cancer" to my mother's inevitable death because the thought of that occurring after reading the letter from the City of Hope was simply too repulsive and unthinkable for me. How would, or could, I even understand that at any level? I never did grasp the City of Hope's fatal prognosis, but for certain, my dear mother had.

So, after my mother was given the rejection for treatment at the City of Hope, we soldiered on with business as usual. While my personal goal was to keep my promise to my dying father, my mother had one simple over-riding plan and goal each day. My mother continued to drive home what my father used to say to all us kids as we went out to play. "We stay together no matter what it takes" had now become my family's much more serious mantra. We all knew it, and we all lived it. We were determined that we would stay together and were always on guard to not ever let the Orange County, California, Social Services agency of cold, uncaring social workers separate us—at least not if we could help it.

As the weeks passed after the receipt of the City of Hope's letter in late summer, I noticed my mom got noticeably weaker and seemed to move even slower. My mom spent much more time in bed and was awake less and less. I was used to taking care of our home, as was the oldest of my younger brothers, Daniel, so we both just doubled our efforts to take care of everyone the very best we could.

My mom had always had trouble maintaining a lower weight and now suddenly, seemingly without any effort at all, when I took my mom for her cancer treatment at the medical center the nurses started telling me that my mom was losing weight at an alarming rate, as much as six or seven pounds a week. I thought this was scary, and instinctively knew that my mom had suddenly started to get much, much sicker; she seemed to be getting frailer and melting away each morning as I looked at her.

In addition, frighteningly, my mom's already slow walking pattern of movement now included an increasing limp, making it even more painful for my mom to go anywhere or do anything other than to stay in our home in one chair, rarely moving, when she wasn't going to her cancer treatments.

As my mom dutifully reported to her cancer treatment at the medical center each week, what my family didn't know was that my mom's rapid decline was also being tracked for a far more disconcerting reason. But we would soon find out, in the most harrowing fashion.

We had only lived in this, our latest new home in Huntington Beach after our last eviction, for about a month. As my brothers were fifteen and thirteen, they would stay with my mom and my youngest brother Michael, nine, and little sister Lisa, four, if I needed to leave for a short while. It was late summer, and the next-door neighbor's family convinced my mom and me that it would be okay if I went to the local beach, about ten minutes away, for just a couple of hours. Mom agreed and I relented, as I had not been there even once for years since my mom got sick. It was like another world—as if I had discovered the beach for the very first time. I felt so free and refreshed the entire few hours I was gone. I also felt guilty for having left my mom and four siblings alone while I had the first fun I had enjoyed in years, even though I was only gone a couple of hours and was only blocks from our home.

When I returned home a couple of hours later, as we drove up I saw my mom sitting all alone in a lawn chair on the front lawn. Where were my three brothers and little sister? They would not all be in the house or backyard and leave my mom alone out front.

Immediately sensing that something was very wrong, I jumped out of the car and ran to my mom, sitting quietly in her lawn chair on the front lawn. My mom calmly explained to me that while I had been at the beach those few short hours, the Social Services social worker had paid a surprise visit to our home. Finding me gone and deciding my mom was too ill to take care of our family—and also deciding that my brothers were too young to care for the younger children—my three younger brothers and baby sister Lisa had been placed in unmarked police cars and taken to the Orange County Albert Sitton Children's Home, the first step to becoming foster children and then wards of the state.

As I had turned nineteen a few weeks earlier, and legal age in California was eighteen, I had escaped being taken away. Also, because I was nineteen, I decided that my mother and I would go and reclaim our family members, no matter what it took to get them back.

I put my extremely frail mother in our family car, and we drove directly to the Albert Sitton Children's Home where—after hours of my mother and I meeting with official after official, then administrators, and then, finally, many social workers—it was determined that as long as I never, ever again left our family alone at home, I could have my three younger brothers and baby sister released back into my custody. It was made abundantly clear to me and my mother that my younger siblings were being released to me and at any time, if the Orange County Social Services social worker decided there wasn't, in her opinion, adequate supervision or provisions, my four younger siblings would, without warning, again be taken away. The only difference, my mother and I were told before we were allowed to take back custody of my three brothers and my baby sister, was that if my four younger siblings were taken away by the Children Protective Services again it would be permanent, and my four younger siblings would go to foster homes awaiting possible adoption.

Finally, my mom and I had my three brothers and my baby sister Lisa brought out to us, and we were allowed to take them and go home. My youngest brother Curtis John Michael remembers his oldest brother Daniel vigorously kicking the door and yelling at the authorities that he refused to let his little brother be separated from his two big brothers and be taken to another facility. We found out that my three younger brothers, fifteen, thirteen, and ten, had been allowed to stay together in the Child Protective Services Children's Home, but my little sister Lisa, five, had been separated from them and my mom's children had been sent to two separate children's facilities.

I felt horrible and very guilty for going to the beach—the only time I had gone—because this had happened while I was away; I felt especially terrible for Lisa, who was so young. Because she was the only girl, she had been sent off alone and afraid.

When all four children had been reunited with my mother and me, we somberly walked to our family car and I drove home without much conversation, as the day's nightmarish events were still fresh in our minds.

My mother felt betrayed by the medical center where she was receiving her treatment. I don't know the exact details of what the arrangements were, but within a few days my mom had made arrangements for our household belongings to be placed in storage and surprisingly, Uncle Carmen—the uncle who had fought so much with my mother after our father died—had graciously arranged and paid for there to be six immediate airplane tickets waiting at the Los Angeles airport for our family, making it possible for our family to return home to Buffalo once again, now in late summer 1972.

Again, neither I nor my four siblings grasped the seriousness of the situation. The plane that took us back to Buffalo was an American Airlines 747, and we thought it was the most fun ride ever. Having never been on a plane, my brothers and I enjoyed the gigantic open area at the back of the plane where we enjoyed snacks and played games. Even my sister Lisa, aged five, who remembers so little of her days prior to our mother's death, remembers: "I was sitting on a really big airplane with all of our brothers and with you. The boys and you got up and went away for a long time, and I was still sitting in the airplane seat next to Mom. Then you and the boys came back and sat in your seats, and in a little while the airplane landed."

Our plane touched down at the Buffalo airport in the early morning hours on the third week of August, 1972. We had arrived back home once again—this now our family's third return from being in Southern California—hoping again for another round of successful cancer treatment for my mother at Roswell Park Cancer Institute.

Whether it was my dogged determination to believe the best, or being too naïve to understand cancer's deadly progression, I did not have a clue that as our plane's wheels were touching down in the misty, early morning in August 1972, my mother had less than two months to live.

Had I realized that frightening fact, I don't believe there would have been anything I could have done. Perhaps God in His mercy didn't allow the truth of what was about to happen to penetrate my thinking and understanding.

What I did know was that my mother's final act of hope for her five children was to return back to Buffalo, to again seek treatment at Roswell Park Cancer Institute and to surround herself with all of our family's relatives—my father's family and her family—believing they would help her keep us safe from harm.

Up until my recent conversation with Julie Moffatt Meszaros in September 2018, I had always wondered if my mother truly understood the magnitude of her illness and contemplated her death. In so many ways, I had hoped she did not. I can't imagine the unbearable thoughts that would have plagued her as she did realize that she would die soon. How did she prepare herself if she did understand that her life was ebbing away?

She and I never spoke of her illness in ways of finality. We only spoke with hope of when she would come home again. I do hope that my mother was spared the agony my father lived through in his last moments of wondering who would take care of his family.

These remain more questions that I will never know the answers to.

But one fact I know with absolute certainly: my mother never knew or imagined that nobody would take care of me. And of course, neither did I.

But the horror of course knew; it knew my family well.

Because horror is a lot like that, I've learned.

But God already knew the horror's plan and had a better plan for me.

Because God is a lot like that, I was to learn, when God heals our orphan hearts.

Chapter 17

"It's Just You Kids Now; Your Momma's Gone Too"

Uncle Angelo, mom's brother, Buffalo, New York, 1972

*"For thus saith the Lord GOD, the Holy
One of Israel; in returning and rest shall
ye be saved; in quietness and in confidence
shall be your strength" (Isaiah 30:15).*

Our American Airlines 747 jet, carrying my terminally ill mother, with only weeks left to live, myself, and my four younger siblings, touched down at the Buffalo, New York International airport in the afternoon sun of late August, 1972. It was deceptively warm, and we were home again after our family's fourth cross-country trip since my father's death in 1967, four short years earlier.

We all knew, even though we didn't talk about it, that we had come home again to Buffalo for my mom to be treated a second time at the world-renowned Roswell Park Cancer Institute; to find out if the doctors there could again halt the relentless spreading of my mom's cancer and bring her back into a state of remission as they had a few years ago.

I don't know if anyone other than my Uncle Carmen knew we were coming back to Buffalo yet again. From the Buffalo airport we went to my Aunt Anna's home which, ironically, was the home that my mother's parents had owned—and that my mother had grown up in—and that my Aunt Anna now owned.

The six of us waited and waited and waited on Aunt Anna's porch as daylight faded into evening, my mom telling us stories about growing up in the house. I don't think my Aunt Anna was expecting us—she would eventually come home to find my mom and her five children waiting patiently on her porch, with no plan or idea as to what to do next. Making our family's plight even more difficult was the same problem that our family continually faced in Southern California: extremely limited funds for housing and food once a plan was decided upon.

My mom's oldest sister, Aunt Connie, and my mom's youngest brother, Uncle Angelo, and his wife, Aunt Mary, seemed to take over as the planners of what was being done and how. Regardless of who showed up to talk to my mom, I was *never* included in any of the talks or plans for our family. I just found out as we went along.

This was quite a weird change for me, as we didn't have a car in Buffalo and I was completely at everybody's mercy as to what was going on—when for so many years I always at least knew what was going on as well. And us three older siblings would drive my mom to her cancer treatments. Now we were just given often-confusing instructions.

Within a few weeks, our family moved into a town-house in the same suburb where my parents had owned their home. But our situation was very different from when our parents owned their home. Our rented townhouse was furnished with the few extra pieces my Aunt Connie, Uncle Angelo, and other relatives gave to us. My mom had a hospital bed in our dining room because she wasn't able to climb the stairs; also, as she spent all her time now in resting in bed, she would be able to feel more like part of our family, being on the lower level where all our activity was.

There were a couple of folding chairs in the living room to sit on, and we had a couple of twin beds upstairs and a cot for the younger kids.

My friend JoAnn Scinta from long ago in junior high remembers, "You had no living room furniture or dining room furniture, and we could only sit on your mom's hospital bed or at the little kitchen table."

My mom only made it to her first appointment at Roswell Park Cancer Institute and never came back home, as her doctors at Roswell Park deemed her cancer so advanced that she was immediately hospitalized. My mom would call us on the phone from the hospital, and we would all take turns talking to her. She sounded weak and frail.

Sadly, I had such naiveté with the deadly progress of cancer, I didn't know that my mother would not ever come home again; I was used to my mom being hospitalized. She would go into the hospital, get stronger, and then my mom would come back home again. We had repeated this pattern numerous times since my mom had gotten sick. I simply assumed, without talking to anyone, that once my mom got stronger she would return home as she always had. Her hospital bed in our dining room was my constant source of comfort, silently attesting to my belief that my mother would return home as soon as she was strong enough to be at home. Nobody ever told me any differently. Nobody really spoke to me very much about anything, but by this time I had grown very accustomed to my quiet, lonely, sad world, so I never thought anything was amiss.

I would sleep in my mother's hospital bed in the dining room, because we didn't have enough beds for all of us to sleep in. We didn't have any lamps—just whatever overhead light fixtures came with our townhouse.

Once a week, Aunt Connie and Uncle Angelo would come over and bring us groceries. It felt so odd not being in control of everything, but again, I assumed this was all temporary—just until my mother came back home.

In a few weeks September came, and it was time for my baby sister Lisa, five, to start school. My brothers would also be starting at new schools again. I would continue to have my usual routine: stay home during the day, tidy our home—making sure our home would be ready and clean when they all got home from school—and make sure meals were prepared. These had been my normal school day activities for years, the same when my mom was in the hospital as when my mom was home, so this wasn't anything more than business as usual.

There wasn't to be any school shopping; our relatives brought school supplies, and we were all grateful for those.

When I eagerly dressed Lisa in her very best clothes, I already had carefully brushed her very curly hair into ponytails for her first day of school. Lisa was all excited, and so eager to be going to school. I looked at Lisa—so happy, so adorable—and wished both my mother and father could see their little girl all dressed up, smiling, and so excited to be going to school. I watched Lisa board the bus so proudly—such a big girl now. She turned, waving and smiling the whole time. Lisa and Michael would ride the school bus together, but as Lisa was only in kindergarten, she would get back home at noon.

It was really a new experience for me to be at home without anyone there. Lisa had always been there, even if my mom was in the hospital. This new freedom allowed me time to walk around our new neighborhood, and I was able to meet two families across the street. I spent more time with the family directly across the street; their mom was home, and I enjoyed talking to her about everyday things. I still hadn't realized the seriousness of my mother's condition, so I didn't say much about my mom other than that I expected she would be home soon.

I didn't really know the other family—the family in the house across the street to the left—very well at all. I was only in their home a couple of times.

What I did know was that their home always seemed peaceful and calm, and to be filled with an almost palpable golden light, as if sunlight was always streaming through their windows. I felt oddly comforted in their home, and that was a feeling I had not known since my father had died.

In 2018, forty- six years later, I found out their names were Randy and Karen Gallatin. Randy and Karen would prove to be the people that forever changed my life; but this time, my life would change forever for the better.

One treat from moving back to Buffalo—in spite of the dire circumstances—was that we were able to see Aunt Stella and Aunt Dolly. My cousin Clara DeFranscisco and her husband Phil were younger than my parents, but I had spent a lot of time around them when we lived in Buffalo when I was younger, so it was nice to see Clara and Phil's family again. I'd always enjoyed them. I was also able to see my cousins Janice, Bobby, Beverly and her brother Chucky, JoAnn and her sister Anne Marie and their brother Joey. That was the one nice part of being back: seeing my cousins and their families.

My very kind cousin, Joanne Miranda—the one whom I had admired when I was thirteen and staying in her mom's, my Aunt Anna's, home—would come as often as she could to our home, pick me up, and make the long drive to Roswell Park Cancer Treatment Center so I could visit with my mom. Joanne usually took me on Fridays. Joanne would always time our Friday visits so that I would be back at our home before noon, so I'd be there when my sister Lisa got home from kindergarten and later when my three brothers arrived home from their school.

I loved visiting my mom at the hospital—always expecting her to be getting stronger; I grew concerned as my mom seemed each week to be getting weaker and weaker, so much so that we didn't talk a lot. Mainly I would sit by her bed and keep her company while she slept.

I remember that my mom had a Bible sitting next to her hospital bedside tray, and she asked me if I could get a hold of Lois from church and ask her to please come and read my mom's Bible to her. I said I would.

I have relived that conversation over and over, always wondering *why* I didn't just pick up my mom's Bible and read it to her myself. Was I that numb to what was going on around me that I didn't respond to my mom's simple request? Was I already that angry?

I don't know why I didn't read Mom's Bible to her myself, but I didn't—and I still to this very day wish that I had.

What I also didn't know was that when my sister started school and my mother was hospitalized, my mother had less than six weeks to live. Had I known that, I believe I would have told my mom how much I loved her and how brave and courageous I thought she was. I would have told my mother how proud my dad would have been at how my mother had fought so courageously to keep our family together and to make sure we always lived in a good neighborhood. Most of all, I would have told my mom how I wished I had been able to make a difference in all of her suffering. But I never said any of those words.

Perhaps my mom and I respected our private worlds of grief and silence—or rather, because I was so used to not saying anything about what I really felt, I wasn't an easy person to talk to. My mom did enjoy talking to her other children, and I could tell my brothers and my sister were able to comfort my mom just with a few words.

I didn't say any of those words, because I didn't know that the horror was to again show itself in a full savage force, snatching our only remaining parent away from us.

On Friday, my usual visiting day, my sweet cousin Joanne picked me up and we made the long drive so I could visit my mother. The day was October 20, 1972. My mom slept for most of our visit, awakening only long enough for me to tell her how all of the kids were doing. My mom was always pleased to hear her children were doing well; it was the one interest she had left.

My mom had always had really beautiful, long fingernails and was very proud of them. The previous week when I had visited her at the hospital, she had told me that the nurses wanted to cut her fingernails, and she had refused. On this visit with my mom on October 20, 1972, she was even weaker—and I noticed that her beautiful, long fingernails were cut short. Seeing my mom's short, stubby fingernails, I felt such a searing pain for her, as her short nails seemed to symbolize how helpless my mom was in all the crushing circumstances happening to her. I felt so bad for my mom, because her fingernails were the one beautiful thing she still had. Looking down at her hands, lying peacefully yet helplessly against the crisp hospital linens, I knew that my mom's long, beautiful fingernails had been cut against her will. So much kept happening against my mother's will. And I couldn't make it stop.

I remember that when I saw her bluntly cut nails—not even an attempt had been made at filing them—they seemed to emphasize our mutual helplessness.

All my mom had had were her beautiful long nails, and now they were chopped off without any regard for her dignity. I always felt so helpless in all that had happened to our family—and this was a small but significant example, as I imagined my mom begging them to please not cut her nails and being ignored, and her being stripped of yet another choice in her life.

When I visited my mom every Friday, I wish I had been brave enough to speak up and ask questions of her doctors and her nurses, to ask what her condition was; but I wasn't brave, and I didn't ask anyone any questions, and so I never realized just how very frail and ill my mother had become.

When I visited my mother on Friday, October 20, 1972, I noticed a suction machine was by her bed, and it had bothered me deeply; I remembered that in the short time I had worked at a convalescent home when I was sixteen, a suction machine had always appeared shortly before a patient died. But again, I wondered, but was too afraid to ask. And again, I did not connect the dots of my mom's impending death.

My mother was sleeping when it was time for me to say goodbye and leave on Friday, on October 20, 1972. I didn't want to wake my mom, who was usually in such pain and was finally resting peacefully, so I quietly kissed her forehead and went home with my cousin Joanne to welcome the four younger children home from school.

Cousin Joanne called the following week and said that she would not be able to take me that Friday, but that we would go visit my mom another day.

Another day never came, as my mom died on Friday, October 27, 1972—the day I normally would have been there. I believe that God in His mercy did not allow me to visit my mother that particular Friday, thereby sparing me the horror of watching my mother also die in front of me.

Knowing my mother had died was stunning – I knew she was sick but when she died I felt little beyond completely stunned- frozen in the horror that had come to envelope my once happy, joyous family.

My three younger brothers, little sister & I were now five very helpless orphans.

I don't remember who called me; I don't remember what they said. I don't remember the kids coming home from school. I don't remember very much at all, other than the phrase *I am an orphan, we are orphans* kept repeating itself in my head.

Silently, I asked questions to no one in particular. *How had this happened?* My mother's hospital bed was still in our dining room, patiently waiting for my mom to come home. *How could she not be coming home?* How could my mother have had to live out such an extraordinarily sad, sad life, when she had loved my father so much and loved her children so much? My mom had tried so hard, always putting her children and family first; why was she not allowed a tiny bit of joy?

Why did my mother have to die? Why didn't I realize that my mother was dying, so I could have said goodbye? *Why didn't I ask?*

It haunted me for decades after my mother died that I should have found a way to be close to my mother. It equally haunted me that I thought I had not been a good daughter. I so deeply wished I had been both. And there was no way to fix my regrets now, no way now to be close to my mother; no way now to try and be a better daughter.

Now, in place of what I wished I could change was the endless finality of my mother's death accompanied only by merciless grief, pain and more sadness for myself and my remaining, quickly-dwindling family.

Whoever said, "What you don't know can't hurt you," didn't know how wrong they were. Because as horrible as becoming my parents' orphans was, my siblings and I still had each other, and we still had our deceased parents' admonition: "You guys are family, and you stick together; no matter what it takes, you stick together." The problem was that the horror was about to raise its ugly head two more, swift, final, bewildering times. Not satisfied with taking away our parents, it would swiftly take away another family member— the most vulnerable and most defenseless—without consultation with or consideration of any of us, the five people who mattered the most to each other and then split we that remained one final, cruel time.

We were now my parents' orphans, and we were now all we had left of our once happy, thriving family. Just five bewildered, alone, orphans; but we had each other, and we intended to stay that way.

Together.

All five of us siblings.

But the horror had other plans—plans that would soon cut us even further apart, dismantling our family even further; paying no attention to our desperate pleas of protest.

But I didn't have a clue as to this alarming, frightening fact looming in our already unsteady and uncertain future;

yet, had I realized that frightening fact, I would have done nothing different.

Why? Because my mother had, in her final act of love, brought her children back home to her family to be safe— because wasn't *home* where the family that loved you took care of you?

I would soon find that to definitely NOT be the case. At least not for me.

Whether it was miscommunication, or assumptions I was already taken care of, I would discover that the stark reality was: no loving family was waiting for me.

Because horror is like that, I've learned; stealing what we think we already securely have.

But God had another family waiting for me.

His family; a family of His choosing.

Because God is a lot like that, I've learned, when God heals our orphan hearts.

Strangers Miciah & Gretchen Purves who
took me in when homeless, 12 days after
being orphaned. Costa Mesa, CA. 1972

Chapter 18

"If You Don't Have A Home, Call This Number; They'll Take You In"

Randy and Karen Gallatin,
Neighbors, Buffalo, NY, 10 days after orphaned

*"'When did we see you a stranger
and invite you in, or needing
clothes and clothe you?'*

*The King will reply, 'Truly I tell you,
whatever you did for one of the least of
these brothers and sisters of mine, you
did for me'" (Matthew 25:38,40).*

I was two months past my nineteenth birthday. I was now the oldest of my parents' orphans. Our remaining family was me, my three younger brothers—Daniel, the oldest, sixteen, Peter, fourteen, Curtis John Michael, ten—and my baby sister Lisa, still five.

Our dad had died at forty-seven years of age, and now our mom had died at forty-three. Both of our parents had died of natural causes.

My overriding memories of my mom's funeral and the confusing days following are of total numbness, of feeling stunned and overwhelmed. I kept thinking about how my mom had been so overwhelmed, and about how deeply my mom had grieved for my father. I knew my mom had fought so hard for her family, and I knew my mom had done her very best; yet I believed my mom had not recovered from my father's death and returned again to having a vivacious zest and joy of life.

We, my parent's children, had been my mother's pride and joy, and she had fought so valiantly and so hard to give us a good life. How could all of my mother's and father's efforts have come to this? My brothers and sister and I were now my parents' orphans. That fact was frightening and numbing, but I figured I had always known how to take care of my siblings, and I figured I would figure it out as I went along.

And *we would* survive.

My brothers and sister and I would not surrender to the horror that had claimed my parents. We were strong, and we would figure it out. We would find a way to not just survive, but we would find a way to *thrive*; thrive, in spite of all the odds against us. We would thrive again.

After my mom's death, I was aware that both my mother's relatives and my father's relatives were talking with each other regarding what would happen to us kids. I was never included in any talks, meetings, or any planning regarding what was going to happen to us five kids.

Within days—to my surprise—I discovered that in 1972 in New York State, at the age of nineteen I wasn't of legal age to keep my siblings. Legal age was eighteen years old in California and twenty-one years old in New York. *Just great!* I didn't trust my relatives, as I didn't really know them. Not being included in any talks or planning left it difficult for me to trust their judgment. I don't believe they even knew how much I had helped my mom before she died.

This nightmare continued. Things kept just happening without any conversation with my brothers, my sister, and me. We were silent players as events kept unfolding around us.

Within days of being orphaned, I was informed that my sister Lisa, now five and primarily raised by me, was to be "taken" by my Uncle Carmen and his wife, Aunt Toni. My youngest brother, Curtis John Michael, now ten, was also to be "taken" by them. A dinner was held at Uncle Carmen's.

My youngest brother Curtis John Michael remembers, "We were all sitting at Uncle Carmen's table and my two older brothers, Daniel, sixteen, and Peter, fourteen, were vehemently expressing their disapproval and fighting with Uncle Carmen that I was not going to be taken away from my big brothers. They told Uncle Carmen, 'Curtis John Michael is staying with us, not you, Uncle Carmen's family,' and my brothers confidently assured all the adults that I was not going anywhere; I was staying with them, period."

I'm very grateful my brothers Daniel and Peter were successful in keeping our youngest brother Curtis John Michael with us.

We were not so fortunate with our baby sister Lisa, five years old. There was such a whirlwind of instructions from well-meaning people that I didn't even have time to grieve my mom; my remaining family's welfare was all that mattered to me, and attempts to split us up after all we had already endured were particularly heartbreaking to me. And coming from every side, those we trusted to help us find a way that all five of us could stay together disagreed with our ideas and refused to help us in any way.

We were entirely alone in our desire and our fight to stay together.

I thought it was monstrously unfair that a state that did nothing to help us all the years we had struggled in California could dictate our actions to my family, but dictate they could and dictate they did.

It was shocking to me and my siblings that there was no way I could keep my baby sister Lisa, five, as I was not of legal age in New York State; I was not in a legal position to fight for her. My brothers and I were sat down and sternly informed of three salient facts. First, my brothers and I were not allowed to tell our baby sister that she was going to be split off from us, as they didn't want her to be scared. Second, my brothers and I were not allowed to say any kind of good-bye to our baby sister or make any promises that we would see her soon. Because, number three, my Uncle Carmen and Aunt Toni were not going to allow any communication between our baby sister and ourselves as they "wanted Lisa to blend into their family as if she was their daughter, and talking to us would make that impossible."

I was hearing such insanity. My sister wasn't a newborn; she was five years old, with memories of me and her three big brothers. They couldn't just wipe out her family; but they sure intended to try. I was told a day would be arranged to pick Lisa up, and my brothers and I were strictly forbidden to say one single word to her of what a traumatic and sad event waited for her on that day.

On the day chosen for my baby sister Lisa to be forcibly removed from my brothers and me, I felt like I was losing my own child; I had not birthed Lisa, but I had raised her. I had started her in school. I had washed and fixed her curly hair.

I had painstakingly handmade her very first pink baby dress on the sewing machine that my father had bought me and taught me to sew on before he died.

This was cruelty heaped upon cruelty. Unimaginable, even in my worst-case scenario. There was no way I was prepared for this latest horror.

My Uncle Carmen and Aunt Toni arrived as Lisa was getting home from school. Lisa had fallen asleep, and this fit well with their plans to take Lisa away from us and to permanently sever all her communication and ties to our family. My Uncle Carmen scooped up my sleeping baby sister and quickly put her in the back seat of their car. Just as they started their car, Lisa woke up. She became very frightened, and seeing my brothers and me at the curb, she tried to get out of the locked car as my uncle pulled away. My last memory of my baby sister Lisa was of her crying hysterically at the back windshield of my uncle's car, desperately hitting the window to try and get back to us.

I stood at the curb long after my uncle's car was out of sight, knowing that I was failing everybody that mattered to me, failing everyone I loved.

That appalling memory would remain stubbornly burned in my brain as I would not see Lisa nor be allowed to have any communication with her at all for many years, exactly as my uncle had planned. When I thought of Lisa, in spite of my attempts to summon my sister's and my happier memories, that horrible scene at the curb—my baby sister crying in my uncle's rear window as he drove away—always surfaced first, and it was always accompanied with my sinking feeling that I was indeed failing everyone.

As I was writing this book my sister Lisa, now a grandmother, and I spoke of what little memories she has of those years. As I mentioned how she was forcibly taken from our family, my sister suddenly shrieked, "Wait! Stop! You mean that really happened to me?"

When I assured her that yes, it had really happened, she quietly said, "I always had a kind of cloudy scene in my head where I'm crying and looking out the back window of a car as it drives away, and I see you and I'm trying to get to you, and I can't stop crying and I can't get out. All these years I've always thought that was a dream I must've had and remembered."

There was a long pause before my sister Lisa said, with as much sadness as I've ever heard her express, "Rosie, you mean that did happen to me—I didn't just dream all that? It really did happen to me?"

Equally as sad, I assured my sister, "Yes, honey, you didn't dream all that—it all really happened to you, and to me, and to your brothers."

Even fifty years after the fact, I still felt just horrible as my sister Lisa learned these new facts about the horror of the circumstances surrounding her being orphaned at five years old and ripped from her family through no fault of her own.

The tsunami of crushing blows continued. Without time to catch our breath at losing our baby sister, my brothers and I were informed that our uncle, who now lived in San Francisco, would fly to Buffalo, and that after the proper papers were signed he would take us back to San Francisco to live with him and his new wife and her six kids.

Again, there was no discussion with my brothers and me; just instructions given.

We had been orphans for less than a week, and we had already lost our baby sister. We were down to just my three younger brothers and me.

It couldn't get any worse, I thought; but of course, it was better that I did not know how much worse my life was really about to become.

In a whirlwind, our San Francisco uncle arrived and the New York family court awarded him custody of all of four of us; I was nineteen years old, Daniel, was sixteen years old, Peter was fourteen years old, and Curtis John Michael was only ten years old. Curtis John Michael had been especially close with our little sister Lisa, five, and so losing her was very difficult for him. It was horrific for us all.

The New York State family court made the decision that it was cheaper to fly my brothers and me *back* to California, rather than to pay for four foster children if placed in the New York State foster system. As bewildering as this unsettling, rapid course of behavior was, at least there would be no further splitting up of my three brothers and me; or so I thought.

In two days, I would learn within minutes of my arrival in California how very wrong I was in thinking that my welfare actually mattered.

Although my San Francisco uncle testified under oath to the New York State family court that I'd live with him, unbeknownst to me my uncle had no intention of giving me a home. None at all. I never knew why, and neither did anyone else I asked; I assumed it had been his new wife who did not want me as my Uncle had always been very kind to me and my family.

All I knew was this: no home for me, and separation from my younger brothers. But God already knew.

A Bible verse I came to live by is: "When my Mother and Father forsake me, then the Lord will gather me up" (Psalm 27:10).

We had been renting for less than six weeks when my mom died. Now, in 2018, after searching for 46 years, I have discovered that Randy and Karen Gallatin were the family across the street who always seemed so different. I didn't know them well, but their home seemed to be filled with a soft, golden light and there was a joy, a kindness, and a calmness always present, even when nothing was being said. I always felt oddly comforted in their home—a feeling I remembered, *but wasn't used to.*

A few days before we were flown back to California, I went over to Randy and Karen Gallatin's home across the street to be polite and say goodbye. They'd always been so kind. As I said goodbye and thanked them for their kindness towards me, Karen gently handed me a piece of paper and said, "I know you're from Southern California. If you ever don't have a place to go, call this number; it's my family, I've told them about you, and they'll take you in."

Little did I know that I was about to learn what homelessness was. New York State put my brothers and me on an airplane and *launched us out of their hair.* My sister Lisa now always says, "Somewhere in the clouds, between New York and California, you magically came of legal age crossing the country in that airplane."

Meeting me at the airport in San Francisco, my uncle said, "You're of age in this state. You don't get any social security money, and you're not staying with me. I'm taking you to your aunt's house." I was driven from the San Francisco airport to the unknown aunt and uncle's home. I never spent a second at my San Francisco uncle's home.

It is interesting how extreme grief steals our voice as I did not protest when I wasn't allowed to speak to my brothers about this latest separation and loss as in less than a week, as my sister was forcibly removed from me. I was now separated from my three younger brothers after being *promised* in Buffalo, New York before we had boarded the plane, that we would all be kept living together in my Uncle's home once we arrived in San Francisco.

Another stunning unexpected blow.

Forty six years later, upon writing this book, my three younger brothers have each told me separately they thought I chose to not stay with them and had they known I was forced out on my own they would have objected.

I had now been separated from my three younger brothers without getting to talk to them and tell them that I was not allowed to stay with them at my San Francisco uncle's home. My unknown new aunt and uncle were both alcoholics with fighting adult children who made it immediately clear that there was no home for me there. I felt so lost. I felt so alone.

I took out my little folded slip of paper, walked to a pay phone, and called that number. In Matthew, Jesus speaks of showing kindness, saying, "For when I was a stranger, you took me in." When the disciples ask, "When did we see you a stranger and take you in?" Jesus says, "For when you have done this unto the least of these, your brethren, so you have done it unto Me." I definitely qualified as "the least of these" at that time.

This was my lowest point. I vividly recall dialing that phone number—standing on a dusty, noisy street, dejected, rejected, bewildered, alone, overwhelmed, unloved, orphaned, a high school dropout, and now separated from my four siblings. I was broke, with the knowledge that nobody really cared at all what would happen to me. Nobody really cared where I would sleep and what, if anything, I might eat. My wonderful childhood seemed to have all been a long-ago dream; truly another life. Was there ever another life, where I was adored and happy? Had it even been *real?*

I stood on that dusty street, listening to a far-away stranger's phone ringing. My mother had died less than two weeks earlier, making me an orphan. I had stopped going to church as my mom got sicker. This was 1972, and the Jesus hippie movement was in full force in California. You can imagine that I did *not* fit into the hippie category.

The phone was answered with an exuberant young women's voice joyfully ringing out the phrase of the day: "Praise God!" I can still hear it! "Praise God!" *Nothing else!*

I was standing on that dusty San Francisco street corner thinking, *Oh? Seriously? Seriously?* This was *just great!*

Such was my introduction to a young family from Calvary Chapel of Costa Mesa, Miciah and Gretchen Purves, who took me in, a total stranger. I rededicated my life to God and entered an entirely new world, fascinated—and I still am—by studying the Bible.

Calvary Chapel Pastor Chuck Smith and his wife Kay, Chuck's personal secretary Mary Wiley, and the family of Tom and Teri Phipps became my family and gave me something I had never known since my dad died: stability—feeling cared for and loved.

In the previous two short weeks my mother had died, my baby sister Lisa whom I had raised was forcibly taken from me, and I had been lied to and separated from my three younger brothers.

What had once been my parents' loving family of seven, had quickly dwindled and become just me, all alone, homeless and scared.

Decades later in speaking to relatives, I would find out that without today's easy means of communication, not all of my Buffalo relatives had known what had happened to me.

Perhaps I could have found a way to call them; in New York, I'd need a Legal Guardian and maybe I didn't think anyone would do that for me. Perhaps I didn't want to abandon my brothers, now living in San Francisco, by going east, where painfully, I knew I could have no contact with my little sister Lisa, only five, whom I deeply loved and dearly missed.

It was all so very confusing.

I was nineteen years old. Had I ever had a picture-perfect, wonderful life?

Now, I was all alone, a tenth grade dropout, penniless. Yet these total strangers—Miciah and Gretchen Purves, with four young children under the age of five: Tina, Jessie, Holly, and Caleb; a young Jesus movement couple who deeply loved God—joyfully welcomed me into their home unconcerned, allowed me to sleep on the couch in their six-month-old son Caleb's room, and heaped on me the loving care I was starving for and had almost forgotten did exist.

I was about to find out that God was capable of loving me and bringing about a plan and a purpose in my life that would astound even me.

But God is a lot like that, I've learned, when God heals our orphan hearts.

Chapter 19

My Brothers Are Back. I Only Have Plan A, and $384 in Monthly Wages

"When God guides, God provides."
Pastor Chuck Smith,
Calvary Chapel, 1972

I'd never even heard about the Southern California hippie "Jesus Movement," and now that I was plunked down smack in the middle of it, I wasn't sure I even liked it. If it was possible, *these* Jesus people were *even more different* than I was! Downright weird, in my opinion.

Yet?

Yet, there was that same comforting, soothing, calming, and loving feeling I'd experienced in my New York neighbors Randy and Karen Gallatin's home. The woman whose little slip of paper with a stranger's phone number on it had started me on this strange journey to unknown people in unknown places, landing me back in Southern California; except I was completely alone, penniless, and bewildered about what to do next.

There was an imposing large circus tent demanding attention. A circus tent! I can't even recall if I'd ever even gone to a circus. What in the world was it doing next to a modest church building in the midst of acres of strawberry fields?

My life was getting progressively weirder, in my opinion. But my opinion was all I had left—so with a suspicious mind, I warily entered the world of the "Jesus Movement" hippies who had found God and celebrated their granola and macramé baskets along with their bare feet and weird, non-traditional ways. But I certainly couldn't deny that there was *something* there. They sure did seem genuinely happy. I surely wasn't anywhere even close to happy.

As bewildered and crushed as I felt, having been forcibly separated from all four of my younger siblings within ten days of being orphaned, I still needed to find a way to just survive.

Within a few days of arriving as a stranger at Miciah and Gretchen Purves' doorstep, a friend of Gretchen's helped me obtain a minimum-wage job at a feather factory plant, making artificial plant arrangements using dyed feathers. I made $1.65 per hour, and I was the only assembly-line worker who didn't have a green card and who had been born in America. At the end of each day I was covered in glue and green feathers. I was so grateful to have a job—any job. A job would always become my launching pad to a better life.

Additionally, as Miciah and Gretchen Purves lived across the street from the sprawling grounds of Calvary Chapel where several daily Bible studies were held each day, I was able to quickly find work as one of the church nursery workers. Tom Phipps ran the nursery and was my supervisor when I became a nursery worker for the two-year-olds.

I would work all day at the feather factory, and in the evenings I would work at the church nursery. As I worked at the nursery I got to know Tom Phipps, who was a very kind, fun man. Tom was very organized and very kind to all of us nursery workers. Tom knew that I lived across the street from the church in the Sunflower Apartments, as I would walk back and forth to work. I got to know Tom's oldest daughter, who was close to my age. I hadn't had a friend in a long time, and his daughter was fun.

One evening, Tom asked if I was available to babysit as he was taking out one of the church members, Teri, and she had two small boys. I said yes, and his daughter Cindy Alderson, a sweet teenager close to my age, also babysat with me.

I was fascinated by Teri, as she knew the names of plants, ate granola, lived the Bible, and went to potlucks with a whole circle of girlfriends. Coming from the last five years of constant evictions and moving, I had not had a plant since my dad died. Teri was very creative in both her cooking and her decorating, and I loved babysitting for her because I could read all her books—which I did the moment her sons, Darin and Jason, fell asleep.

Tom and Teri continued to date, and every week I continued to babysit for them. I also continued to meet more friends through Gretchen and Miciah Purves and others at Calvary Chapel church. Tom and Teri decided to marry—and as I did not have any money at all to buy an appropriate gift, I decided to be very creative and gave Tom and Teri a gift certificate for one free year of babysitting.

Little did I realize at the time that my gift to Tom and Teri Phipps on their wedding day was actually a gift to myself of something I desperately needed. For in giving Tom and Teri a year of free babysitting, I unintentionally ensured for myself a whole year of being loved by Tom and Teri. Tom and Teri simply loved me in ways that made me feel that I was genuinely cared about and that I belonged. While Tom and Teri knew I was orphaned, they did not know how recently it had occurred, nor did they know any but the smallest, most basic details. Everything since my dad's death had been just too horrific to talk to anybody about. I just stayed quiet. It never did any good to complain.

With the Gretchen and Miciah Purves and Tom and Teri Phipps families, it was nice to laugh again. It was nice to be able to plan on the simplest events and know I could follow through with my plans. I still felt immense sadness and grief at being orphaned and at the disillusionment over being separated from my siblings, but at least I knew I was loved by stable families who really did seem to have my best interests as heart, which felt good after so much chaos.

At this time in 1972, I had no communication with my two older living half-brothers. They had both always been loving and kind, wonderful big brothers, but I hadn't seen them in years as they were living their lives and I did not know how to contact them. When I did reconnect with them years later, I was delighted to have my big brothers again in my life and continued to love and adore them as I always had.

Living in Southern California in 1972, we didn't have access to the types of communication we have now, and so I had extremely limited communication with my younger bothers. Any communication with my baby sister Lisa was completely forbidden, exactly as I had been told when she was forcibly taken from me. I did not have any contact with any of my Buffalo relatives, as it did not occur to me to try and contact them for help. As the majority of my life had been spent in Southern California, except for the few short months while my mom was sick, I didn't realize that if I had told my east coast relatives what was happening, it is likely that my aunts, uncles, and older cousins would have reached out and made arrangements for me to go back to Buffalo, and I would have been helped by them.

Perhaps, in retrospect, I unintentionally still believed my mom's instructions to not let people know how badly I was doing. I knew I couldn't see my sister, and I knew I did not want to leave my brothers; I would then be further abandoning them if I were given an opportunity to go back to Buffalo. Additionally, if I returned to Buffalo, I would need a Legal Guardian. I don't remember why I told no one I was now homeless. Perhaps I was still too stunned and exhausted at losing all my siblings to two different home coupled with the reality of being orphaned.

Soon, Gretchen and Miciah Purves presented me with an older, basic car, and I was astounded at their generosity towards me—plus, I was so happy to have a way to get from place to place. The very first weekend after I was given my car, I drove straight to San Francisco to see my three younger brothers.

While I remain grateful that my uncle took my brothers into his home—saving my brothers from possible further separations—I was saddened by the conditions I saw. Unlike my Uncle's clean, organized home in Buffalo, this home seemed very chaotic with his six step-children and my three brothers. My three brothers were not living in his main home; instead there was a very small, cramped, tiny camper trailer in his backyard, and that was where all three of my brothers lived. The two older of my younger brothers had each other and could go do things together, but I felt especially bad for my youngest brother Curtis John Michael, as he now seemed withdrawn and quite. The pants he had on were several sizes too big for him, and there was a ragged, scuffed-up bottom on each pant leg instead of a neat hem, as someone had cut the bottoms off of Curtis John Michael's pants instead of having them properly hemmed. Not my fastidious uncle I used to know. I don't know why things were so bad, all I knew was I hurt for what my youngest brother was experiencing.

My brothers and I were ecstatic to see each other, and we enjoyed our weekend together. Oddly, we did not talk at all about being orphaned and having our baby sister forcibly removed from us.

It would be almost fifty years before my siblings and I would be able to speak to each other about the horror we had lived through, and the price that horror had exacted from all of us.

When Easter vacation came a few months later, the two older of my younger brothers hitchhiked the nearly eight-hour drive, covering 425 miles, to visit their friends in the little town of El Toro, where for a short time we had been more like a traditional family before my mom's cancer had returned to take her from us. I enjoyed seeing my brothers during that visit.

In early June of 1972, orphaned now eight months and still in quite a tailspin with all the unexpected forcible separations, I continued to work at the minimum-wage feather factory with the green-card, Spanish-speaking employees. And in the evenings and weekends I worked as many hours as I could at the Calvary Chapel Costa Mesa Church nursery, making $2 an hour. Every Friday evening I had the luxury and joy of babysitting for Tom and Teri Phipps, to allow them to use my wedding gift of one year of free babysitting. I continued to bask in their genuine love of God and their genuine, healing love of me.

Coming out of church in June of 1972, I found my three younger brothers and my San Francisco uncle in the church parking lot; each brother was quietly standing there holding two paper bags of clothes each. My San Francisco uncle said, with much distaste, "You want your brothers, you've got your brothers. Here, take them, they're all yours."

I had not been called, consulted, or notified in any way—just again "informed," the way I had kept getting informed of each major life-changing event in my life since my father had died five short years earlier.

I was to find out from my brothers decades later that they had planned, in their youthful resolve, to hitchhike back to Southern California when school was out. So, we all assume now that those intended travel plans were the reason why my uncle dumped my brothers at my church parking lot without consulting or informing me. Additionally, I don't imagine it was very easy for my San Francisco uncle to be managing his own home with a total of nine children—the majority of which were lively, hormone-racing teenagers.

While not a wealth of money by any means, my brothers did receive a meager death benefit from my father; it totaled less than $300 a month for the three boys.

When my San Francisco uncle dropped my brothers at my church parking lot, he refused to give me any money at all from my father's death benefit that was intended for their support.

I know my uncle's new wife had six children of her own—all teenagers except for one, and of course teenagers are expensive—but I was nineteen years old, working two minimum wage jobs and renting a room in a mobile home park from a church friend. I did not have any money, place, or means to care for my three siblings, aged seventeen, fifteen, and ten years old. I felt that old sinking, no-choice feeling I always felt when the responsibilities of my parents' children fell squarely on my young shoulders; there simply wasn't anybody else. If there was, I didn't know who that person was.

As I mentioned, there are questions in my story that will not ever be answered as the people involved have died, and no one else knows the answers to my painful questions.

For whatever reason, my San Francisco uncle and new wife not only refused to give me any of our father's death benefit money that he had received that month—and which rightfully belonged only to my three brothers—but he and his new wife continued to keep the next six months of my father's death benefits for himself and his new wife's family, even though my brothers were with me in Southern California. My uncle had always been so kind towards me and my family, I was very confused by this action.

In retrospect, maybe if I had notified the Social Security Department that I now had physical custody of my three brothers, they would have stopped payments to my uncle's family. But at nineteen years old and with no understanding of how the administration of their funds worked, I did not know what to do except to figure out it out.

Taking care of my three younger brothers would be business as usual. I set about immediately to find a place to live for the four of us and to figure out how to pay for a home, utilities, school expenses, and food for our family.

When my San Francisco uncle abruptly dropped my brothers off without notice seven months after we were orphaned, it never, never, *never* in my thinking *ever occurred to me to call social workers* and ask the obvious, glaring question: "Exactly what am I supposed to do with these three orphaned brothers who just showed up?"

I was still nineteen years old, still with a ninth grade education and two minimum wage jobs; now I had three extra people to support all alone. So, I got three more part-time jobs. I now worked one full-time job with medical benefits for my brothers, and four part-time jobs—often overlapping, with little to no sleep. Both Peter and Curtis John Michael remember, "You were always gone working, one job or another, always gone working."

Two of my brothers were aged seventeen and fifteen, and I enrolled them in Estancia High School. Pastor Chuck Smith of Calvary Chapel gave my youngest brother Curtis John Michael, age ten, a full scholarship to the church's Maranatha Christian Academy so he could attend a private Christian school.

I found a small one-bedroom apartment in Costa Mesa, across the street from a convalescent hospital. The apartment property manager was also the director of nursing for the convalescent hospital and gave me a job as a nurses' aide. The apartment rented for $200 a month, and I made $66 a week at the convalescent home; my take-home amount after taxes was $53.75 a week. I earned another $30 a week working four days a week at the church nursery. My total income was $384 a month, and the apartment with utilities was $250 a month. Somehow, I had to make this work; there was no Plan B. I had Plan A—and only Plan A—which was me taking care of three siblings while making $384 a month.

The next years would prove to be the most challenging of my life. My brothers were aged seventeen, fifteen, and ten, and their ability to have a home and be able to function in school was up to me alone.

All I knew with 100% certainty was my parents were gone and my baby sister had been forcibly taken from me. My brothers *had* been taken away and placed in foster care for one day while my mother had still been alive and whatever it took, I was certain no social worker was ever going to take my brothers away from me again.

I had a strict food budget and if I spent one penny over my budget, food items were returned to the shelves from my basket.

I was used to young parents at church talking about how broke they were, and I was also used to not whining and complaining—so I never told anybody how incredibly broke we were and that there wasn't enough money left for food. I became extremely creative with money and food.

There was no choice, and my family deserved my best efforts to give them the life I believe my parents would have made for them.

Even though I was nineteen years old and of legal age in California, I needed the Santa Ana Family Superior Court to award me sole legal guardianship of my three younger brothers so that I could enroll them in school and see to their medical needs. The California courts had a law that there must be seven years between the legal guardian and the person they were the legal guardian of. Due to this law, I needed to appear before the court seven different times before they would finalize the court order.

While continuing to petition the Family Court to appoint me to be my brothers' Legal Guardians, I was unexpectedly told by my San Francisco uncle that he would not send me any of my deceased father's monthly Social Security death benefit of $300 that was for the care of my three younger brothers until I became their court-appointed Legal Guardian. My uncle gave me no explanation for his decision. This was shocking to me, as I had full physical custody of my three younger brothers with no more help from or contact with this uncle and his new wife.

It remains a mystery to me why our San Francisco uncle and his new wife's six children received—and spent—my deceased father's Social Security death benefits meant for my three younger siblings for those six months. Our uncle and his new wife, kept and spent my brothers' money for the six months it took me to convince the California State family court that there simply was no one else who could be legally responsible for my three younger brothers. It was brutally emotionally hard and physically exhausting trying to figure out each day how to make this work and avoid being reported to Social Services for not providing a proper home and adequate food for my family. I lived with fear of losing my younger brothers and exhaustion of working so much. Although the older brothers were more self-sufficent, the hard reality was they could just as easily be scopped up and taken away from me if I was reported to social workers if they were even one day short of being 18 years old.

Each of the seven court appearances ended with the same judge saying, "There *must* be someone else who can be legally responsible for these kids." Finally, with all three younger brothers in the courtroom the judge admonished my brothers, saying, "I don't like doing this and I don't want to do this. But it appears to this court that there is no one but your nineteen-year-old sister who can take you. I promise you, if I get one single report of any of you getting in trouble or being a problem in school, I'm having you picked up and you're going back into the foster care system."

Finally, the judge spoke the words I had fought so hard to hear: "This court appoints Rose Mary George-Ann Finocchi as sole Legal Guardian of the three minors in the Petition before the Court. It is so ordered."

And so the judge finalized his order. I had to buy a bond for $240 to ensure that I would take proper care of my brothers. I had finally succeeded in finding a way to keep part of my promise to my dying father, made six years earlier.

I was now the court-appointed sole Legal Guardian of my three younger brothers, Daniel, aged seventeen, Peter fifteen, and Curtis John Michael, aged ten.

I was still nineteen years of age. I still had only a ninth grade education. But I had three of my deceased parents' children legally and permanently with me, and they were never going to get taken away and separated ever again by anyone. We were family, and we would stay family. I would see to that no matter what I needed to do and how many jobs I needed to hold.

In 1972—months after being orphaned and homeless, when my San Francisco uncle had dropped off my brothers at my church parking lot—my life became extraordinarily hard, but I never said anything to anybody, because it really was what I had always done: kept my promise to my dad to take care of our family.

I had no choice, and I was as determined as I could be that while we did not have an easy life, my brothers were going to get to attend school and be allowed to graduate from high school. I felt great pride when my brothers began to take part in traditional high school sports and activities and made friends.

But there was always one relentless question I faced each day: *exactly how do you feed, clothe and properly care for three teenage boys on $384 a month?*

I continued to work full time for minimum wage at the nursing home, and nights and weekends in the church nursery another twenty hours. I babysat and gave guitar lessons. With such low wages and growing teenage brothers, I felt so bad that I did not do a better job of providing for my brothers. They never, ever complained, and the two older boys eventually were helpful in getting part-time jobs. Both of my brothers got part-time jobs at Burger King, and I was secretly relieved that they were allowed to eat the food there, as my efforts barely kept up with their teenage boys' appetites.

Although I was now only twenty years old, I was always so exhausted; I never told anyone—just did what I had always done: figured out how to pay our rent, keep meager food on our table, and keep my brothers in school.

Daily, I continued feeling overwhelmed and feeling ill-equipped. But I kept on keeping my promise to my dad. My brothers were teenagers, and my endless seven days a week of work was very, very hard.

We just scraped by—always out of money, never an extra dollar, eating the famous Kraft orange macaroni and cheese, which I made with buttermilk because I did not have enough money to buy both milk and butter. I also made use of ramen noodles and powdered milk.

My best surprise was to discover that the Chef Boyardee homemade pizza box had a 25 cent coupon on the back, so I would carefully count my pennies and buy one box of Chef Boyardee pizza and cut out the 25 cent coupon and repeat the same process day after day, for months on end. I would also buy a potato, cut it up, and cook it with the tiniest amount of precious milk and serve potato soup. I bought powered milk and would mix it with a small amount of real milk to try and mask the taste, but my brothers always hated the powered milk.

I made Hamburger Helper endlessly, always using less ground hamburger than needed and stretching the finished dish by adding more noodles. I would make large pots of stew and spaghetti and also made homemade bread by hand as there were no bread machines then. I always made two loaves of white bread and two loaves of wheat bread each week. I would buy enough bananas for each brother to have three a week, and when the bananas kept disappearing earlier than planned I took a pen and labeled each banana with each brother's name and wrote #1, #2, and #3 directly on the banana skins.

Our friend Steve Hernandez remembers my brothers as always being hungry, and me trying so hard to find creative ways to feed them with our meager funds. Steve remembers I would make large quantities of spaghetti and meatballs and invite all their high school friends over and have everyone sit at our table and say grace.

Steve laughs, remembering, "You wanted so much to have a traditional family atmosphere, and you would ask one of us to say grace. We were teenage boys and we felt awkward saying grace, but you insisted, so we always said 'Rub-a-dub-dub, thanks for the grub, amen.'"

I preferred my brothers' friends to hang out at my house because I knew what was allowed, and so did my brothers. Steve also recalls, "Everybody hung out at your house because you were always gone working, but we knew you were strict. We always washed our cars with your bathroom towels and you'd get really mad because you said it cost money to launder the towels. One time we were hanging outside after 10 p.m., and after 10 p.m. if we had the music on in our cars outside your neighbors would call the police. We saw lights up the street and someone said, 'It's the police.' As the car got closer, another friend said, 'No! It's worse! It's Rosie!'"

I did apply for Food Stamps but was told I made $10 too much a month to qualify. I guess they didn't know how much teenage boys eat. It didn't occur to me to quit one of my part-time jobs and collect the food stamps instead of working.

We were so poor, I'd come home to find bags of groceries and dollars tucked in our apartment door. My brother Curtis John Michael remembers the wobbly two and a half chairs and tiny table and my little rabbit purse people would sneak money into. I did not let my east coast relatives know how desperately poor we were and how hard this was for me. I was too afraid of losing my brothers again to tell anyone how hard it was. I couldn't take a chance of losing my brothers again.

I received no financial help from anyone—it was just me, working and raising the kids as best I could while still a teenager myself. Jobs are not real great with a ninth grade education and zero skills, but the kids all knew the Lord. Tom and Teri, who continued to love me as my spiritual parents, continued to provide a constant source of love and caring, yet I never told even them—or anyone—how exhausting and hard it was.

One very bright spot of those very difficult, extremely poor years was that I learned to trust God for money.

It wasn't that I was trying to test God; it wasn't that I was trying to be super spiritual and holy. I did not have a choice. We were always out of money, and we were usually out of food.

So, I would wait for God to provide—and He always would, often in funny ways.

One evening, I did not have any money for dinner other than a potato. A friend of my brothers' came by and said that he had left his book in his locker at school, and if I could drive him there, just a few miles away, he would give me $5! I was elated! My brothers had food when I came back after driving him to get his homework from his locker.

My younger brothers finished high school, yet I kept trying to make up for them being orphaned—feeling like I had not done a very good job of teaching them successful life skills, as I didn't have those skills myself.

I never dated, I never went anywhere, and I did not have any hobbies. It had been a decade since I had ice skated. All that my brothers and our friends remember about those years is how much I was always working. I had to carry my Guardianship Order with me, because when I would go to the high school to get my brothers for a doctor's appointment I would get asked for my hall pass—the high school would think I was one of their students. I was able to get my brothers free basic dental work at the local dental clinic for financially challenged families, but since the free dental work was only for children under eighteen, my teeth got brushed by me, I never saw a dentist.

In response to the relentless stress, instead of gaining fifty pounds as I did when my father died, I gained another seventy pounds—now weighing close to 260 pounds.

My brothers and I still had not been allowed to speak one single word to my baby sister Lisa, whom I had raised, since the autumn day in 1972 when she was forcibly removed from our family, days after my mother had died and we were orphaned.

In August of 1974, I finally turned the magical age of twenty-one years old; twenty-one years old was the magical age, because New York State had mandated twenty-one years of age as its legal age.

I was now twenty-one years old, and I was going back to Buffalo, New York, to reclaim my baby sister Lisa, now seven years old.

My decision to go back to Buffalo to try and reclaim my sister Lisa would play out as one of the most painful periods of my life—for her and for me—because the horror was still functioning in my family, unabated.

And horror is still a lot like that, I've learned.

But God still continues to work in the midst of our great pain with great gentleness and tender, loving care and mercy.

Because God is like that, when God heals our orphan hearts.

Chapter 20

"I'm Twenty-one Now, and I Want My Little Sister Lisa Back"

Me, back in Buffalo, New York.
1974, three weeks after I turned 21 years old

*"What shall we do for our sister in
the day when she shall be spoken
for?" (Song of Solomon 8:8).*

"I'm twenty-one, and I want my sister back."

To say that my Uncle Carmen and Aunt Mary were furious is an understatement.

I was now twenty-one years old, the age at which New York State considered me to legally be an adult. That meant that I could be legally responsible for another person. And the person I fully expected and wanted to be legally responsible for was my baby sister Lisa, now seven years old. My Uncle Carmen had made good on his word not to allow me any contact with my sister, and that did not sit well with me. In addition, I had found out that when it had not worked out for my sister Lisa to remain at my Uncle Carmen's home, he had—without notifying me—sent my sister to live with his oldest sister, our Aunt Mary. They had one daughter, Rosemary, who was about twelve years old. The problem was, our Aunt Mary was well-known to be the crazy aunt, always yelling and screaming, and I believed her to be physically, verbally, and emotionally abusive to my sister Lisa.

In order to reclaim my sister Lisa, I would need to take my Aunt Mary to New York State Family Court and break their current order of her Legal Guardianship of my sister. I was unsuccessful in communicating with my Uncle Carmen. I was able to contact my mom's oldest sister, my Aunt Connie, and she agreed we could all come back to Buffalo and stay at her home while I tried to get my sister back.

Once again, my brothers and I packed our suitcases on the west coast in Southern California, put them in my car, and made preparations to return to Buffalo, New York, on the east coast. We were determined to reclaim our baby sister Lisa, now seven years old, and reunite our siblings. We had not had any contact at all with our baby sister in any form. What my brothers and I lacked in understanding the formidable resistance we would face in Buffalo, New York was made up for by our sheer determination to get our baby sister reunited with us.

My youngest brother Curtis John Michael was the only one of my three brothers who would need to be enrolled in school once we were living at my Aunt Connie's home in Buffalo. The plus of the move back to Buffalo would be to see our relatives on our mom's side, as many of them still lived in Buffalo. None of us thought it was odd that we had given up our nice, comfortable Southern California home to reclaim our sister Lisa in Buffalo, New York. Lisa was our sister, and Lisa belonged with us, as a family.

There was no debate or arguments. We were 100 percent in agreement from the moment I told my brothers what I was doing. As my two older brothers were done with high school, I gave them the choice to remain in Southern California if they wanted to live with their friends or their friends' families. They both wanted to go with Curtis John Michael and me back to Buffalo.

My brothers and I thought that we would have a better chance of getting our baby sister returned to our family if all four of us appeared in front of the New York Family Court judge and requested that our remaining family be reunited with our last and youngest sibling.

In expectation of spending the winter in Buffalo and to further my efforts to get Lisa back, I had purchased— for me at that tenuous time, very expensive—steel-studded, steel-belted radial tires. My previous experiences in buying a "new" tire had been begging tire establishments to sell me the old tires they were removing from a customer buying new tires. The tire store would sort through the discarded tires of customers who had bought new tires to find the tire with the most tire tread left and *sell* it to me for $15. Before I bought my brand-spanking new snow tires, I had never bought more than one tire at a time—and I'd never replaced a tire without seeing the tire tread steel and white threads showing through in multiple patches, or having a flat tire from the perilous condition of my tires.

So, I saved for several months and boldly bought those four snow tires in the blazing August sun in Southern California. Every time I looked at them, I experienced the twin feelings that not only I had done something really unusual to have really good tires on my car; but also, and far more important to me, was the feeling that started with those new tires—that I was now taking concrete steps to go back to Buffalo and planned to fight to reclaim my sister Lisa and to make our family complete once again. I would keep my promise to my father and also honor my mom's valiant efforts to keep our family together up until the day she died.

My brothers and I were soon packed into my used car with the brand-new snow tires and on our way across the United States—again a drive of almost 3,000 miles—with every intention of not returning until our baby sister Lisa was next to us in my car. It was a somber, uneventful trip; we talked of nothing in particular, staying focused on the uphill battle that that lay ahead of us when we arrived in Buffalo and informed our Uncle Carmen and Aunt Mary that we not only wanted our sister back, but that we were willing to take them to court if they refused.

Upon arriving in Buffalo, New York, my mom's oldest sister, our Aunt Connie, graciously allowed all four of us to live with her in her home. Our Aunt Connie lived in one of the larger, older homes in the Italian section of Buffalo, and living in the city was an entirely new experience for all of us. I gave my Aunt Connie a small amount of money to help with living expenses, but the extra stress of having four new people in her home was a gift my Aunt Connie gave to us that I will always be grateful for.

My Aunt Mary's home, where my baby sister Lisa now lived, was in the country on a picturesque road on acres of wooded grounds; it was a beautiful home that my dad had built when I was five years old. I had spent many happy days and special occasions at the home during my childhood, when we lived in Buffalo. I fondly recalled children's parties and special holiday meals at my Aunt Mary's home.

I had loved visiting Aunt Mary's home. My Aunt Mary's front walkway and porch were majestic, and every holiday our family, dressed in our holiday best clothes, took our family photos. But that was another lifetime; now, I was forbidden in her home.

The day after I arrived in Buffalo I looked up the grade school for my Aunt Mary's home address, and I drove to the school without first contacting anyone. I hoped I would be able to find my sister Lisa at the school and speak privately with her, to tell her that her brothers and I had come back to take her home with us but that we might need to go to court to accomplish this.

I parked and went into Lisa's grade school. The halls were all empty, and I was thankful that no one was there to ask me for identification, or why I was at the grade school.

I believe God in His grace and mercy allowed Lisa to be in the hallway all alone, walking to use the bathroom. Lisa was very, very excited to see me, and we hugged for a really long time.

I'll let Lisa tell her memory of my surprise visit to her school. Lisa, then seven years old, is now in her early fifties and recalls, "I vividly remember your arrival and our long hug. I was like, *wow*, I knew it was you—and I remember being super, super excited."

I explained to Lisa that Uncle Carmen had taken her forcibly from us when our mom had died, and that I had not been old enough to stop him from taking her away from us. I also told her that Uncle Carmen would not let any of us talk to her after he took her from us, and that he did not tell me when he sent her to live with Aunt Mary. Then I explained to Lisa that her three big brothers and I had all come back to Buffalo, and we planned to bring her back home to Southern California with us. Lisa smiled a lot and nodded as I quickly explained our plans. She also looked nervous, as she knew how volatile Uncle Carmen and his sister, our Aunt Mary, would be once they found out that I had come back to reclaim Lisa from our Aunt Mary.

I didn't want Lisa to get into any trouble, so I didn't stay a very long time. I was happy that I had found Lisa, and I quickly explained what had happened when she was taken away—without me telling her what was about to happen— two years ago, and why none of us had been able to talk to her for the last two years. I was also very happy that Lisa wanted to see us and come back home to Southern California with my brothers and me. I knew that my Uncle Carmen and Aunt Mary would have a huge fit when they found out I had secretly gone to my sister's school, but I was willing to pay that price, as I knew I might not get a chance to talk privately with my sister for a very long time.

My sister Lisa and I have recounted this incident now that decades have passed. Lisa remembers being surprised to see me there in the hallway of her grade school in 1974, two years after being taken away from me and not understanding what had happened. Lisa recalls that when she got home from school that day, my Uncle Carmen and Aunt Mary weren't very happy when they found out I had snuck into Lisa's grade school and secretly visited with my little sister Lisa. I really did not care how upset they were. I kept thinking, no matter how well-intentioned their behaviors were, how foolish they both were to think they could make Lisa forget her biological family when they stole her away from us when she was five years old.

I did not know that my secret five-minute grade-school-hallway visit with my sister would be my last conversation with her, as seven years would pass before our next conversation.

I needed to work full-time and quickly found the only kind of work that I knew: taking care of an elderly person. I was again working for minimum wage, as I still only had a ninth grade education. I only knew that I needed a full-time job, as I needed an attorney—because my Uncle Carmen and Aunt Mary informed me in no uncertain words they would not even consider a visit between my sister and me.

I would spend every dollar I earned on my attorney to petition the New York family court to have my baby sister Lisa returned to me. My cousin Anna Marie Palmeri gave me the name of an attorney she knew from college, and he graciously, after hearing my story, agreed to represent me in family court—and even more graciously, charged me a very small amount.

Every Friday, my routine never varied. I would pick up my minimum wage paycheck, cash it, and drive directly to my lawyer's office where I would give him $25 towards my legal bill. I was thrilled to have a very good attorney and the start of court efforts to get my sister Lisa back to our family, where she belonged.

I had waited the requisite two years required of New York State to be twenty-one, and now I was determined to make it abundantly clear that I wanted my sister back.

As expected, Uncle Carmen and Aunt Mary absolutely refused to allow me any contact or visits with Lisa. I rationalized that at least my sister Lisa now knew that, regardless of what lies she was being told regarding our family's sudden disappearance, for certain she had not been abandoned and unwanted by her siblings.

As with most legal situations that have to wind through the legal system, the process to have my sister Lisa returned to me was a very lengthy one. As had happened with my three younger brothers, this legal decision was not going to be made in just one court appearance.

It was soon very apparent that many, many months would stretch into more than two years before a judge would make a final decision. Months went by between court appearances.

At the first court appearance, I saw my sister sit frozen and trembling as our Aunt Mary glared at her the entire time. At this first hearing, the judge awarded me supervised visits with my sister Lisa. These were to take place at my Aunt Mary's home with one person from each side supervising my visits with my sister, the child I had raised. Our Aunt Mary's daughter Rosemary, twelve, and my Aunt Connie were present for each visit.

Even though my father had built my Aunt Mary's beautiful large home, and I had spent numerous birthday parties, holidays, and visits at this home as a child, I was only allowed entrance through the back mudroom door, and all visits took place in the back playroom—my punishment for trying to get my sister Lisa back.

My sister was too terrified to speak to me, staying silent and keeping her head down during the entire two excruciating hours that I visited; she was staring at the ground during the entire visit, trembling, as the minutes agonizingly ticked by.

We sat inches from each other, my Aunt Connie sweetly chattering away trying to get a reaction from Lisa, and me just swimming in the absurdity and enormity of the fact that my sister—whom I had raised for five years—was now too terrified to even look at me.

At the end of the two hours, I would leave without my sister and I even making eye contact. The end of each visit was announced by our Aunt Mary shrilly screaming, "Lisa! Get back in here this minute!" Although I knew that my sister was under great stress from my visits, I needed to keep showing up while I was petitioning the court for her return. Yet the visits were awkward and painful for both of us.

At the end of a year in Buffalo, Daniel, as the oldest of my younger brothers was of legal age made the difficult choice to return back to what we all considered our "home" state of California to pursue work and a more traditional life. He began working a full-time job and rented a home with another friend from high school in the El Toro area, which was the area where we had lived the most normal life and knew many families before our mom's cancer had returned.

Another year passed and Peter, my middle youngest brother, now almost twenty years old, made his choice to also go back to Southern California, where our other brother Daniel had a home and Peter would now also live with him. I was glad that both of my brothers were having an opportunity to live more traditional lives, even as I missed them because they were so far away.

Still, my fight in Buffalo, New York, to reclaim my sister dragged on for me, with no end in sight any time soon. The New York judge hearing our case next ordered a home study—which, with all the additional delays, took almost another year to complete.

The traumatic supervised visits between me and my sister continued, with Lisa silently trembling and staring at the floor during each visit; our two hours always ended with our Aunt Mary screaming, "LISA! Get in here this minute!" and Lisa, quaking, complying.

Our Aunt Mary, my father's sister, never had one single civil word to speak to me. The court fight continued moving with glacier speed into another year, dragging on with motions and delays, and new motions and new delays.

After almost two years of court appearances and still no end or final decision in sight, my brothers and I decided it was in my youngest brother Curtis John Michael's best interest to also go back to Southern California and live with his two older brothers. We did not think the Buffalo schools were a place where he could thrive and do his best schoolwork as the weather also bothered his knees plus we all believed now that Curtis John Michael was a teenager, he needed some male influences in his life. His older brother Daniel would provide a stable environment, plus Curtis John Michael would again be friends with the families he had known when our mom was still alive, and I knew them to be good, solid, traditional-values families.

With great sadness, I talked with Curtis John Michael about what his brothers and I thought was best for him, and he agreed that he would like to go back to Southern California and live with his two older brothers, while I stayed in Buffalo and continued the fight to get our sister back.

Curtis John Michael went back to Southern California and was taken care of by Daniel, the oldest of my younger brothers in his home, where our brother Peter also lived.

My siblings and I will always be grateful that our Aunt Connie allowed us a place to live for the several years it took to try and reclaim our sister. She was very good to us.

In an odd twist, while trying to reunite our family, we were now in three different homes separated by 3,000 miles. I consoled myself, thinking, *At least my three brothers are all together,* and I hoped Lisa and I would be back in Southern California very soon. I had no control over our court dates, or whatever additional information or investigations the judge wanted.

There was one unexpected and strangely comforting outcome of my youngest brother Curtis John Michael returning to Southern California. For the very first time since my dad had died in 1967, I suddenly had no one but myself to supervise or cook for. For the very first time in my teenage and adult life my time was my own, to spend as I wished when I wasn't working.

I have heard Dr. Phil McGraw say that once a tremendous responsibility is lifted or a big life change is made, such as losing a large amount of weight, a person will often revert back to behaviors they either missed or enjoyed at a younger age. This can manifest as good behaviors, or as more rebellious behaviors.

In my case, once the stress of taking care of all my siblings was temporarily removed, I remembered how much I used to love to ice skate. Although I had not skated since I was sixteen years old, I found an ice rink, rented figure skates, and had so much fun that first evening, skating away all by myself. I weighed over 250 pounds that first evening. I rented ice skates, not even knowing what size I should get, and was thrilled to be skating again. I still remember overhearing a teenager say, "How can she be so fat and skate so good?" I wondered if his words were an insult or a compliment.

I did not care—all I knew was that as fat as I was, and as long as I had been off the ice, I still skated fairly well, and enjoyed myself with a deep personal joy I had not experienced in many, many years.

I also joined Weight Watchers, and ever-so-slowly I began to feel like I wasn't drowning in so much pressure and sorrow. I slowly lost weight and enjoyed learning new foods. As I kept skating, I made friends, and I only knew that at the ice rink I had again found a safe place where I could relax and put away the cares of my uphill battles with my relatives to regain my sister.

The bright light that was my return to ice skating in the evenings after work was to be a lifeline I would come to cling to. I was having simple fun, something I had forgotten how to do. It was only for an hour or two each evening, a couple of evenings a week, but I found that one clear breath which would allow me to keep fighting during the weeks and months ahead of me, as the horrible tug-of-war for my sister Lisa played out in my Aunt Mary's home and the Buffalo courtroom.

My slow return to ice skating was to become my bright light, my lifeline.

Though the horror might seem to be winning, God will always throw us a lifeline.

Because God is like a lot like that, when God heals our orphan hearts.

Chapter 21

I Have Fought the Good Fight, I Have Finished My Course

"I have fought the good fight, I
have finished the race, I have kept
the faith" (2 Timothy 4:7).

The horrible, supervised visits with my sister continued through another winter, and Lisa continued to stare at the floor, trembling, for the entire two hours that I sat visiting with her. I knew that our Aunt Mary was physically, emotionally, and verbally abusive with my sister, and I hated that no one who saw it would report our Aunt Mary and protect my sister Lisa. Our Uncle Carmen never knew of the abuse my baby sister was experiencing at our Aunt Mary's home. He would have put a stop to it had he known.

Although Lisa does recall her teachers whispering about the bruises on her arm, and authorities were called at some point—sadly for Lisa, nothing ever came of it.

At our final court hearing, Lisa was taken into the judge's chambers to talk with him privately. Lisa recalls, "Aunt Mary, firmly and sternly, simply said, 'Anybody says anything, anybody asks you anything, anybody tells you anything, you are to answer "No," and nothing else.' Aunt Mary kept saying this to me, right up to the time the judge took me into the back chambers to talk to him. Due to the prepping from Aunt Mary, when the judge asked me a question I didn't understand, I simply responded as I had been instructed to say: 'No,' and that was what I told the judge, 'No.'

"I immediately realized I should have said 'Yes,' because the judge had said, 'Is it true you don't want to see your family?' Once I got home, and after Uncle Carmen left our home, Aunt Mary made it known that I was in huge trouble—and I realized my mistake meant that I had said I *did* want to see you. So I was really happy I had said the wrong thing, and I was happy I would get to see you."

Lisa remembers that although Uncle Carmen was very angry and infuriated with the court proceedings, he was always very kind to her, and never raised his voice to her.

Finally, after almost three years of court hearings, the judge gave us his final ruling. Because our Aunt Mary had an established home and Lisa had been there for three years, the judge said he was not willing to remove Lisa and reunite her with her siblings. Our Aunt Mary had also lied, telling the judge I would have wonderful visits with my sister if she kept my sister.

As my sister Lisa, now ten years old, had told the judge she wanted to visit with me, the judge also ordered that we would indefinitely continue the torturous two-hour supervised visits, where Lisa was terrified to speak to me and trembled, shook, and stared at the floor the entire two hours, until our screaming Aunt Mary dragged her to her room.

What a horrific, tragic decision for my family and me, and especially for Lisa, now ten years old.

Now the judge's order was final. Lisa was not going to come back home with me and be reunited with her brothers. I had no recourse but to accept the judge's heart-rending legal decision. How could the legal process keep our sister from our family?

Deeply disappointed, I prayed and prayed and prayed as to my next steps.

I had known my Aunt Mary was physically, verbally, and emotionally abusive to my sister Lisa, even though I never witnessed it. Once my Aunt Mary had prevailed in our custody hearing, her screams at my sister Lisa became louder, more shrill, and more often. She repeatedly screamed at my sister through the wooden kitchen door that separated us from my screaming Aunt Mary, disrupting our already distressing, two-hour supervised visit.

Just seeing how my sister ducked and flinched at the sound of my Aunt Mary's shrill screams, I knew in my heart—and years later, as an adult, my sister Lisa confirmed—that our Aunt Mary had increased her abusive behavior towards my sister once she prevailed in the court custody hearings and she knew I could not remove Lisa from our Aunt Mary's home.

The pressure I felt was suffocating. Did I stay here and see my sister, ten years old, for our tortuous two-hour supervised visits, knowing she was being physically and emotionally abused before and after every single visit? Did I continue with these court-ordered visits where Lisa continued to sit, shaking, trembling, and staring at the floor—and flinching so much it looked like she was having a seizure—as our Aunt Mary's screams grew bolder each week from behind the kitchen door physically separating our Aunt Mary from our visits?

Every visit, I'd watch with horror as my sister's ten-year-old face would turn white as a sheet when, at the exact two-hour mark, our Aunt Mary screamed at the top of her lungs, "Lisa! Get back in here right this second!" I would watch Lisa slowly walking, shaking and trembling, into the other room. I would see the door shake as our Aunt Mary slammed it so hard and would hear our Aunt Mary screaming at Lisa, knowing she was to be punished later because I had visited. What were my visits doing to my baby sister? My intent had never been to cause my sister Lisa more harm.

I kept praying and seeking God's wisdom and guidance. All through the almost three years I had now spent in Buffalo, Tom and Teri Phipps and my Southern California Bible study friends continued to write weekly letters of encouragement, assuring me of their prayers. I deeply counted on their wisdom. With each visit I felt worse and worse as our Aunt Mary's abusive behavior continued to escalate.

After one particularly painful visit with Lisa, I came home and started sobbing uncontrollably over my Aunt Connie's sink. That was where my Aunt Connie found me hours later, still sobbing. In response to her question of what had happened, all I could repeatedly say was, "I don't know what to do. I don't know what to do." Over and over and over. "I don't know what to do."

All I could think of was that my sister was being hit for my mere presence, but how I could I voluntarily leave her again—and in leaving, lose her again? *How* could I do that? But *how* could I stay and continue to see her every two weeks for my horrible, monitored two-hour visit, *knowing* she was beaten each time after I left?

I feel asleep, still crying and still wrestling with my lose-lose dilemma.

I spent the next day, and the day after that, being very quiet; continuing with reading my Bible and relentlessly seeking God's guidance. Because either God really does guide us through His written Word, our Bibles, or else I might as well just flip a coin and live with the results.

Late in the afternoon, I came across this scripture: "I have fought the good fight, I have finished the race, I have kept the faith" (2 Timothy 4:7).

This verse in 2 Timothy resonated in my heart so deeply that I once again began sobbing quietly, not out of confusion, but out of deeply defeated grief—for I now knew exactly what I needed to do, and I knew I needed to do it very quickly, before I lost my nerve.

I know now that what occurred when I read that verse in 2 Timothy was what Bible teacher Joyce Meyer explains: that when God speaks to us and when God guides us, there is a place deep inside our hearts where a shift occurs; where we know we are now different, because we know we have heard God's voice speaking to our hearts. This is also true when the guidance given is in true conflict with what we really want to do in a situation or decision-making scenario.

I had asked God to show me the very best decision for my sister Lisa's well-being, for her happiness. After reading this verse—and how moved I was deep in my heart—I knew with 100 percent certainty exactly what I would do, and what was the best thing to do.

I would return to Southern California and leave my sister Lisa in the home and hands of our abusive Aunt Mary. I would trust God that the hallway talk with my sister at her school, when I first came back almost three years ago, would allow my sister Lisa to know in her heart exactly what had happened—and that, most importantly, I did not abandon her when our mom died four years ago, and I was not abandoning her now.

Leaving my sister Lisa in Buffalo, New York, was the only way I could ensure that I could do my part to lessen the abuse our Aunt Mary was subjecting her to. The judge had reduced me to doing very little, but I was determined that I wasn't going to bring my sister Lisa more pain and abuse— not brought on by my presence.

And so, with an extremely heavy heart, in the early morning hours of October, 1976—four years after my mom had died in this town of Buffalo—I once again packed all my meager belonging into my used car, said goodbye to my kind relatives and my few ice skating friends, and solemnly made the drive back to Southern California. I took solace in the fact that at least I would not be the reason for or the cause of my sister being abused physically and emotionally every two weeks.

I took comfort knowing that God was real, and that my sister Lisa knew without a shadow of a doubt that she was loved by me and she was wanted by me. I knew she would find me as soon as she could.

As Buffalo faded in my rear-view mirror, I pondered my times in Buffalo. First, I had watched my dad die in 1967, when I was thirteen years old. Then, I had returned to Buffalo for my mom's last days of her deadly, terminal cancer treatments in 1972; I was nineteen years old. My sister whom I had raised, then five years old, had been forcibly taken from me in 1972, within days of my mom's death. And now, I had again returned to Buffalo and had spent the last three years engaged in a sad and tragic custody battle, which I had lost—ensuring that if I stayed in Buffalo, my sister Lisa, now aged ten, would continue to be emotionally, verbally, and physically abused.

I felt as battered, bruised, and deeply wounded as I had ever been, and every heartbreaking event had occurred in Buffalo. Whether consciously or subconsciously, I just did not have much of a heart for the city of Buffalo. I wanted no part of Buffalo any longer, despite really loving my relatives such as my Aunt Connie, Aunt Stella, Aunt Mary, and Aunt Dolly, my Uncle Angelo, and my cousins Clara, Joanne, Anne Marie, Janice and Susie and their growing, loving, caring families. They and their families were all quite wonderful to me; but once I walked away from my baby sister Lisa, I just didn't have it in me anymore to drive down a single street in Buffalo or to be in close proximity to anything that reminded me of all my family's tragic, unavoidable losses—all of which had occurred in the space of a few short years there in Buffalo.

I didn't decide it right then, leaving Buffalo in my rearview mirror, but I never again had any desire to visit Buffalo. Buffalo held no happy memories for me.

Understandably, forty-four years of the anniversaries of my parents' deaths would come and go before I finally admitted that I desperately needed the emotional healing which only another trip to the homes where I had been so happy would bring—to the homes where I had watched my parents' lives ebbing away—culminating at my parents' gravesides where, on another rainy day, I finally forgave myself for all the places I felt I had failed my parents, and all the times I felt I had failed my brothers, and especially for the times I felt I had failed my sister.

So, the horror had won for now; I was defeated and quite emotionally unhealthy, physically unhealthy, and financially unhealthy. I was all of twenty-six years old, having spent the majority of my life helplessly fighting the consequences of my parents' deaths and trying to give my siblings a semblance of a better life—to give them a small amount of the stability that I had always yearned for.

It would be more than four decades before I was even strong enough to want to face the horror once again and to tell it, "No more—your horror controls me no more, your fears control me no more. God wins now, not you, not the horror of the scraps left of my shredded, once-wonderful life."

I had so little left; but I really had everything. I had three loving brothers waiting for me, and a loving sister who I knew would find her way back home to me; our hearts would meet again when she was older. I had Tom and Teri Phipps, who loved me as deeply and lovingly as my own parents once did.

Most importantly, I still had a God who loved me as a father loves his daughter; a God who still had a plan and a purpose and a great love for me. I was completely defeated, but God wasn't.

In the years to come God would still triumph, in ways I never even imagined.

But God is a lot like that, I've found, when God heals our orphan hearts.

Chapter 22

<hr />

My Little Sister Lisa Finally Comes Back Home to Me

"When your life's been out of control, you can't trust not being in control."
Rosie George Finocchi 2017
Bethany Celebrate Recovery

I arrived home in Southern California and stayed with my three brothers who had returned before I did. My brothers were all doing very well, and I was very proud of the lives they were building for themselves.

Curtis John Michael was now fifteen, and eventually he came back to live with me as his brothers lived close by. Money was still tight, as I still only qualified for minimum-wage jobs and he was a typical teenage boy. I worked one full-time job and several part-time jobs. I found a small one-bedroom apartment in the little beachside community of Laguna Beach, an artists' community. He and I kept track of whose "turn" it was to sleep in the only bedroom on a calendar. As I often worked nights it worked out well. Curtis John

Michael was a gifted artist and cartoonist, and we liked that he could live in an artists' community. Curtis John Michael also played varsity football at Laguna Beach High School. It was refreshing to see the bright blue ocean as I drove around town.

We often had company over for meals. A neighbor saw how financially difficult it was and offered to become Curtis John Michael's legal guardian so he would also qualify for California state foster child monetary benefits, but I refused as I felt it was not honest.

During these years, although I was denied any contact with my baby sister Lisa, I would save my money, and at her birthday and Christmas I would go to an expensive store like Macy's and buy and mail Lisa really nice outfits to wear—including sweater sets and good winter coats—because I knew my Aunt Mary wasn't so crazy that she would throw them away or give them away. I knew that Lisa would not be told the nice clothes were from me, but I didn't care; I just wanted Lisa to have nice clothes, as Aunt Mary dressed her in hand-me-downs and Salvation Army clothes even though she could well afford to buy Lisa nicer clothes.

As Lisa recalls, "I always knew what was from you, because Aunt Mary would never, ever buy me anything new that was nice—so I always knew the really nice clothes were from you."

Curtis John Michael graduated from high school, and I was so very proud that all three of my brothers had finished high school, as I never had. Curtis John Michael decided he wanted to move back with his brothers who lived close by. I wish I had encouraged Curtis John Michael to go to college and continue his education, but I did not.

I remember standing in the street as Curtis John Michael, now eighteen years old, drove to his brother's home to live, and thinking, *They all have a high school diploma, and I'm still a 10th grade dropout.* I thought that school was Monday through Friday from 8 a.m. to 4 p.m., and that was the only schedule possible; so I thought I couldn't go back to school.

After Curtis John Michael moved, I decided to move closer to work. I was still attending Calvary Chapel of Costa Mesa, and Senior Pastor Chuck Smith's secretary Mary Wiley gave me a room to rent. Mary became like a mother to me, and I absolutely adored Mary. She remembered the Great Depression and was industrious and very hard-working, she herself holding down several part-time jobs in addition to being the church's full-time secretary and coordinator.

I loved living at Mary's and looked forward to our evening talks, as she deeply cared about me and was sassy and wise. I had continued to ice skate occasionally when I came home from Buffalo, and I still found this to be a great joy in my life. I still made very little money and was on a very tight budget—but all that was about to change.

Tom and Teri Phipps, who were also close to Mary Wiley, continued to love me and include me in their family functions, plus I'd have the treat of seeing them at church each week. I had taken a home nursing job that gave me the unusual hours of twelve hours all day Monday; twenty-four straight hours on Wednesday night through Thursday night, and then another twelve hours Friday night until Saturday morning. These hours enabled me to still work other part-time jobs and temporary jobs. I would go straight from one home nursing job to the next, often with very little sleep. Many jobs allowed me to nap in a chair next to my patient's bed, as long as I awakened when the patient needed me during the night.

I had developed sensitive feet as an ice skater, and I would take off my shoes, and wearing fresh socks I'd place my toes between the mattresses on the patient's bed. Any movement by the patient would awaken me, so I was glad when I could take little naps at night at work and still keep my patients happy.

One afternoon I was talking with Tom, and he casually mentioned that Teri had made $300—to me, a huge amount of money—in just one day. Teri had worked as a hair stylist, and I didn't know any hair stylist that made the kind of money Tom mentioned. When I asked how, Tom said that Teri had learned how to apply and fill the new acrylic fingernails, also called false nails. I called Teri, and she explained that these nails were a mixed liquid and powder directly applied to a lady's individual fingernails with a slender artist's brush, shaped while wet, then additionally carefully shaped with a nail drill and nail file, and then polished. The artificial nails lasted from two to three weeks, and then the lady would return for a fill. The initial application was $50 and the fills were $20, usually every two to three weeks. With returning, steady clients, it was easy to imagine a decent income.

Teri said I didn't need a high school diploma to attend beauty college and become a licensed manicurist. I immediately found a beauty school near my home. I contacted the beauty school, and my unusual work hours allowed me to attend the beauty college each week on Tuesday, Thursday, Friday, and Saturday. I was placed on a weekly payment plan so I could start the following week. I needed to complete 400 hours of instruction and pass the state exam.

I quickly mastered the art of applying artificial nails and did all the beauty school clients, as the other manicurists found the technique too messy and difficult to master. The entire manicurist's course took about four months to complete, and I was so happy to be learning a new way to make a living.

During the last few weeks of my beauty college manicurist training, I received a call from my Aunt Mary. My little sister Lisa was now fourteen years old, and I had had no contact of any sort for four long years. Daily, I prayed to be reunited with my sister Lisa. I answered my phone; there was no caller ID in 1980. I heard the instantly recognizable, shrill voice of my Aunt Mary calling me from Buffalo, New York. She had never called or written me in the five years since I had left Buffalo after losing my custody fight to have my sister returned to me.

"Do you still want your sister Lisa?" She curtly and shrilly said, without any preliminary, polite statements of civility.

"Yes! Of course! What is going on?" Stunned, I stammered the only words that came to my brain, with little thought of where and what I would do with my sister Lisa, who was now a teenager. All I heard was that I could possibly have Lisa again!

"I'm putting her on an airplane, and she'll be at Los Angeles airport tonight on this flight. She's all yours."

As Aunt Mary started to hang up, I shouted into the phone, "Wait! I don't even know what Lisa looks like anymore!"

Again, shrilly and even more abruptly, Aunt Mary spit out the words, "She's wearing her school uniform." That night I would find out from Lisa why.

Lisa, now an adult, recalls, "I think Aunt Mary heard me telling cousin Rosemary that I was going to run away and find a way to get to Southern California, and find you and my brothers and be with you. I overheard Aunt Mary tell Uncle Carmen that she was thinking of sending me back to you in California, and I could tell that Uncle Carmen did not like that idea at all. A few days later, Aunt Mary picked me up from school and had a small suitcase with a few of my things in it. Aunt Mary drove me straight to the airport and put me on the plane. She told me you would pick me up at the Los Angeles airport. For the second time in my life I got ripped away from school and my friends, and I never had a chance to say goodbye to anyone or was even told what was happening or why."

Now, as I hung up the phone that day in 1980, I was ecstatic. Finally, our family would be together again after all these years of waiting. Mary agreed that Lisa could stay at Mary's home with me for a short time, but I would need to find a new home for both of us.

My Uncle Carmen's daughter Susie Finocchi Alagna and her husband Joseph are kind, deeply committed Christians. I remember playing with Susie when we were both little girls. Susie has told me now in 2018 that her father, my Uncle Carmen, had wanted to keep Lisa living with him, but it had not been possible. Uncle Carmen never knew that our Aunt Mary was planning to send Lisa back to me, and he was very upset when he found out. Uncle Carmen appears to have been in a difficult place of loving Lisa; yet when Lisa could not live in his home, Uncle Carmen tried to keep her close by with his sister, our Aunt Mary.

I still needed to finish my manicurist beauty college training and take my state licensing exam. When I finished school and passed my state licensing exam, Teri Phipps personally trained me at the salon where she was working, teaching me all the little intricate details of looking at all the angles of a nail, and proper nail techniques that allowed me to provide my clients with a superb quality set of artificial nails.

I quickly found a job with a small, family-owned hair salon with a regular clientele. Teri also taught me marketing tips and appointment strategies as a manicurist, so that I quickly developed a clientele of my own with approximately 150 regular clients. I cut back on my home nurse's aide jobs, and finally was able to give up the home nursing completely—as very quickly, I was making more than $300 a day on my busier days. I averaged about $600 a week, which was almost as much as I used to make in a month of all my nursing jobs combined. Teri continued to give me tips on manicuring and promoting my business and my business thrived, and I was beginning to also gradually recover from all the horror of my early years.

At least I could make a plan and choose to stick to it. Failures were my fault; no one else's.

I found an apartment for Lisa and me, and together we enjoyed a life for the two of us. It was wonderful for all of my siblings to be living close to each other. Lisa and I enjoyed our time of getting reacquainted and Lisa, now fourteen, was a pretty typical teenager. But all I cared about was that Lisa was finally home again and our family, our parents' orphans, were whole as far as our family was concerned. I loved Lisa dearly and deeply, and was so grateful that God had brought Lisa back home to us—her loving, praying, and waiting family. Oddly though, my siblings and I *never, ever* discussed either of our parents' deaths; not what we saw, not what we heard, and not what the results of their deaths had been.

Neither of us, nor did any of my siblings, ever speak again to our Aunt Mary, although I did continue to send Aunt Mary Christmas and birthday gifts.

In retrospect, I wish I had been more mature and had tried to maintain a civil relationship once I got Lisa back, as Aunt Mary was my dad's sister—no matter how broken and mentally unhealthy she may have been

When I had returned to California from Buffalo—completely physically, financially, and emotionally spent—I was twenty-six, and instead of enjoying a carefree life I developed crippling panic attacks, feeling that I couldn't breathe; severely limiting my work. Travel was non-existent except for short distances to limited jobs, such as the nurses' aide home care jobs that I held even with that kind of panic.

One of the unexpected and unplanned joys of owning a manicuring business with 150 clients was that several of my clients were psychologists. As I grew to be close friends with one of them, I shared my personal fears and insecurities. As I was beginning to have a tiny bit of breathing room financially, I made one of the best decisions of my life: to seek professional, private counseling. It was not easy, but the panic attacks I suffered from were so crippling. I read everything I could about panic attacks and learned how certain behaviors and even diet changes could help, but I was still so limited.

These panic attacks that I was experiencing were so baffling to me, as I incorrectly believed that as a Christian I should not be experiencing any abnormal problems or issues. I thought that if I just believed hard enough, my panic would be gone. I was to learn that having a panic attack did not mean I did not love God enough or have enough faith to be healthy.

Pastor Alan Jackson teaches: "Life is not as easy as I would like. Life comes fully loaded with challenges." These panic attacks presented my greatest challenge now. Instead of being free of my early, age-inappropriate responsibilities, I was now a prisoner to my own misfiring nervous system, compounded by my deep feelings of inadequacy in so many areas.

Fortunately, owning my own business allowed me to regulate my own hours, and so I was always able to take a break after a few hours. When the panic attacks were at their worst, I could not even stay at work for more than two hours without needing a break. I could not drive in anyone else's car, and I could not date. I had distressing stomach issues as a result of the panic attacks, so I always needed to be near a bathroom and carried medication with me at all times. It was a horrible way to live. But I figured out how to manage. I always figured out how to function. That's what I knew to do.

Surviving was all I did; I was secretly miserable. I reasoned that I was alive, and I could seek professional help, and I could heal. I still believed, as dysfunctional as I was and felt; I knew I could get better, even if very slowly. I decided eventually that incremental progress would be better than getting worse.

My professional counselor and I began to look at some very early traumas in my life. Specifically, she and my counselor/client gently walked me through the pain and shame of the extended family member that sexually molested me when I was not yet a teenager. I understood why it upset and affected me so much, and why I had felt so broken and not okay as I got older. I came to learn that my shame was absolutely normal, and she helped me to realize that what was done to me was not an indicator of who I was.

As I continued with healthier friends and the constant love of Mary Wiley, Tom and Teri Phipps, and another sweet motherly client, Jeannie Solum Perry, I began to slowly, incrementally get better. I never quit seeking ways to get healthier. I kept trusting God to help me.

Pastor Steven Furtick teaches on Exodus 23:20: *"See, I am sending an angel ahead of you to guard you along the way and to bring you to the place I have prepared."*

He teaches from his "Waymaker" series: "God will guard us along the way, and God will bring us to the place where God wants us, because God is very good at getting us to the place God wants us to go. We have been positioned for a purpose of God's. But God can't take our steps to that place of healing and purpose for *us;* we must do that for ourselves. Doing the work ourselves to get to where God wants us to be is God's kindness to us. God will guide us along the way, but we will only see that looking back."

This teaching by Pastor Steven Furtick was extremely helpful to me in understanding my own life's journey of seemingly incomprehensible, cruel twists and turns.

I have heard one of my favorite Bible teachers, Joyce Meyer (who I have daily listened to for decades), explain, "We live life going forward, but we understand life looking backwards."

As my sister Lisa grew restless with me, she would be taken care of by her oldest brother, my oldest of the younger brothers and his family. They also provided Lisa with a loving, stable, fun home where she could explore her own unique gifts and talents. Lisa also graduated from high school, and I was happy to see Lisa enjoying her own life. During the time Lisa lived with me, she made friends with a young woman at high school, Sue Correa, who is still to this day Lisa's and our family's beloved, sweet friend.

Once all of my siblings were making their own lives, I decided to vigorously pursue the two areas of my life that I had enjoyed before all the horror had come to stay: figure ice skating and, reaching back many years to happier times, my own education.

Sadly, there were still many unhealthy behaviors that I stubbornly held onto that deeply impacted my life and my own happiness. I would continue to spend money and try to rescue my younger siblings, often with the only result being that I was very frustrated at my loss of time and money and at seeing no changes taking place. But I could not stop rescuing, because I felt such sadness that they had been deprived of parents—and always, there was my resonating promise to my dying father to "take care of his family."

I knew I needed to change, and I knew I was very emotionally unhealthy. I became diligent with Bible studies requiring me to search the scriptures myself, not just to sit quietly in a church seat. I loved the Old Testament, with story after story of God's second chances, of God's endless compassion, of God's willingness to heal and restore.

As I learned God's scriptures for myself, my circle of belief in myself started to widen; and my panic attacks were under enough control that if I controlled every single moment of my day, I would usually not have a panic attack. It was a small start, but a small start was all I needed.

I had a ninth grade education, and a persistent belief that I could succeed in school, and a love of pushing myself. These two loves would compliment each other as I resolutely pushed forward, asking God day by day for His guidance in this, my journey in uncharted waters.

I have always made decisions by following Pastor Michael Youssef's teaching: "When needing to make a decision and seeking God's guidance and wisdom, pray, asking God to *shut* every single door and just leave *open* the door that you, God, want me to walk through."

Dr. Youssef's teaching was a confirmation in my heart of my favorite Bible verse, Isaiah 22:22, *"I will place on his shoulder the key to the house of David; what he opens no one can shut, and what he shuts no one can open."*

I determinedly held God's hand and powered forward. Had I known that my journey for education and healing from all my traumas and grief would take thirty years, maybe I would not have started. But with my usual belief in my ability to figure things out, no matter how complicated, and to keep taking one step after another, I made two life-changing-for-the-better decisions.

First, I decided to ice skate a little bit more, as it relaxed me and was fun.

Second, I decided to find out where to get my GED.

My two seemingly small decisions—to ice skate more and to get my GED—would prove to set me on a wondrous path to the first Adult USFS National Ice Skating Showcase Championship gold medal and a Master's Degree in Theology and Minstry. Each feat was accomplished by God's miracles of loving kindnesses and tender mercies, every step of the wondrous way.

The horror had done its best and left brutal tragedies in its blazing path.

But I was still the woman God had fashioned in my mother's womb with unique abilities and strengths that God would now cause to come into full bloom.

But God is a lot like that, I've gratefully learned, when God heals our orphan hearts.

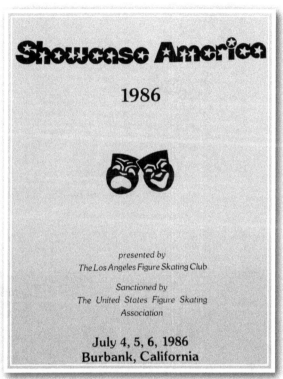

Inaugural-First Ever "USFS 1986 Adult National
Showcase America"-1st of my 5 straight National wins

Me - Layback Spin - Gold Medal
Performance 1991, California

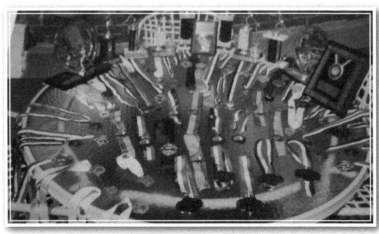

My 5 National USFS Gold Medals in Front,
Los Angeles, California 1978-1993

Chapter 23

⊷————⋅————⊶

My United States Figure Skating National Championships and My College Degrees

*"Therefore, since we are surrounded by
so great a cloud of witnesses, let us lay
aside every weight, and sin which clings so
closely, and let us run with perseverance the
race that is set before us" (Hebrews 12:1).*

*"Know you not that not all who run
receive a prize, so run that you may
achieve" (1 Corinthians 9:24).*

"Congratulations on winning your gold medal—and I don't mean to be rude, but weren't you dead last in your last ice skating competition?"

The adult female ice skater politely speaking to me was still wearing her ice skates and her sequined competition dress at the San Diego ice rink.

"Yes, I was, and I didn't like being last one single bit," I answered with a smile.

The lady was silent for a few moments. Finally, she gestured towards my gold medal hanging around my neck from its pretty red, white, and blue ribbon, looked me earnestly in the eyes and said, "What happened?"

Back in Southern California, after my unsuccessful attempt to get my sister Lisa returned to me, I remembered that the one joy of being in New York had been ice skating in the evenings, as I was able to leave all my cares behind. I started skating every couple of weeks. I didn't have money for lessons, but I enjoyed asking skaters questions and teaching myself again.

As I was making a little better money from manicuring and progressing through my professional counseling, I began feeling better about myself and opening myself up to additional activities. I became friends with some of the ice skating instructors at the Costa Mesa Ice Chalet where I skated. My first coach ever was Cheryl Smith, who encouraged me to compete and choreographed my first skating routine to my favorite piece of classical music. I practiced during the public sessions until the day of competition.

I bought a used $15 competition dress from an adult skater and recorded my classical piece of myself, at home on a cheap cassette player, literally splicing together music cuts with recording sticky tape. I just ignored the thumping sound and hoped the judges would not realize it was from my homemade music splicing.

I felt really nervous when I stepped onto the ice, but as my music started I executed all my moves with the same deliberateness and patterns I had practiced for months and was rewarded with my first gold medal for the event. I still remember my first routine. I loved feeling graceful and soaring across the smooth ice to beautiful music.

When I'd get to the public ice skating sessions early, I always noticed the elite skaters practiced a skating form called School Figures: intricate patterns made and repeatedly traced on the ice of difficult edges and turns, increasing in difficulty, skated both forward and backwards. As a skater passed the first test, the Preliminary Figure Test, they continued to the Eighth Figure Test, known as the Senior Figures Test. There were corresponding freestyle tests that were also passed as skating skills increased.

I soon met a lifelong friend, JoAnn Schneider-Farris, a gold medal coach running one of the figure skating programs. When JoAnn's children were born, JoAnn taught all three of her children, as they became Elite USFS National Figure skaters going on to hold numerous USFS records. JoAnn was an excellent coach when we met in 1978 and encouraged me to compete.

The elite figure skaters at every ice skating rink in the United States are members of the United Skates Figure Skating Association, commonly called the USFSA. Usually, each ice rink has a USFSA Club affiliated with the USFSA. The USFSA was the American national governing council for all standardized figure skating tests—the qualifying tests given to determine at which skill level a figure skater would compete in competitions.

The USFSA sanctioned and accredited all the local USFSA ice skating clubs' individual figure skating competitions as either qualifying or non-qualifying competitions.

A qualifying competition for elite ice skaters meant that the three top medalist finishers—from, in my case, the USFSA Southwest Pacific Regional Championship, which included Arizona and Nevada—would advance to the Pacific

Coast Sectionals, and the top three medalists there would advance to the United States National Championships. The top finishers there would advance to the World Figure Skating Championships, and in an Olympic year, to the Olympics.

When I started figure skating competitions in the late 1970s, there were not any United States Figure Skating Association (USFSA) Adult Skaters competing, as the USFSA was only open to younger skaters with the possibility of being National Champions. I later heard had been USFSA Adults competing locally in the Mid-west and east coast areas, but none that I knew of in Southern California and Adults were not allowed in the USFSA qualifying regional competitions anywhere in the United States.

The USFSA made it very clear that ice skaters over the age of eighteen were not welcomed into the elite National Figure Skating ranks of the USFSA. We were simply banned from all their competitions by virtue of the fact that there were no Adult Skating events offered for us to enter on the competition announcements and entry forms. So Adult Skaters could not enter, and we were effectively omitted from USFS competitions, even the non-qualifying ones, other than a local club competition if one could be found.

That's the way the USFS had always treated Adult Skaters.

The USFS informed us Adult Skaters that we could compete in the new Ice Skating Institute (ISI) organization, which was intentionally formed for beginning recreational ice skaters and welcomed Adults.

The ISI had Adult Skating levels, but the judging, rules, and levels were very different, with severe restrictions in each level. So if a skater, such as myself, was able to perform advanced-level spins, they could not do all of their more advanced spins without penalties, which seemed quite harsh to us. Other Adult Skaters and I started in the ISI doing all their competitions, but we wanted inclusion in the prestigious and elite United States Figure Skating organization— including unheard-of Adult qualifying events leading to Adult National Championships.

This was the late 1970s, and the USFS made it very clear that their organization was elite and prestigious—and we Adult Skaters were not, in their eyes.

But I was not deterred and set about finding others to help open USFS to adults.

I was very fortunate that the Costa Mesa Ice Capades Chalet was home to one of the sport's legendary coaches, Mr. John Nicks. Mr. Nicks and his sister Jennifer Nicks were the 1953 World Champions in Pairs. His Olympic students have included Peggy Fleming, Pairs team Tai Babilonia and Randy Gardner, Kristi Yamaguchi, Sasha Cohen, and Ashley Wagner. Mr. Nicks was coaching 1988 Olympic Pairs Bronze medalists Jill Watson and Peter Oppegard, and Jill, Peter and I quickly became friends. Jill and Peter's friendship and encouraging suggestions to improve my skating were so helpful, as were Julie Keen's, whose son Jonathan would become a U.S. National Champion.

Other skaters and their families very supportive and helpful in my Adult Skating were International coach Roger Bass, Les and Dee Goldstein, whose children Troy Goldstein and Dawn Goldstein Eyerly were U.S. National Medalists and an International Elite Pairs team, as were Katy Keely and Joey Mera. Katy's mother Mrs. Jane Keely was a USFS judge, so Mrs. Keely's advice was very helpful. Annette Hurd and so many other advanced skaters were so friendly and helpful.

Adam Jim Swift was a superb Adult figure skater and was having success in winning several of his competitions. His coach was Lorin O'Neil Caccamise, himself a U.S.

National Gold Medalist and Elite International skater who became one of my dearest friends—not to mention, my biggest cheerleader. Sadly, the USFS formally changed the cut-off age to 18 as the limit to compete, and Adan Jim Swift needed to change to another category in order to continue competing.

Adults were *not* wanted in the USFS in the early 1970s through the early 1990s.

As I became more serious about competing and advancing in my skating skills, I began to take figure lessons and freestyle lessons. Figures were intricate tracings of edges meticulously skated on the ice, and freestyle was the more well-known spins, jumps and footwork choreographed into a routine or program set to music.

As Adult Competitive Figure Skaters were so rare in the late 1970s, there were no other Adult Skaters on the ice with me. So to my huge benefit, I trained every day next to the elite National, Olympic, and World Champions and their coaches, who were practicing their triple jumps when I was practicing my own single jumps.

Fortunately, as an act of kindness, I was gifted my training for much, much less than other skaters. I would not have been able to skate had I been charged regular prices.

Daily, on the private figure skating ice, the elite skaters, families, and Olympic coaches welcomed me, the lone Adult Ice Skater, with friendship, support, and encouragement onto the private ice each day. The atmosphere was electric, and being caught up in such a hard-working environment, very quickly both my figures and my freestyle improved dramatically.

I was able to join the USFS; usually parents were allowed to join as Skating Adults, but we just weren't allowed to compete in their competitions.

I was also extremely fortunate to have as my coach Sondra Holmes, herself an Elite International competitor and United States National Medalist. The unique element about Sondra was that she trained me as a young, competitive skater, not as a recreational ice skater. This meant Sondra pushed me and expected excellence in everything I did. Sondra knew I wanted to compete and hated to lose, for any reason. We both wanted me to win.

Upon passing my Preliminary Figure Test, I was eligible to compete in the San Diego competition which had eleven Adult Skating competitors, including myself. I was so excited, and proudly laid out my figure tracings on the clean, smooth ice, skating between the watching judges. The problem was that I completely lost track of where I was on my last figure, the Waltz 8, which required a one-foot turn from front to back and then again to front, all on one skate—so when I turned around for the last part of my figure, I could not find my center starting point on the ice. This resulted in a wavy, wobbly skate around the ice instead of the round circle, as I frantically searched until I found my center—desperately running out of speed and trying not to put my second skate down on the ice.

This unplanned skate around the ice resulted in a dead-last finish. I was upset and demoralized; I knew I had it in me to be a good skater.

The next morning, I told Sondra my results. She listened quietly and said something I've never forgotten. Sondra said, "There's a big difference between being good enough to pass a test and winning a competition. Which one do you want?"

I answered, "I want to win."

"Good, now we can get to work," Sondra said.

And we did.

Sondra Holmes was the best thing that could have ever happened to me, as her skating lessons were equally applicable to winning in all areas of my life.

I now skated with fierce determination and expectation, and Sondra expected no less. I was on the ice at 5:00 a.m. and skated three figure sessions and three freestyle sessions, practicing right next to the 1984 and later the 1988 Olympians. They respected me, and I respected their tremendous talent and competitive drive.

Sondra and I worked on all the tiny, small, intricate parts of my figures and my freestyle programs, over and over and over, hour after hour after hour—with attention to detail, never with an attitude of "nobody else can do that as good as you're asking me to skate it." Instead, our shared attitude became: "I'm going to concentrate and learn this better than anybody else, so there will be no doubt I will win." I came to crave being able to trace my figures as if only one tracing had been done, as I knew this was a highly scored skill.

As my close friendship with Olympic and World Pair Bronze Medalist' and Hall of Fame Skaters and United States National Champions Jill Watson and Peter Oppegard continued, I was afforded the unique and rare opportunity not only learn the mental toughness and work ethnic training and competition nuances from Olympic Champions but also to travel to and experience extended backstage and weekend time at the elite Tom Collins World Tour which each year traveled the United States with each of the Figure Skating World Championship medal winners from Ladies, Mens, Pairs and Dance. Because of Jill and Peter, I met and spent time with every single 1988 Olympic medalist including my very favorite Katarina Witt, 1984 and 1988 Olympic Ladies' Champion, an achievement only mastered one other time by Olympic Ladies Champion Sonja Henie.

I will always remember Katarina telling me "I will not be second," when I asked her in 1987 about the upcoming 1988 Olympics. And she was not; winning her second Olympic Gold medal, relying heavily on her artistic mark to win her second Olympic gold medal.

In the following year I had the high honor of meeting Peggy Fleming at a charity skating event and giving Peggy one of my long skate laces when she needed something to tie around her waist to keep her $5000 Bob Mackie gown in place when it proved to be too long. Simply to most, but I felt like a queen helping my childhood idol.

I tried to emulate Katarina Witt as well as Jill and Peter in my own freestyle programs, there was a technical mark for the elements and an artistic mark for the overall presentation. As the artistic mark would break a tie, as I learned from Olympian & World Bronze Medalist and Hall of Fame skaters Jill Watson and Peter Oppegard, I had music that always suited my skating style, which allowed me to have difficult connecting moves that garnered precious extra points. Additionally, I have always found spinning quite easy, and so I was able to build on my natural spinning ability and core strength. I developed specialty spins with positions no other skater was doing, as well as developing five-position combination spins, utilizing spinning both forward on my left foot and backwards on my right foot, which also allowed the judges to award me very high points.

Adding to my pleasure and determination to win were the daily encouragement and additional instruction the elite skaters offered me as we trained together. There was hardly a day that one of the elite International skaters at my home rink didn't offer a quick passing tip to an element I was learning that quickly produced results. In addition to Sondra Holmes exemplary and extraordinary coaching and attention to details, the help from the elite skaters helped me to believe in my ability to train harder than anyone else and win.

I won my next figure competition, the one at the San Diego ice rink, by a large margin, also winning the freestyle event.

I loved my two gold medals and the trophies I was awarded.

I competed in the ISI recreational competitions and met Melissa Parker, a strong, beautiful Adult Skater who is still a wonderful friend. I only met other Adult Skaters at ISI competitions, so these other Adult Skaters were like bonus friends. Melissa was gifted and hard-working, and often the podium was me and Melissa, first and second, or vice versa. We often traded those two places, as Melissa's strength and artistry in her skating was beautiful to watch then and still are today. I never minded placing second to Melissa.

Simultaneously with developing my ice skating, I began to want to further my education. Most of my close friends had college degrees, and I kept silent as I was deeply embarrassed at being a tenth grade dropout. I always believed that education was only Monday through Friday, 8 a.m. to 4 p.m., and since I worked full time I was not aware of other options—until a friend enlightened me, saying there were night, weekend, and TV classes.

A whole new world opened up to me when I learned there were alternatives to standard classroom hours. I went back to my old Huntington Beach High School and again started onto the familiar, beach-breezy campus.

It was 1987, and instead of joy I felt only absolute heart-pumping terror and panic. Those were the unexpected and very unwelcome emotions I suddenly experienced as I stepped foot onto the grounds of Huntington Beach High School. I had only attended for a few months in 1968 before being expelled for continued truancy, as I stayed home as much as I possibly could—partially out of need to help with my family, and partially out of a complete disinterest in school. Either way, my school truancy had cost me dearly.

Truth be told, back in 1968 when I was expelled, I really truly didn't have a clue why I was being forced to attend school. But now, in 1987, I was determined to change my life and was continuing with my resolve to get my education—no matter what it took, no matter what it cost, and most importantly, no matter how seemingly forever my education might take me. I had always held onto and trusted God's promises, and today wasn't *any* different.

And so, my education process began with a less-than-stellar start! As I forced myself to simply keep taking one more step at a time—to accomplish *only* walking in the *door* of the records office—two thoughts persisted in fighting with each other in my mind: the first, *How can I do this if I'm terrified, with massive panic attacks?* and the second, stronger thought, *I'm doing this, somehow, some way, with God's help. I'm not quitting; even if I have to do this with massive panic, I'm not quitting!*

So, I did what I'd learned to do so many decades earlier—I kept walking, one determined step in front of the other, one focused step in front of the other, until I reached the door to the school's Office of Records. I stood there, memories of the horror and immense sadness of my short-lived high school years flooding my brain—reminding me of my teenage memories of always feeling so different from every other student, all of which started the first day back at school after the day my father had suddenly died.

As the scripture says, *"David encouraged himself in the Lord" (1 Samuel 30:6)*, I resolved and repeated to myself that

God would help me like He had always helped me, and I didn't quit walking until I reached the records counter.

Explaining that I was a dropout, I was given the phone number and location of the High School Equivalency GED Center. I attended the next evening and learned that first I would take a practice exam in the four areas of the GED: reading, math, science, and social studies. I needed to pass all four areas of the GED exam to receive my GED. This preliminary testing would show which areas were below passing standards, and those would be the areas I would study. Although all four areas would be tested on my first attempt, if I passed one area, then on my future attempts I would only be testing on the areas I had not passed until I received a passing grade in all four areas.

At the end of the practice GED exam, the teacher gave me the documents and told me to go and register to take the real GED exam. I said I didn't understand; what did I need to work on?

The teacher smiled and said, "Nothing. You scored high enough in each practice section of the four areas of study on the GED that you don't need to study anything. Just go take your GED exam; you should pass with no problem and be fine."

As I walked to my car, the sky was a deepening blue with streaks fading into sunset. For some reason I kept thinking of my mom. She had passed away fifteen years earlier. I had been a tenth grade dropout for nineteen years, and I had always been so deeply embarrassed and ashamed, thinking how "stupid and uneducated" I was. I was quite stunned by my practice GED results. I kept thinking that I really hadn't been stupid for nineteen years; I finally said out loud, looking at the sky, "Hey Mom, look, I'm as smart as a high school graduate. Imagine that."

As with so many things, I wished my mom had been alive to celebrate with me.

The next month I took my GED exam and was shocked, *absolutely shocked*, to score in the United States' top 98% for the GED High School equivalency exam. I never had a clue I even had a brain.

I then took the classes necessary to complete my Associate of Arts Degree, intending to become a nurse.

My first class was anatomy, and not having a clue how to study—or the discipline—I got an "F" on my first exam. I spoke to my professor and he pointed out the student with the best grade in the class, a woman who lived close to me. I went to her home and was surprised that she was studying in the middle of the day, as I only squeezed in studying at night, after I got home from work and classes. She showed me how to outline the chapters and said to learn the chapter study questions at the end of each chapter, as our class exam questions usually contained several of these book questions.

Her study tips and my professor's offer of extra credit papers were all I needed to figure out how to do college level coursework. I finished with a "B" grade and used those study tips the rest of my college days.

Additionally, I took a speed-reading course, dramatically *reducing* the amount of time I spent studying. College was expensive and I could not afford all my books, so I took several classes without the books. Every school's library is required to have one copy of each class' required book, so I would copy the pages I needed for ten cents a page every week after class, or read the class assignments in the library.

After my first semester, Mary Wiley offered to pay for my books. She said she didn't pay for my first semester's books as she "wanted to make certain I was serious." I would then resell my books and buy used books, but I still used the library copies, as books cost $150 each and I needed as many as four books per class.

Even though in the first semester, I never bought the microbiology book because I did not have the money to pay for the $150 textbook, I excelled in microbiology and really enjoyed identifying, tracking, categorizing, and systematic identification of all the various germs.

Although I did not realize it then, God was directing me when my microbiology teacher took me aside and said, "If you ever change your mind, you'd make an excellent paralegal with your love of detail and investigation."

When I said I didn't know what a paralegal was, she explained that a paralegal was a lawyer's assistant and was certified by the American Bar Association, the same association that licensed attorneys nationwide. As my physician and nurse friends were leaving the medical field for various reasons, I changed to a business law major using my nursing and paralegal classes for my electives.

As I was still a competitive ice skater, my biggest problem was finding school classes to fit my work and skating schedule. There were six junior colleges within an hour's drive, so each semester I would get each college's paper class schedule, then figure out which schools had the classes available at a time I could attend. I attended Saddleback, Irvine, Orange Coast, Golden West, Coastline, and Long Beach City Junior Colleges to attain my Associate of Arts degree, often as many as three schools at once during one semester. This was not forbidden—it just became more expensive, as each school required non-class fees. I figured out the costs as I needed the particular classes.

Although every semester I received numerous scholarships for my high GPA, school still was very expensive for me, and I needed to be very creative in attending and paying.

For TV courses, I knew that the neighborhood public library was required to carry a videotape of the TV classes. I couldn't watch the TV classes, as I was working and there were not yet DVR recorders, so I would check out the full TV classes' series of videos from the library and watch each week's video classes consecutively for an entire weekend, and do all the homework and mail in the exams in one weekend. I did this every four weeks. I would attend the classes' finals reviews and using a $20 hand held tape recorder, I'd record the teacher's finals review, type it out from the recording, and study from the teacher's review I typed out.

As an independent manicurist, I made my own hours, so if a much-needed class was anywhere near a time and day I could manage, I'd offer my clients free appointments for that semester if they would agree to move their appointment to another day just for the sixteen-week semester. My schooling was a win-win for all!

My clients were very supportive, and the four teachers who were my clients spent *their* appointments tutoring me while I did their nails, and then paid me!

Simultaneously with my education, I continued to turn my attention to getting Adult Skaters into the closed doors of the highly-restrictive elite USFS.

I met Adult Skaters Donna Fountain and Nancy Horton, both visitng from Northern California and they told me to join the USFS Los Angeles Figure Skating Club.

The USFS Los Angeles Figure Skating Club (LAFSC) is one of the oldest, most elite, and most prestigious USFS Clubs in America, and one of the few USFS Clubs nationally willing to include Adult Skaters in their closed, club-members-only competitions. These were not qualifying competitions, but they were sanctioned and accredited USFS events, and we had our foot in the door by competing in these USFS events.

Jack and Eleanor Curtis were on the Board of Directors, and the LAFSC Board was an early champion of and approved of opening the USFS to Adult Skaters including a national event. Other highly supportive members were Morry and Elda Stillwell, Wayne Hudley, Kim Cozean, Sharon Watson, Laura Chinook, and Mary Roof, all of whom served diligently on the elite Los Angeles Figure Skating Board in capacities as judges, accountants, and referees. We remain deeply indebted to them and the other members of the LAFSC club and their Boards for all their diligent efforts to open the USFS qualifying competitions to Adult Skaters wishing to compete on an elite level.

I am proud and honored to still count these exemplary people of the Los Angeles Figure Skating Club as my friends today.

To this purpose the LAFSC's Club competition was closed to non-club skaters, and if you joined their skating club, they would have an event for Adult Skaters. Donna Fountain, Nancy Horton and myself were now United States Figure Skating Los Angeles Figure Skating Club members, and we competed as Adults in one of the first-ever Adult Skating USFS sanctioned and accredited events. The Curtis' daughter, Denise Curtis, is a beautiful and strong Adult Skater who also competed, winning many Adult Skating medals for her elegant and powerful skating.

Donna Fountain instructed me that every time there was a USFS skating club competition anywhere in California, we would all first join that club as new members, then we would take the competition entry forms, *write in* an Adult Skating event, and submit all our applications *together* in one envelope. This was done because often the club excuse was, "We need two Adult Skaters for an event."

There were often figures, freestyle, interpretive, and Showcase of light entertainment and dramatic performances as separate events. So with our three new club memberships at $65 each, with each of us entering a minimum of three events—$60 for the first event, $50 for the second and third events—this totaled up to a *lot of money* given to the struggling skating clubs.

As Donna Fountain said with a huge grin, "No club is going to return hundreds of dollars." On our request to be included we would politely state that we did not need clean ice, we did not care what time of the day or evening we skated, and we would comply with any conditions the club wished to provide us with, *please just let us compete somewhere in your competition.* Reluctant as the clubs were, we were never refused inclusion in a USFSA Adult Skating event. And the three of us often skated in terrible conditions—but the important fact was, we were competing in *USFS sanctioned and accredited* ice skating competitions.

Starting in 1980 and using this method repeatedly, Donna and Nancy would travel to Southern California to ensure a USFS Adult Skating event, and I would travel to Northern California to ensure their USFS events. Additionally, Donna and Nancy were the first adults to be doing double jumps in Adult Skating competitions; this was thought to be possible only for younger skaters. We also continued competing in ISI competitions.

I have every one of the programs, judges' score sheets, medals, trophies, and videos from every one of the early years of our Adult USFS ice skating adventures.

During the years of 1980 to 1994, although Donna, Nancy and I *did not start Adult Skating* in the USFS—utilizing our original, unique method of joining the individual USFS clubs, then writing in Adult Skating events on the clubs' competition entry forms for often four events each, and sending hundred of dollars of our combined club and entry fees—Donna Fountain, Nancy Horton and I were able to inaugurate, compete in, and win USFS Adult Skating gold medals and Adult Skating podium wins in the very first ever Adult United States Figure Skating competitions. These competitions were added to the following TWELVE United States Figure Skating Clubs' elite skating competitions— Adult Skating competitions which continue today for hundreds of current adult competitors:

All Year Figure Skating Club
Chabot Skate Palomar Figure Skating Club
Conejo Valley Figure Skating Club
Culver City Figure Skating Club
Golden State Figure Skating Club
Golden West Figure Skating Club
Mesa Verde Figure Skating Club
Orange County Figure Skating Club
South Bay Figure Skating Club
Pasadena Figure Skating Club
San Diego Figure Skating Club
San Fernando Valley Figure Skating Club
Van Nuys Figure Skating Club
West Covina Figure Skating Club

In order to bring attention to the desire to have Adult Skaters added to the USFS, Nancy and I would often skate two completely different USFS competitions on a single weekend, with three events each, for a total of six events each weekend. It was not unusual to skate in competitions for four weekends in a row. If we could get an Adult Skating event, we showed up, and we skated. We competed at least once a month for years doing multiple events each. Whatever it took to keep Adult Skaters in the USFS public eye, we did as there were often just the two of us in the entire event.

In 1986 our hopes, dreams, and goals came to life as the Los Angeles Figure Skating Club hosted the inaugural, first United States Figure Skating sanctioned and accredited United States Open National Showcase America.

Knowing I could use spotlights to highlight my dramatic effect, I called Olympian Jill Watson as I had never skated in spotlights and asked Jill's advice as I would not have any opportunity to have even one practice using spotlights. Jill said, "The spotlight effect is very dramatic but you can't see where the ice ends so you run the risk of running into the boards. Don't look directly at the spotlights. You can take a chance for the effect and try not to run into the boards or play it safe and see where you're skating!"

I decided to take the big chance and go for the win, informing the organizers I would be skating in the spotlights! I was so thrilled to not run into the boards and also to win the inaugural, first-ever United States Figure Skating Adult National Open Showcase America gold medal and I repeated as the United States Figure Skating Adult National Open Showcase gold medalist in 1987 through 1991.

The judges and accountants at the beloved Los Angeles Figure Skating Club knew how thrilled I was to win the inaugural, first Adult National Showcase and presented me with their original judges' score sheet, where I still to this day proudly read the "1" next to my name on the list of 12 competitors, as I was awarded first place by the five USFS National Judges and verified by the USFS National Referee. I was thrilled.

In later years Donna Fountain, Nancy Horton and I were joined in our USFS competitions by exceptionally beautiful Adult Skaters CeCe Frankenhusen, Kathleen Powers, and Melissa Parker as the Adult Skating contingent slowly grew through the 1980s and 1990s, as more Adult Skaters joined and discovered the joy of ice skating competitions within the elite USFS.

Additionally, the Los Angeles Figure Skating Club continued to champion opening the USFS for Adult Skaters to compete in the highly prestigious and elite Southwest Regional Qualifying and the Pacific Coast Sectional events.

Both my friend Adam Jim Swift and I had the unique privilege and the honor to compete and medal in the inaugural, first USFS Adult Southwest Regionals, qualifying as a medalist and advancing to the inaugural, first USFS Adult Pacific Coast Sectionals.

Adam and I again had the honor and privilege of repeating as a qualifying medalist in both the second Adult USFS Southwest and second Adult USFS Pacific Coast Sectionals.

There were no Adult Nationals at the time I skated; if there were, Adam and I and the other medalists for both Men and Women would have advanced to Adult Nationals.

In 1995, through the efforts of Joe Kaplenk and Rhea Schwartz, and with help from my original skating friends Nancy Horton, Donna Fountain and the indomitable team of Jack and Eleanor Curtis and the backing of the distinguished Los Angeles Figure Skating Club and others, the United States Figure Skating Committee restructured the old 1986-1994 United States Adult Nationals competitions— first accredited and sanctioned by the United States Figure Skating and held at the Los Angeles Figure Skating Club in 1986—into a new, tiered Adult Skating track, and held the first newly restructured Adult Nationals in 1995 under their new system.

Upon written verification requests to the Governing Board of United States Figure Skating and in-person meetings, my first ever Adult USFS National Titles starting in 1986 are still recognized by the USFS, although the dates fall outside of the later, current Adult Skating track.

I was forced into retirement from competitive skating in 1993 by my intervention in a skating mother beating and punching her young daughter in the ice rink, which resulted in my own assault, battery, and severe concussion when attacked by the skating mother. I was unable to continue skating. Police response, intervention by LA Child Protective Services, and my intervention and attack were reported by Dana Parsons in the Los Angeles Times in 1993, in an article titled "Coming Between Parent and Child can Be Risky Business." My attack was reported a second time when a local reporter did an article on the consequences of being a Good Samaritan.

Although I was saddened to leave competitive ice skating—and all ice skating—due to the severe injuries, I left knowing I had changed the sport I loved for the better, knowing I had helped to open wide the door of USFS Adult Skaters' inclusion to qualifying events.

As iconic legend Billie Jean King has said, "We paved the way and made it much easier for today's women to compete." I attend today's numerous USFS Adult events fondly remembering the fight to open the door for these, the Adult skaters that would follow Donna, Nancy and myself.

At the time I retired from USFS and ISI figure skating competition in 1994, I held more United States Figure Skating Adult National gold medals, Adult USFS National and Adult Regional and local competition podium medals, as well as holding the record for the most combined USFS and ISIA Adult gold medals and podium medals than any other Adult Figure Skater in the history of both the United States Figure Skating and Ice Skating Institue associations.

My friend JoAnn Schneider-Farris still an active ice skater says, "Everywhere I skate, everybody knows Rosie George Finocchi because you did every single competition they ever had for decades!" That many competitions do add up to a lot of medals and trophies!

The United States Figure Skating organization confirmed to me in 2018 that my competitive ice skating accomplishments still stand today. Nancy Horton and Donna Fountain hold the second and third place records, respectively, for the most USFS Adult gold medals and podium wins.

Today, amazingly, Adult figure skating pioneers Adam Jim Swift, now a coach, Nancy Horton, Kathleen Powers and Melissa Parker still compete just as powerfully and beautifully, in both the USFS and ISI competitions, again winning National medals in addition to continuing to pass difficult Gold tests in all disciplines. CeCe Frankenhusen is a talented coach, successfully guiding her students to their own wins. They are joined world-wide by more then 30,000 adult figure skaters, as there are now International Competitions for Adults.

Today's Adult skaters display a beautiful combination of power, elegance and artistic, musical expression. In addition to my pioneering Adult skater Adam Jim Swift, my favorite skaters include Jennifer Jones, Carolee Kness, Elizabeth Palomeque, Kathleen Westmoreland, Paula Ky Santos, Lauren Day, Cbella Vida, Deana Crisso Sroka, Scott Davis and Jose Antonia Hinojos. Each performance more breathtaking than the last. A new acquaintance is the incredibly gifted Rohene

Ward who lights up the ice with his innovative and unique skating. Rohene is the 2015 and 2017 Choreographer of the year and his performances show why.

Additionally, with today's social media I have the privilege and honor of being friends with Olympic gold medalist Trixi Schuba and Olympic medalist Barbara Roles-Williams, long considered one of the best skaters and coaches in the world.

The older discipline known as School Figures is also enjoying a comeback and NancyBlackwell-Grieder is the 2017 Ladies Gold Medalist of the 2017 World Figure and Fancy Skating Championship skated each year on unique black ice in Vail, Colorado.

Although the early years of Adults being allowed into the United States Figure Skating were met with pockets of resistence, todays Adults are a welcomed and thriving, important part of the USFS. Adults are known for their world-wide friendships and unparallel camaraderie as seen by the friendships seen at competitions.

As the needs of adult skaters differ from those of their younger counter parts it's no wonder master costume designers such as Natasha Estrada of Los Angeles is recognized as one of the top custom designers for adults. Nastasha understands the differences and advices Adult skaters, "Have fun! Picking a costume for your adult figure skating experience needn't be a stressful experience. Don't feel the pressure to wear what the younger skaters do. Instead chose your costume so you can showcase your skating at its best. When it comes to bling let taste be your guide. There really is no right or wrong, only personal preferences."

Small wonder with such fun advice Natasha adds to the fun of skating with her beautiful and elegant sparkly dresses.

Interest in Adult Figure Skating continues to grow world-wide as evidenced by Alexandra Sell's beautiful movie that chronicles learning to ice skate and compete as an adult, "Die Anfängerin" (The Beginner".) Alexandra was honored as Winner of Best Director at the 2018 Ft. Lauderdale Film Festival.

Figure skating gave me a daily sense of purpose, goals and accomplishment which mirrored my thinking regarding my continuing education. Throughout my exhilarating adult competitive ice skating accomplishments, I still kept attending my college classes. Finally in 1993, when I was forty years old, I received my first college degree—my Associate of Arts degree—with honors, and also I became a Certified American Bar Association paralegal, also with honors. I was crazy proud of myself.

It was also very important to me that from the very first class I took at my local junior college, I always received merit scholarship based on my grades which greatly encouraged me to continue my goal of higher education and job skills.

This was very new to me—starting to be proud of myself—as was achieving my goals. I was so happy when friends and family attended my college graduation and later my party, including my ice skating friends: 1988 Olympic & World Pairs Bronze medalist Jill Watson and my longtime training partner, Adam Jim Swift.

In 1999, my constant and pounding headaches which I thought were caused by allergy and stress lent themselves to the discovery that I had a possibly cancerous tumor suspected of having been in my head for at least 10 years as it was now the size of a tangerine. My surgeon was facial reconstructive specialist Dr. Robert Woods and he was nothing short of miraculous. The tumor had fingers and strands deeply woven throughout my head and attached to the base of my tongue, my upper pallet and numerous other places as it was located behind the bone surrounding my right eye and had in fact eroded the bone underneath my right eye to the extent that had I been hit on that bone it would have snapped like a twig.

Dr. Woods carefully explained I would have a four hour surgery as Dr. Woods would need to move out of the way my jugular vein, my carotid artery and my trigeminal nerve in order to access the tumor. Dr. Woods could not guarantee me that he would be able to even remove the entire tumor and detailed the possible scary potential side-effects of the operation I was facing including facial paralysis and reduced arm movement. I would not be able to talk or swallow without great difficulty following the surgery and should expect to be hospitalized for several days.

As my day of surgery approached I was quite terrified as I'd never had even a stitch. I was comforted to know more than 1500 people were praying for a safe and successful surgical outcome.

Upon coming out of the anesthesia effects, I had no pain and no difficulty either talking or swallowing and Dr Woods and the floor nursing staff were quite amazed.

Dr. Woods asked me how many people had been praying for me. When I told Dr. Woods the number of people praying for me was around 1500 people I asked him why. Dr. Woods informed me their prayers had not been in vain as Dr. Woods said the operation had gone much quicker than he expected as when he had gripped the tumor with his forceps and wiggled it to see gauge how firmly it was attached to my head in all the places the MRI had indicated, the tumor had slid out of my head in one very heavily encapsulated piece. Dr. Woods informed me there had not been the need for any additional surgery. I had no pain at the hospital and went home the next day.

I was so grateful my tumor tested benign.

I continued working but was still limited in earning potential as my attitude and work ethics did not combine to make me a perfect employee.

As I continued in school and working I was on an extremely tight budget. I was determined to stay in school and while my scholarships helped, it was still expensive to attend but I became very creative including attending the local food bank SOS where I lived.

I chose to live in a run-down trailor in a trailer park that I bought for $2000. The trailor did not have any heat and as it was close to the street and the large garbage bins for the property. I was frightened every night as I heard the local drunks using the garbage cans, always afraid someone would wander to my trailer which was a couple feet from the large commercial garbage bins.

As scared as I was, I kept working and attending school, finishing classes and staying always forward-focused.

Every week I would drive to the local food bank early in the morning and be given a number for my brown paper bag of food. There were piles of day old bakery breads and other baked items stacked on a table we could take for free. I filled my bags with those items in addition to receiving one large paper bag each week filled with various food perishables and cans.

As odd as it sounds, each week I looked forward to the possibility of two actions happening which always brightened my otherwise weary day at the local food bank.

First, on occasion, the SOS food bank would add to my brown bag a lump of cellophane-wrapped unlabeled meat that resembled a cut of beef and I would be absolutely thrilled to know I would have a little meat that I could stretch for my week. Second, there would sometimes appear at the top of my brown paper bag of food items a single long stemmed rose. I was to find out someone would anonymously drop off bouquets of long stemmed flowers and the SOS food bank would place them in the bags of their female participants. I was super happy when my bag would include a cellophane-wrapped lump of meat AND a single long stemmed rose.

Additionally, I qualified to receive a few dollars in County Food Stamps which I was very grateful to receive as every little bit allowed me to continue my goal of furthering my education and adding more job skills.

I continued doing all I could to improve my life and I continued to receive more healing, growing stronger every year, but my final healing would not come until 2010, when I read Johnny Baker's book.

At that time, in 2010, I was a perfect example of what Joyce Meyer describes when she states, "When your foundation is broken, everything you attach yourself to is broken. Allow God to do the full work in your life and do what God has called you to do."

James and Betty Robison had a guest couple on their program *Life Today*, Aaron and Amanda Crabb. They spoke of how their album *Restore* came to life. Aaron Crabb said, "There is no condemnation to ask God 'why?' We need God's grace and mercy. Invite God in and He will restore. Why is it so hard to say, 'I need help?' There is nothing cool about being tough."

Aaron's words resonated and described perfectly why I had continued my quest to be fully restored and fully healed. And I did not care how long it took; God was helping me to heal, and I knew it.

Because God is a lot like that, I've learned, when God heals our orphan hearts.

ROSIE GEORGE FINOCCHI

"Accepting things I cannot change is
central to experiencing serenity"
Living Serenity: The Serenity Prayer and Scripture
Deborah Galasso, R.N., M.S.

Chapter 24

Unresolved Trauma Bleeds into Every Area of Your Life, and I'm Really Not Okay

*"Your ears shall hear a word
behind you, saying, 'This the way,
walk in it'" (Isaiah 30:21).*

The movie "Denial" says it best; "The trouble is what feels best isn't always what works best."

I was now forty years old, and I had already journeyed quite a distance from my homeless, ninth grade education days. I had succeeded in changing many of my feelings about myself that were birthed in my past—as simultaneously, during the last fifteen years, I had completed my Associate Degree with honors, had become an American Bar Association paralegal with honors, and had won the very first United States Figure Skating National Adult Showcase gold medal. As verified by United States Figure Skating, I also held the most USFS Adult National and Regional gold medals and combined USFS and ISI medals—a record that still stands today.

During this time, I met Arnette Travis, a licensed stock broker who changed my life forever for the better. After investing a very small amount of money with Arnette she patiently answered all my questions regarding investments, and it is Arnette's patient instructions and life-long friendship that have allowed me to wisely invest small amounts of money with good returns.

I had quite a bit to be proud of. As I continued to believe education would be a way out of abject poverty, I continued with additional training and classes. I traveled to another state and studied for a year and became a licensed stock broker and financial advisor. I added a course in taxes by H & R Block and was now certified to prepare taxes. I learned as much as I could and became an accomplished American Bar Association senior trial paralegal.

However, in spite of all my new accomplishments, I still enabled and tried to rescue some family members and friends, leading to extreme financial losses and immense frustration on my part. I was driving up and down the state and sleeping very little as I tried to take care of everybody but myself in a really healthy way.

What I had slowly discovered was that unresolved, only-covered-up grief, coupled with unrealistic expectations, produces a less than emotionally healthy person, and I became that person.

Grief's twin is fear.

Grief and fear had become my two best friends, and no amount of outside accomplishments and awards and accolades made a difference.

My unresolved griefs and fears made themselves known in my life in subtle but very destructive ways. I did not realize that I harbored and protected my secret, deep, unresolved grief, as that had been all my deeply damaged orphan's heart had known for decades.

As unsteady as I felt, these feelings felt familiar and brought me an odd comfort. I continued to become healthier in some areas, but my deep orphan's grief remained stoic, untouched, and buried—and most importantly, it was therefore unresolved, locking me into continued patterns of well-meaning but very self-destructive behaviors.

This continued year after year and soon, decade after decade. I was continuing to get healthier in many ways, yet I felt I still had so many broken places deep inside of me—like I wasn't really a whole, healthy person. I still had issues with being overweight, trouble with work authorities, financial issues, panic attacks if I didn't control everything—and I sure didn't trust very many people.

Bible teacher Joyce Meyer teaches, "The very best gift you can be is to present yourself as a healthy individual, as it's very hard to be all broken inside and the other person you are with is walking on eggshells."

I began to discover that *unresolved trauma* has a way of making itself at home in your life and then *bleeding into every other part of your life.* I hid it very well, but I *knew* I still wasn't healthy emotionally, physically, financially, or even spiritually.

When your life's been out of control, you can't trust not being in control. I hid all this very well. I'd learned to be very self-sufficient when my father died. Feeling I didn't matter at all, in spite of all my exterior accomplishments, I knew I had gotten really good at the façade, but the façade was hard to maintain especially when you know deep down, *you're now the one that's really not okay.*

As emotionally unhealthy as I was, I always knew I'd be made whole. I constantly felt like I lived on two mountain tops. Over here, on this first mountain top, I was doing my best, attaining goals and accomplishments; this looked good from the outside to everyone looking at me—but I knew that inside, in my heart, there were a lot of broken places in me still.

Then over here, on this other mountain top, this was where wholeness and joy and contentment lived and thrived. I always *knew* I'd get over to the other mountain top of joy and contentment there, but there was this chasm between the two mountains. No matter what I did, no matter what I accomplished, no matter how diligently I worked, I could not ever figure out *how* to get over to that other mountain top of true wholeness; to live in the calmness of real, authentic joy, where I was as peaceful inside as I appeared outside.

That was what my heart longed for: authentic peace, joy, and contentment as an everyday way for me to live; but I couldn't bridge that gap between what my reality was and what I believed a healthier me would look like.

I've always liked the scripture in Ezekiel that says, "I, God, looked for someone to stand in the gap." I always liked that scripture because first, God acknowledged that there are gaps, and second, because God also acknowledged that we sometimes need help to get over our personal gaps, whatever they may be.

For me, year after year, I just couldn't figure out how to get over that gap. *But I knew –* God promised healing. *I knew it and I clung to that.* I kept running after my healing, yet still struggling with gross obesity, financial issues, problems with work authorities, and getting fired—which, of course, totally stemmed from being in control at a young age and having to take on adult responsibilities, endless issues of control and self-worth, and feeling overwhelmed and ill-equipped. But I never gave up hope.

Never.

On vacation during Thanksgiving of 2009, I read John Baker's book *Celebrate Recovery* and learned of Celebrate Recovery's free, year-long Step Study program which, in a same-sex weekly group meeting, gently walks you through the twelve steps to healing and wholeness. *Celebrate Recovery* is a Christ-based twelve-step recovery program based in Rick Warren's Saddleback Church, using Christ's teachings of the Beatitudes to implement the twelve steps to healing.

Every *Celebrate Recovery* location welcomes anyone with a "hurt, habit or hang-up," so the emphasis is not just on the more traditional drug and alcohol participants. *Celebrate Recovery* is usually held at a church location, but it is not a church service.

I was determined to find one. I found a *Celebrate Recovery* Step Study at Los Alamitos Cottonwood Church. Celebrate Recovery's Ministry Director, Pastor Gene Pitrini, has been assistant pastor at Cottonwood Church for over twenty-eight years. Pastor Gene and Kimberly Carlile founded *Celebrate Recovery* at Cottonwood Church eleven years ago. Kimberly had come from a background of heroin addiction and prison and now was celebrating a clean and sober, changed life— because Jesus Christ gave her the power to change.

I came that first night to Cottonwood Church *Celebrate Recovery* and asked, "Where's your Step Study? I want in that Step Study." The Step Studies close after the first month, as the participants bond and it's too difficult for a newcomer to feel like they fit in and feel safe with strangers. It was the last week before the ladies' Step Study would close and the leaders said, "Well, you're coming in at the middle." And I said, "I really need your *Celebrate Recovery* Step Study. If you will let me in the Step Study, I promise I'll follow all your instructions."

Graciously, my Step Study leaders Kim Eliff and Joy Cuciak allowed me to join in June of 2010. Kim and her husband Mark were the *Celebrate Recovery* ministry leaders. My life would never be the same, as I would find the peace and healing that had for so long—up until that moment—eluded me.

I remember that from the very first *Celebrate Recovery* meeting, every single time I'd park my car in the parking lot, and before I even had my car turned off, I'd start to cry because I knew, *I knew, I knew* that I'd found the place where, if I didn't quit, I would be made whole.

I felt like I had found the place where I could partner with God and be healed. I never, ever doubted that I was in a safe place for my healing and a safe place for my restoration from all the traumas and grief I had known. I would think, *God, you know I love you and I know you love me; I'm going to hold Your feet to the fire, and now You will heal me because You said You would, and I'm going to hold on here and see that You do*!

Every single week, every Tuesday morning from 9:30 a.m. to 11:30 a.m. for the entire first Step Study, as I said, I cried—every single week. I made myself one promise: "I will do my weekly *Celebrate Recovery* Step Study homework, and I will show up every week, and I will not quit."

In this Step Study I met Karen Ramsey, who was to become a dear, beloved friend.

For every week of the first year of 2009 – 2010, I kept showing up; I kept doing my homework, and I kept following the *Celebrate Recovery* program. I graduated the *Celebrate Recovery* program and, along with Karen Ramsey, was asked and decided to become a Step Study leader. Karen and I started with twelve ladies, and we ended one year later with the same twelve ladies. Karen and I have been told we were the first Step Study to start and end with the exact same participants, as life happens and participants will often drop out for unavoidable reasons.

Karen Ramsey and I went on to lead nine more year-long *Celebrate Recovery* Step Studies as servant-leaders, for a total of ten Step Studies now completed.

I have loved every one of the ten *Celebrate Recovery* Step Studies I have attended. True trauma and grief resolution takes time—nothing happens overnight—and I had lived so many years damaged; going forward I would be healthier every day and every year.

As I moved forward in directly addressing my grief and traumas I would remember what Bible teacher Christine Caine taught: "I decided to make what Jesus Christ had done for me bigger than anything Satan had done to me."

I knew I had a lot of issues and griefs to address, and in *Celebrate Recovery*, I found a safe place in which to look at the griefs I've known and the sadness and aloneness I have felt. I found that the people in *Celebrate Recovery* are people who totally believe in you and are totally behind you as you seek your healing.

As Karen and I continued each year to lead another *Celebrate Recovery* Step Study group, my issues slowly resolved, and I realized that my horrific panic attacks had subsided as I was addressing and admitting the truth about myself.

Bible teacher Joyce Meyer teaches, "The scripture 'You shall know the truth and the truth will set you free,' means we are to know the truth about yourself, and to allow God to heal the broken places and bring wholeness."

I found the year-long homework books of *Celebrate Recovery* to gently guide me through the process of honestly looking at the truth about myself, my responses, my attitudes, and my survival and defensive behaviors to trauma that were self-destructive to my hope of a healthy life.

Step Four of the *Celebrate Recovery* program says, "We made a searching and fearless moral inventory of ourselves." This meant I was to write about my painful issues and share them with a trusted person: my sponsor, my Step Study leader Kim Eliff. With so many issues, I decided to write mine as a chronological autobiography.

One cool, quiet morning I cleared my glass table and put pen and paper on it.

I then sat down at my table and I wrote one sentence: "I was born in Buffalo, New York, in my happy house," and I started weeping and weeping and weeping. I could not stop weeping.

Then I remembered years earlier, when I had attended Pastor Jentezen Franklin's Free Chapel church in Irvine, California, Pastor Franklin had taught that a man had traveled cross-country to his father's grave to offer forgiveness to his father.

My close Christian friend and mentor, Hodges Pickens, has always told me to pay attention to the scriptures and sermons that come to mind as you are praying, as they are often God's guidance and direction for a matter.

Weeping and remembering Pastor Jentezen Franklin's sermon on forgiveness, I knew with instant clarity that I needed to go back to Buffalo and make peace with my parents' deaths and all the chaos of the ensuing years.

I had not been home to Buffalo in thirty-six years. Thirty-six years had passed since I drove west to California, leaving my parents' graves and my little sister Lisa behind.

Buffalo wasn't a place of great memories. I had thought my relatives didn't care about my family, and the panic attacks I had endured for almost thirty years did not let me travel; there simply was no way for me to get on an airplane for five hours when I had been terrified to sit in a friend's car for even two minutes.

There had been very little contact with my relatives in Buffalo, New York, except for Christmas cards from my kind cousins at Christmas. In 1976 when I left Buffalo after failing to have my baby sister Lisa returned to me, there was no Facebook, or cell phones, or any other easy, cheap means of communication that exist today.

Further, whenever I thought of Buffalo, I had nothing but an endless, gaping hole of deep sadness where anyone or anything connected to Buffalo had been concerned.

I had not made any effort to stay in touch with any of my relatives in Buffalo since my return to Southern California thirty-six years ago.

In truth, in 1972 when I had been nineteen, the year my mom died—five years after my father—I had been a mouthy, stubborn, know-it-all, determined person who listened to nobody. I had thought, *If I don't get done what needs to get done, it's not going to get done.* This independent attitude had been reinforced by the crushing poverty my siblings and I had endured all alone, with me working four jobs when I was nineteen years old and struggling to simply feed and house my family. Through no fault of theirs, I thought my relatives were kind, extended family—and I felt like I had alienated them, and therefore I felt I was useless to them. I was used to taking care of everybody and struggling alone. I really thought no one in Buffalo cared about me or my siblings at all.

Strangely, ten years earlier with my panic attacks *completely* restricting me from even riding in a friend's car, I had signed up for Citibank American Airlines miles. I flew nowhere! *Never!*

Scripture says, "Before you have asked, I, God, have answered." I was healthy now and could fly without any issues, and I realized I should find out what happened to all those Citibank American Airlines miles that I had signed up for ten years earlier.

American Airlines requires 50,000 miles for one person to fly coast to coast. I was hoping I had enough miles to fly to Buffalo by myself. I needed to make several phone calls over several days, but American Airlines finally tracked down my airline miles and confirmed *that lo and behold, I had 155,000 miles available to use for flights, anywhere and anytime I wanted to fly!*

So I called my brother Daniel, and we were ecstatic to make plans to go back to Buffalo, New York. The roundtrip Los Angeles to Buffalo flights for my brother and me would not cost me a penny, thanks to Citibank and the American Airlines mileage plan! We were so excited to go home!

Life mentor and teacher Alica Bett Chole teaches, "Doors allow us access to questions, questions that then allow us answers."

The American Airlines miles which I had now discovered were mine to use would become the doors that would make it possible for my brother and me to journey back to Buffalo, New York—allowing me the luxury to access the doors as to why these events had happened.

After I had made plans for a hotel and car rental for our return visit to Buffalo in the summer of 2011, I called my cousin Joanne, who still lived in Buffalo, asking to see her when I visited. Joanne had taken me to visit my mom every

Friday while my mom was at Roswell Park Cancer Institute in 1972.

To my complete surprise and delight, Joanne insisted that my brother and I stay with her and said our other relatives wanted to see us. I was so very surprised.

I had not seen my cousin Joanne or any of my Buffalo relatives since 1976. 36 years had passed.

But that was soon to change; as were a lot of old, deeply engrained, incorrect beliefs that were about to be challenged and healed by facing the truth of my life's events, enveloped in God's steady love—the truth of what had happened during the years following my parents' deaths.

As Joyce Meyer teaches, "I can't promise you that when you give your life to God and become a Christian, you will never have another problem. But I can promise you, you will never face another problem alone. You'll face your problems with God's help."

The horror's grip was ever-loosening.

I knew I would not be alone. God would closely walk this latest journey—towards more healing of my orphan heart, step by precious painful step—with me.

But God is a lot like that, I've learned, when God heals our orphan hearts.

Chapter 25

You Can Go Home Again; the Path To Healing is Through *Celebrate Recovery*

Beloved family home in Buffalo, New York, 1967, where my father died, where I returned 36 years later, to make peace.

MY PARENTS' ORPHANS

*"In returning and rest you shall be
saved, in quietness and confidence shall
be your strength" (Isaiah 30:15).*

"My Buffalo home has been only five hours away for the last thirty-six years. It's been right here, five hours away, for thirty-six years."

That thought kept repeating itself over and over as our American Airlines 737 jet that had left Los Angeles at midnight the night before and carried us across the country was skimming over the trees in the foggy, early morning, on approach to bring my younger brother Daniel and me home to Buffalo. It was thirty-eight years since we were orphaned; thirty-six years since I had lost my court battle for my little sister Lisa. I had left all the grief of my Buffalo memories behind as I returned to Southern California, determined to keep the promise to take care of my father's children that I had made when I was only thirteen—a lifetime ago.

As the ground came up to meet us, my heart jumped at the recognition of the quaint little homes of Buffalo—the big backyards, the quiet, tree-lined streets—so very different from the fast-paced housing tracts of cookie-cutter homes so popular in Southern California.

As we approached the Buffalo airport runway, I was looking out at the trees and pondering the immensity of the startling fact that I was really, truly seconds away from touching down, back in the place I loved and hated the most. I had loved Buffalo because I had been so delightfully, carelessly happy in our happy home that my father had built on Thurston. I had known unselfish love from my parents and siblings and had reveled in that amazing love.

Yet, I hated Buffalo with all that was within me—because every shred of security, every shred of confidence, and every shred of normalcy had been stripped and wrung out of me. I had watched my beloved father die before my eyes; I had watched my beloved mother valiantly and courageously battle for her life as she finally succumbed to cancer's horror; and there, in Buffalo, I had had my baby sister Lisa, whom I had raised, forcibly taken away from me and my siblings.

In October of 1972, the legal authorities in Buffalo had put me on a plane when I had been orphaned days earlier and had falsely assured me that I would be part of a loving family again—a family where I would be loved, protected, and cared about.

Instead, upon my arrival in California, I had been left homeless, broke, and afraid, unexpectedly separated from my three remaining younger siblings and needing strangers to rescue me, needing strangers to give me a home and a hot meal.

Silently, as the American Airlines jet descended into the town of my greatest love and most wretched pain, these thoughts tumbled through my brain—memory after memory after memory flashing before my mind's eye. They reminded me of how wondrously happy I had been, how securely loved I had been. And with equal force, I saw flashing across my mind's eye my father dying before me, me promising my dad I'd take care of his family, us losing our family home, all the chaos of constant evictions, my mom's death, and my frightening homelessness that I had no choice but to endure.

But most importantly, and with equal certainty, I knew that the me that was about to touch down on Buffalo soil was the me that had graduated from the one-year *Celebrate Recovery* twelve-step program, and who had learned that pretending like none of this had ever happened and pretending that none of these numerous traumas had ever occurred only deeply harmed me further.

Relief washed over me; I was so deeply grateful that I was back home, so deeply grateful that I could walk again the streets of my happy home and the sad streets where my parents had died. I would again visit my father's and mother's graves. *I was all of these memories*, not the selected few I pulled out when I needed to be a victim; and I also wasn't the memories which I pretended did not exist when I needed to be strong for myself and to be strong for others.

Living in California for thirty-six years, and not returning to Buffalo for those thirty-six years, had mercifully allowed me enough distance from the horror of my parents' deaths. I had needed that distance because I just could not face seeing the peaceful, quiet streets of Buffalo belying so much horror that had happened to me.

As I felt the unmistakable sound of the tires contacting the Buffalo airport's cement runway and the jarring impact of the engines in reverse thrust, suddenly there was an eerie quiet as we had landed and now would slowly taxi to our gate. The plane's actions matched my own emotions: flying at lightning speed, a ferocious-sounding touchdown, a sudden reversing of energy, and then welcome calm.

Still gazing out of the American Airlines jet's windows, I took in the beauty of the Buffalo trees as we rolled peacefully towards our gate. I had never thought of Buffalo as pretty. I had never thought of anything about Buffalo—other than to stay away as long as I could. To stay away as far as I could.

Yet, that same thought kept repeating: *I'm back home. It was here all along, only five hours away.* Like a song looping in my brain that I could not get out of my head.

Another turn by the jet slowing rolling on the runway and I could see the pretty, well-kept Buffalo homes near the airport—and it just hit me that it was all really real. It was real, and I had done it; I had come back to Buffalo thirty-six years later to face all my fears, face my grief, and face my sadness. Watching the trees and homes roll by, it felt very surreal, and I kept thinking to myself, *Buffalo has been only five hours away for the last thirty-six years. It's always been this close to me, yet it seemed a lifetime away.* I kept thinking of *The Wizard of Oz*, when Dorothy is told, "You could have always gone home."

Buffalo had always been there; home had always been there, *but I wasn't ready* to make the journey. It had taken me thirty-six years to make the five-hour journey home again; but I had done it and here I was, ready to face full-on whatever Buffalo held for me now.

I had succeeded in connecting my past to my present.

Although I had rented a car, my cousin Joanne insisted on meeting my brother and me at the Buffalo airport, eagerly running up the ramp to meet us. Within an hour of our arrival in Buffalo, all my Sicilian aunts and cousins had descended on my cousin Joanne's home with food.

Two of my aunts were still alive who'd known my parents. It was so much fun to hear my parents simply talked about; to hear memories of conversations, family gatherings, and family adventures they remembered. It was delightful to hear my parents called Aunt Margie and Uncle George. I had not heard my parents called those endearing names in thirty-six years. I was basking in so much joy.

After almost five decades of feeling like the oldest, most in-charge person in my family, it was such fun to be the baby cousin, and to be told, "Oh no, honey, don't worry, we have this." I had forgotten how fun it could be to be surrounded by a loving, extended family who shared memories of both good times and bad.

I had the most fun time and wondered why I had waited so long; I loved these relatives of mine and could feel that they loved me back. My hardened, broken orphan's heart was healing by the minute.

Because of *Celebrate Recovery*, I finally understood my mother as they spoke. There wasn't any exact moment when my questions about the "whys" of my mom's behaviors melted away; there simply came a peace and rest in my soul from a deeper understanding of my mom, and even of myself, than I had ever known.

I felt bad that I had waited thirty-six years to return home to Buffalo when I was so warmly welcomed by my loving relatives. Now, sitting at the table surrounded by my aunts and cousins and having so much fun, the pieces of the puzzle fell into place. My first return to Buffalo in 1967 had ended with my father's death and losing our family's home. My second and third return visits to Buffalo had centered on my mom's cancer treatments and her death in 1972, coupled with my sister being forcibly taken from me at that time. My fourth visit in 1974 had ended with the court refusing to return my sister Lisa to me.

I had the epiphany, while sitting at my cousin Joanne's table surrounded by so much fun and laughter and love, that I had never spent time in Buffalo that wasn't crisis-laden, with horrible, sad consequences ending my return visits.

Buffalo had never felt happy to me, so why bother to ever come back?

And as suddenly as I realized why I had not returned home in thirty-six years, because of *Celebrate Recovery* I realized that the uncaring behavior I thought I was witnessing from my relatives when I was so young, after each of my parent's deaths, was really my loving relatives' helplessness at my mom's circumstances—a poor young widow with cancer and five young children.

As *Celebrate Recovery* taught me to make amends, I sat at the table with all my relatives and said I was sorry. I said I was sorry that I hadn't known they cared, and I apologized for being a mouthy, stubborn nineteen-year-old know-it-all.

They all said, "Oh honey, no, don't worry, no you weren't," but my 94-year-old aunt—who had been driven by my sweet cousin Janice from Atlanta, Georgia, just to see me and my brother—caught my eye and nodded, "Why, yes you were."

Later that day, my brother and I simply drove around what had been our old neighborhoods, and we went to the little white church where we used to sing. We sat out in front of the closed, still-picturesque little church. It was raining. We both were silently looking at the church, lost in our memories, and just very spontaneously we both went, "Da Da Dad Da To DAH"—and we just burst out singing, "Onward Christian soldiers, marching off to war." We sang the song, and we were smiling with wet eyes. We didn't say a word to each other, we were just remembering sweet times at what had been our family's childhood church. I had tears running down my face. God heals. Laughing was good.

Before I went home my sponsor, Kim Eliff, had said, "When you go to your parents' graves, I want you to take five flowers, one to represent each of the family members, including yourself" (because I had never seen myself as someone who needed to be taken care of, because I was taking care of everybody). Kim instructed me, "I want you to take one for each child to your parents' graves to symbolize that you are finished keeping your promise to your dad for all of you. You've done all you could do; they are in God's hands now, and now you get to have your own life."

My dad loved petunias, and I would help him plant and water them when we lived in Buffalo and in California.

The next day I got up early, before anyone, and bought ten petunias: five for each grave down the street where our happy house was. The cemetery had just opened, and because of the rain, no workers were working. It was about 7:00 in the morning; there was still a light, drizzly rain, reminding me of the day my dad had died and been buried.

Rounding the small hill, I remembered driving this route in the cemetery so many times, sitting next to my dad to visit his mother, my grandmother; and then later I made this same drive, sitting next to my mom, visiting my father's grave.

Soon the familiar shape of my dad's tombstone came into view, and I was suddenly very overcome—it had all been very, very real. I had really, truly had a dad once who adored me, someone who thought I was special and lovely and delightful exactly as I was. There really, truly, *had been* all that joy once. I had not dreamed that joy or made it up.

I suddenly realized, looking around, that I had nothing to dig the ground and no way to plant the petunias that were so symbolically important. Not even a pen. My dad's family headstone is a foot thick and four feet high.

As I started to walk up the hill the sun broke through, and through my tears I saw something really shiny glinting in the sun. I thought it was another gravestone in the back, with glittering flecks in it.

I was completely wrong; the shiny glittering was not another gravestone.

As I got to my father's headstone I felt drawn to the shiny, glittering spot and saw that there was a bright silver, hand-sized, brand-new gardening tool sitting *as peacefully as could be on the top of my dad's headstone*. Not a speck of dirt or a scratch on it. The gardening tool was brand new; it had never been used.

301

After Jesus' death and burial, Mary goes to Jesus' grave and finds the giant stone rolled away with an angel waiting there. When I saw that gardening tool resting on the top of my father's headstone, brand-new, shining in the sun, I immediately felt in my heart that an angel had been sitting on my dad's headstone for many years, patiently waiting to welcome me home so I could be healed, made whole, and restored again.

God had provided the gardening tool, just as God had provided for me every second since I had witnessed my father dying in front of me.

The moment I looked down and saw my dad's name actually on his gravestone: "George Joseph Finocchi, December 24, 1919 – April 20, 1967," I collapsed on the ground next to his name plate, crying uncontrollably, saying over and over and over, "It was so hard. It was so hard. It was all so very, very hard." I couldn't stop sobbing, and I kept repeating, "It was so hard, it was all so very, very hard."

Now I acknowledged what I had stoically denied all the years I needed to be strong for everybody else, so I could be there for everybody else: my father had been real. My mother had been real, and it wasn't my job to do what I had decided to do.

I'd never, in all the decades since my dad had died, *ever* told anyone it had been hard. But I told my dad over and over and over, for a very long time.

Finally, I planted each flower next to my dad's grave's name plate, using the gardening tool that had been left for me, crying and telling my dad about each of his five children, including myself; telling him details of his children's families, and his grandchildren and great-grandchildren.

Later that day, my cousins Joanne, Clare, and her husband Phil took my brother and me to our mom's grave; and again, sobbing, I repeated planting flowers and telling my mom how her five children were doing.

All I remember of my mom's burial was numbness—and my own silence, compounding my grief.

Later in the afternoon, my younger brother and I went back to my father's grave so that he also could spend some quiet time together with his memories of his father, whom my brother always calls "my hero."

Because we had so many homes and memories to visit, my brother came up with the idea that we should visit in chronological order. Starting with Grandpa's home, we visited there first, and then we excitedly went to our childhood happy home in Buffalo.

I had been able to contact the current owners prior to our trip, and they had agreed to meet us and let us go inside. My "Happy House" was as perfect as I remembered, each room exactly as I had remembered living in them. We went into the basement, and I saw my dad's workshop where he had refurbished my shiny new bicycle all winter, spring, and summer when I was five years old.

I stood in the kitchen where my mom had baked apple pies, and the bathroom where she had braided my long, dark hair. I walked in the grass where I had my swing and my dad had frozen an ice rink for me.

I stood in the living room where I used to twirl and say, "Daddy, watch me dance!"

Next, my brother and I went to the other homes, ending at the home where our father had died.

As we entered the neighborhood we had not seen for 44 years, my brother Daniel asked to go into his grade school alone, and as I sat in the car, my heart was touched watching my brother enjoying a return to his old school.

I remembered how both he and my brother Peter had told me that they remembered walking to school and talking about whether Dad would make it; what a sad conversation for two young brothers, nine and eight years of age. They had both told me how, when the school aide brought a notice in, they each—separately, in different classrooms—knew the note was for them, telling them their beloved Dad had died.

I sat in the car watching my brother walking in and around the grade school and tried to imagine how hard the walk to school—and the harder walk home from school—had been for my younger brothers so long ago.

I have absolutely no memory beyond the phone call where my Uncle Angelo had said only, "Baby, your Daddy's gone."

I don't remember my brothers or my mother coming home, or anything until I was crying myself to sleep that night.

Finally, my brother and I were again standing on the driveway of the home in Tonawanda where we had had so many dreams smashed and never regained. Again, we stood silently, lost in our own thoughts and memories.

Unlike our childhood "Happy House," this house was owned but not lived in, and that seemed oddly fitting for our feelings towards it; it was like it was a ghost house—only a mere shadow of what it once was to my family. It was only a pretend home now, not really a home to another family, because it still held so much overwhelming sadness—too much to overcome to allow joy inside its walls again.

It really was a pretty home—the grass was so green and so lush—yet so lonely; like the home itself was still grieving, all these years later. I walked to the backyard where I used to garden with my dad and then water his garden and flowers, and I peeked over the fence.

When I did, I saw the big, plate glass windows where I used to iron my dad's white business shirts and then hang them on the living room four-foot-high curtain rod that ran across the windows. I was always so proud when I could count ten ironed white shirts belonging to my dad.

This time when I looked at the big plate glass windows, all I saw was a cold, empty shell of a home that represented such horror and grief to me.

There was a large, empty pool taking up the backyard where we had once placed a tent to camp out at night, and where we had so many birthday parties and family meals.

But now the gardens were gone; the only remnants were dead, left-over flowers and lots of dead grass—a backyard completely unkempt and completely unloved.

I could see across the highway behind our home's backyard fence to the white-roofed community center building that in the winter time held the outdoor ice rink where I loved to skate, listening to the popular music of the movie *Romeo and Juliet* and enjoying moonlight skating under the clear, cold, winter nights.

Finally, I was brave enough to go to the front of the house and walk on the front porch, where again so many parties had been held and where I had stood when my Uncle had come to quietly tell me that my mom and dad's little dream home had been foreclosed and then auctioned off, and that we needed to move.

I was able to see into the large living room windows to the exact place where my dad's black and white recliner chair had stood. I could see everything exactly as I remembered it: the doorways, the distance to the kitchen door, the distance to my room down the hallway. I could see all of it.

Looking into that living room in 2011 was to be again in 1967, standing in front of my father's chair, watching him die and having my last-ever conversation with my dad, and making my promise to care for his family—my thirteen-year-old self, making such a serious vow.

I looked through the glass and saw myself at thirteen, and my father in his chair, and my mom in the kitchen.

I felt like I was watching a play onstage, but the actors were my father, my mother, and myself; all alive again, yet unable to stop the inevitable, final, tragic scenes being played out in this owned, yet unlived-in home.

It seemed fitting that although there was furniture in the home's living room, the place where my dad's white and black recliner had been was strangely empty of furniture—like the space had been waiting for a new chair, or the chair had been recently removed. Either way, the spot on the living room rug was devoid of furniture, conveniently allowing me to picture my dad's white and black recliner sitting in the exact place as it had in 1967; sitting there where my father had died in his favorite white and black recliner chair, tragically surrounded by his six-months-pregnant loving wife and four loving children.

My brother Curtis John Michael, only 5 years old, remembers seeing my mom standing at the doorway to the living room, looking at my dad laboring for breath. John Michael remembers, "Mom was holding a plate. Mom looked at Dad, then her face turned white as a ghost and she dropped the plate and it shattered on the kitchen floor."

I felt such sadness knowing that my family's horrors all started in this home; the home with so many unattained hopes, plans, and promises when it had been bought by my parents.

I stood looking through the glass windows, seeing every inch of the living room where my life had changed in an instant, and *I allowed myself to feel every single feeling of sadness slowly gripping me.*

This home was why I was broken for so long. This home was why I had felt unsafe, insecure, and broken for most of my adult life. This was the home that gave birth to my panic attacks, and this was the home I now needed to confront and make my peace with God over.

This was the home for which I had traveled over 3,000 miles, to make my peace with God about the events that had unfolded in this living room; now inches away from me, yet frozen in my memory from a lifetime ago—*a lifetime of consequences* that had unfolded for me because of the horror that occurred in this room, right before my eyes.

This was the home that had ruled my life. This was the home that had held the grief and the secrets and the vows made by me which had driven me in 2010 to *Celebrate Recovery*, to make peace with my past and to find a way to escape from this home's terrible grasp and the vow it had extracted from me at the most agonizing moment of my young thirteen-year-old life.

I was looking directly at the very spot on the rug where my father's chair had been; I was looking directly at that spot on the kitchen floor where my mother had turned white as a sheet and dropped and shattered her plate. Finally, I was looking directly at the spot on the rug where I could visualize my thirteen-year-old self, listening to my dad say, "Oh, God, who's going to take care of my children?" and I saw and heard my thirteen-year-old self, promising my dying father: "Don't worry, Daddy, I will," and I understood it all.

Standing there, watching my life's defining moments from 1967 playing out in my mind's eye, I suddenly and clearly understood my desperate attempt to alleviate my father's immediate pain, and I suddenly and clearly understood my desperate attempt to keep my unrealistic promise for decades—doing my very best, taking care of my four younger siblings until they each became eighteen years of age and went out on their own. But even more importantly I also understood, conversely, *why I had needed* to stay frozen in time and had needed to hide behind my promise to my father.

I had needed to hide behind my promise to my father so in effect, I could hide from having my own life—and thereby avoid the possibility of being vulnerable and being as hurt and grief-stricken as my mother had been, and as grief-stricken as I and my siblings had been.

I realized that after an extended family member had sexually molested me, the only time I had ever felt safe was when my dad was around; and once my dad had died, there was no place in the world that was safe enough.

I understood that it had been the conversation with my father and the events I had witnessed in this living room that had left me falsely believing I could not risk being vulnerable—falsely believing I could not emotionally ever let anyone in—and so for forty years, I had always found something wrong with every man I had ever dated.

From the day my father died, I had falsely believed that I needed to protect myself—as my protector, my father, was gone—and it was much safer for me to overeat. It was much safer for me to gain a lot of weight, because somehow the sexual molestation I had suffered and survived had become entangled with the loss of safety I felt at my father's death—leaving me with the twisted belief that it was not safe for me to be pretty; it was not safe for me to be attractive.

I continued standing there, looking through the window into the living room where my father had died. I was not upset at these revelations occurring to me; rather, they just finally allowed me to make sense. *It was like a blindfold had been removed* and all the dots of the events in my life for the last forty-four years had connected, and my choices and their underlying reasons for all these years just made sense.

As I was looking through the window, I understood with total clarity that the ways in which I had chosen to adapt and survive—at age thirteen, through my teenage years, through my twenties, until the time I came to *Celebrate Recovery* in my late fifties—had been then, and still were now, the "problem" I sought to understand and fix.

I had always known that somehow—in so many ways, if there was a problem in my life, I often felt that I was the problem. But now, for the first time, I really understood the "whys" and the "hows" of my life; how sad the early years had been, combined with my behaviors since my dad died and then my mom died, and why I felt like I needed to take care of everybody except myself. It all just made crystal clear sense now.

And because God had allowed me to come home and had gently helped me to see the truth about myself so that I now understood myself, I knew unequivocally that I could ask God to help me to change into a healthier, more complete version of myself.

As these thoughts continued to fill my heart, a type of blissful, deeply satisfying sense of relief flooded me—and I understood why I did what I did, and why I could not make myself do what seemed so very easy and natural for everybody else.

Vern Perry, my sweet mom Jeannie Perry's husband, knowing of my promise to my father, once told me, "Honey, you made a promise your Daddy never asked you to make and never expected you to keep."

I don't know how long I stood there gazing through that window, watching my life-shattering morning of April 20, 1967, playing before my mind's eye.

I do know that as each epiphany and understanding kept breaking through my long-established patterns of fear, grief, and denial, I felt as if heavy chains were dropping off of me—chains of fear and rejection that I had carried for decades.

God continued speaking softly and clearly to my heart, and I clearly saw that my misguided, self- protective behaviors had become deeply ingrained, self-destructive thoughts and beliefs that had left me with unwelcome and undesired outcomes.

As Bible teacher Joyce Meyer has taught, "Life and death are in the power of the tongue." I finally looked directly at the place where I knew my dad had sat in his white and black recliner as his life had ebbed away, and where I had made my life-defining promise, and said, "I love you, Daddy, and I miss you, Daddy. I wish you had not died; I miss you so much. I am finished with my promise; it's all over, and I am finished. Your family is all grown, and I did my very best. I wish you were here, and I love and miss you and Mom dearly. Good bye, Daddy; I can't keep living out the promise I made to you—it's all over. I love you, I miss you."

I turned from the window, ending my conversation with my beloved father, and went to find my brother—who was roaming our old home's grounds, lost in his own poignant memories.

My brother and I walked the neighborhood and talked of long-ago days and happier times and reflected on how they had all suddenly ended.

On my last day in Buffalo, I drove again to my happy house and I stood there a very long time. Standing on the street gazing at the little house that symbolized all the happy love I had once known, I said out loud, "I was very happy here. I was loved here. I am going *back* to California and I'm going to be every single bit as happy in California as I was here. I'm going to be *every bit* as loved in California as I was here."

I went to the playground down the street that my dad had built me, and it was still there, looking exactly as it looked in my memory from when I was five years old—because nothing changes in Buffalo. There was a light, drizzly rain falling, and no one else was at the playground. My dad's playground has little hobby horses, so I again rode the little hobby horses.

My sister and I share a love of swinging on swings, and even though my sister Lisa does not remember much about our mom, I always tell Lisa that we get our love of swings from her. I remember we never went to a park that our mom didn't swing on the swings, with the biggest of smiles on her face.

I smiled to myself as I actually swung on *my swing* that was still there, thinking of my mom and my sister Lisa and how my life had come full circle, back to the home I dearly loved and knew I was dearly loved in.

There was sweetness to the stillness surrounding me at my dad's playground. I once again found the comfort of being loved. It felt as if my parents were hugging my heart. As the rain continued to drizzle, it felt as if the gentle rain was helping to soften my heart and soften my attitude, and the need to always be in control. I could feel my heart opening up to vulnerability, and feel confidence being born in me as my orphan heart was finding solace, comfort, and hope in the destinations and discoveries where my journey home had taken me.

A deep peace pervaded my heart, and I knew I had been restored. Certainly, there were still issues to be faced, and some hard times and probably angry thoughts I still needed to address, but I knew the lion's share of my healing had been completed with my trip home to face my saddest fears.

I also knew I could trust God to continue to bring to the surface whatever harmful thinking still resided in my heart. And I knew that as more painful memories and attitudes surfaced, I could trust God to also heal me of them.

Above all else, I had faced all that the horror had to throw at me, and I was loved.

God had won.

But God is a lot like that, I've gratefully learned, when God heals our orphan hearts.

Forgiving God

*"Yea though I walk through the valley of
the shadow of death, I will fear no evil,
for you are with me" (Psalm 23:4).*

"Seriously? Really?" These were God's plans for me?

It was 2015, four years after I had gone home to Buffalo, and I was again going through another year-long *Celebrate Recovery* Twelve-Step Study class, knowing I still had stubborn issues I needed God's help to heal.

I had no goal in attending, other than to become as emotionally healthy as I deeply believed God desired to help me to become.

My Step Study leaders were Debbie, a kind, caring woman and Ruth Osborn —an editor who came to know Christ in 1989 at age 32. Both are sweet, knowledgeable women who made us all feel very safe and very loved an atmosphere I desperately needed at that crucial moment.

I was sitting in a shaky plastic chair in a child's Sunday school room in a metal trailer on another hot, sunny May morning in Long Beach. This was my tenth time of journeying through the *Celebrate Recovery* year-long Step Study. My tenth commitment to taking a year, fifty-two weeks of Sunday mornings—sunny Sunday mornings, cold and rainy Sunday mornings, and all the Sunday mornings in-between—with the never-fading hope that God was changing me, God was changing my heart; and continuing to hope that I would have more healing, and that more healing would bring about more joy.

This Sunday's question in our workbook was simple enough. It asked about our thoughts about God's plans for us. I remembered the scripture Jeremiah 29:11, "For I know my plans for you, plans for good and not evil, plans to give you a future and a hope." And without a second passing, the anger I'd long suppressed and refused to acknowledge—believing "a good Christian *can't* be angry at God"—flashed like a lightning strike, giving birth to deeply and secretly held thoughts. They flooded my brain as I was unable to stop the rush of words, finally acknowledged and set free from their dungeon of forty-seven years of carefully hidden, white-hot anger.

My rage erupted silently in my brain and tumbled out, finally unlocked and set free.

Seriously?

Really?

Inwardly I raged at God, still sitting quietly in my shaky plastic chair. No one around me had a clue as to the momentous healing about to take place this morning, as my thoughts continued raging at God faster than I could process them.

I was sexually molested, and I only felt safe with my dad, and You took him when I was thirteen, so I lost all my safety; then, I had to watch my mom slowly die. I was left an orphan at nineteen, my sister was forcibly taken from me, I was separated from my remaining siblings, and I was left, days after I was orphaned, homeless, alone, and very afraid.

*It was so very hard to take care of my family at nineteen,
with a ninth grade education.*
These were Your plans? You planned this?
How and why could You? Why did You do this to me? You!
How?
Why?
What did I do wrong?

I still hadn't said a word, yet I instinctively knew my
charade was over, my façade was irreparably cracked. I knew
I had a choice in which answer I chose to give to my ladies'
group when it would be my turn to speak.

It was not unusual for me to take notes for myself
regarding a painful memory or situation that arose during
the others' responses each week. In fact, my workbook and
notebook were lined with "just for me" notes that I would
write about and later share with just my sponsor.

Through each successive Step Study, I had learned that
I was only as damaged, unhealed, and emotionally sick as my
secrets. In my previous nine Step Studies, as I had done my
homework and then participated in my ladies' group giving
my answers—also listening to the other ladies' answers—I
would sometimes experience a sudden, stinging sadness that
quickly brought tears to my eyes which I fought to hold back
during the remainder of our class.

Each time these tears appeared, they were always in
response to being stung by the suddenness of an unexpected
and deeply painful emotion from a shame and a hurt I had
experienced. I also had the dual awareness that something
incredibly powerful and wonderful was taking place at that
moment of finding and feeling that particular unique pain,
for I knew God had again helped me to uncover an area of
emotional pain. Now that I knew the pain had made itself

known, *if I chose to reveal this painful discovery to another, I could experience healing from it.*

But this was different; this was *big!*

I instantly knew I stood at a crucial, defining crossroads in the complex healing of my orphan heart.

Travis Cox, my *Celebrate Recovery* ministry leader and *Celebrate Recovery* state representative, taught us that our secrets are like a deck of cards—each secret holding a perceived value, which decides how willing we are to share that particular secret with another.

Travis taught us, "We will share our number card secrets, maybe even a Jack or a Queen card secret; they don't have a lot of value. But we sure aren't telling anybody our King and Ace card secrets; those are the really big, ugly, shameful secrets. Yet it is those crucial secrets that are doing the most damage to our hearts, feelings, emotions, and behaviors."

Celebrate Recovery's Pastor Gene Pietrini is a favorite pastor of mine and he teaches the story of "The Trash Man" from Max Lucado's book *Next Door Savior.* An allegory of how we are weighed down by the "trash" of sin, guilt, shame, and regrets but Jesus took our trash. 11 Corinthians 5:21.

Now I was stuck with an important decision to make as the ladies were continuing to answer, working their way around our circle, slowly making their way to me—when it would be my turn to answer. Or I could choose not to answer and pass, or give a less revealing answer.

I had professed to be a Christian for over fifty years; I had been in church leadership and a chaplain for more than nine years. I was known as kind and compassionate.

And now I was to admit I'm *furious* with God?

Admit I'm *angry* at God?

Who says *that o*ut loud?

Yet, I knew; I knew deep in my heart that I had finally come to a crossroads in my life, where I had gone as far as I could go in my healing. I knew I could go no further without being willing to tell my ugly, shameful secret of being angry and mad at God.

I also knew, looking at my small circle of Step Study classmates, that this *Celebrate Recovery* room was the place where I felt the safest. This *Celebrate Recovery* program was the place where, in a room exactly like this room, I had healed from other painful hurts.

Acknowledging how much I trusted my *Celebrate Recovery* program, leaders, and classmates; knowing this was my safe place; knowing that here I felt so safe and so loved; I knew, right at this crossroads of emotions, that I needed to say out loud what had been buried so deeply and had been my profoundly hidden anger now for decades. I needed to say it out loud, so that my anger at God would loosen its grip on me.

I chose to trust God's words of promise to heal my heart if I did my part.

I chose to heal as I waited my turn to speak my answer.

My turn came, and the stillness of the ladies waiting for my answer settled and hung in the air, slowly settling around me as I gathered the courage I had not been able to find in my previous tenth Step Studies. Gathering my composure, I quietly gave my simple, two-sentence, explosive answer.

"I was sexually molested when I was young. At thirteen, I watched my beloved father die in front of me; then at nineteen I watched my beloved mother die in front of me and was left alone, homeless, scared, uneducated—and left raising four siblings because we were all orphaned without any help. *This* was *Your* plan for me God? *You* planned this?" and I stopped speaking.

The silence hung like fog and continued; this time more of an awkward silence for me than anyone else.

Finally Debbie, the leader, said, "Thank you for sharing."

My deepest, saddest thoughts and feelings had been laid bare in front of women who knew and respected me, and I sat quietly with my conflicting emotions. Sad, as I truly loved God—so how could I be so cruel in speaking such angry words out loud about *God?*

Perplexingly, as starkly alone as I felt at that moment, I also felt profoundly joyful—as I had finally said out loud what I had kept hidden for almost fifty years.

The brick walls inside my heart, containing my carefully hidden anger and disappointment in God, had finally begun to crumble. I felt so intensely relieved and took the first really deep breath of total and complete honesty, lacking the shame of needing pretense.

Finally, the totality of what I had said reached into those dark places—the locked, sad places of my heart—and I was once again left with the hope of more healing for my orphan heart.

In the fable "Pandora's Box," it is said that after Pandora's Box is opened and all the ills of the world are released—when Pandora's Box has been totally emptied of every imaginable cruelty, horror, and grief—the bottom of Pandora's Box is lined with hope.

Now all I had left was hope; hope in God, and hope in my Bible verses that I loved so much and clung to.

I sat with my vulnerability completely exposed, yet I had never felt more hope of God continuing the healing of my orphan heart, as I knew this latest admission of my secret thoughts and feelings would continue to move me along my personal pathway to freedom.

Later, at home, I again sat with pen and paper—writing another painful, personal, honest, and searching moral inventory. Slowly, and without explanation or excuse, I began to list and unflinchingly tell God all the events which I had hated that I thought He, God, *could* have stopped, and didn't.

On my paper I wrote:

"Dear God, I hated it. I hated having watched my father die. I hated being only fourteen years old when my mom took me into the small bathroom and showed me her breast mastectomy scar; I hated seeing my mom's angry, bright red, thick, jagged scar that went up into her armpit, across her now-flat chest where her breast had been. I hated being sixteen and remembering my mom sitting alone in the doctor's office, with her head hanging down, her hand covering her eyes, too stunned to even look up when I entered; my mom—who had already been through so much, fighting for her family—now sitting there all alone, because the doctor had just told my mom her cancer had returned; and in 1970 when that happened, when you were told your cancer had returned, you put your affairs in order and prepared to die.

"I hated all my brothers telling me that they also remember on a windy, cold winter's day in Buffalo, New York—in front of our family church of all places—

319

seeing our mom's wig blow off her head. I hated remembering how we all stood horrified watching my mom, her head bald and pale from chemotherapy, chasing after her wig as it continued rolling sideways down the wet, dirty, slippery streets, running after her dignity in full view of her kids and the church members. I hated that my youngest brother John Michael remembers going to the hospital to visit our mom before she died. I hated my mom's hospital bed in the dining room as a constant reminder of how fragile and terminally ill she was. I hated seeing my mom's hospital bed empty in the dining room, as it said she was slipping away from us. I hated seeing my mother in a casket, and I hated burying her also.

"God, I want You to know, I hated it all. Every single second of it. Every single second that I had to see, experience, and live through these horrors vibrated with my hatred. But I also stuffed all that hatred towards You down. I was a Christian. I loved You, God. I really did. And I *knew* You, God, loved me.

"But, God, I hated that I had no choice but to witness all these events. I hated the gross helplessness I always felt, starting with watching my father die, and watching my abysmal life keep crumbling around me, completely powerless to make it stop, even for a brief moment. I stood by helplessly as people died, and my life got harder, and more and more horrible images burned their way into my already-crowded brain—and I couldn't make it stop.

"God, I am so angry that these images are burned into my brain—these heartbreaking, poignant images shaping every word I said and more importantly, every word I didn't say. I always knew there was no one to help me, no one to talk to—or at least that I knew of—so instead I ate immense quantities of food to ease and quiet the aching pains inside.

"God, I remember when I was thirteen, my dad took me school clothes shopping by himself, and my dad bought his chubby thirteen-year-old daughter school clothes that fit me, that were pretty—and I felt pretty.

"My dad bought a really old sewing machine and then my dad sat next to me very patiently and taught me to sew in the evenings when he got home from work. I hated that I had such a loving father—and You took him home and then left me alone.

"God, I hated standing next to my dad's black and white recliner chair; hated that I remembered seeing and watching my dad gasping for breath. I hated that I heard my dad desperately asking You,

God, who would take care of his family. I hated remembering that I knew about my dad's nitroglycerin pills, yet my mom was there and I wasn't in charge—so I hated always living with the guilt that I had not given my dad his pills, feeling I could've saved my father, but I couldn't. I even hate knowing now that his pills would have done nothing to save him had they been given to my father, by me or anyone else.

"God, after my dad died and my sister Lisa was born, I was still thirteen years old and I saved my money and I bought a pretty little newborn baby dress pattern and yards of pink, fluffy, puckered material. Ever so slowly and meticulously, I pinned the petite dress pattern pieces to the material, cut them out, and sewed my newborn baby sister Lisa the prettiest little pink dress with lots of ruffles, thinking how happy my dad would've been if he'd even known he was having a baby girl. And as I sewed my newborn baby sister Lisa's pink dress I hated thinking of my dad, remembering how he had taught me to sew, missing him with every stitch of the sewing machine he had bought me, sewing the little pink baby dress for the daughter my dad would never know, and thinking how my newborn baby sister Lisa would never know my loving father.

"God, I hated not having enough food to feed my brothers; I hated being uneducated and not being able to earn enough money to feed my family more than twenty-five-cent boxed pizza and watery, powered instant milk. I hated leaving my sister Lisa behind in Buffalo, knowing she was being abused by our Aunt Mary when You didn't give her back to me.

"I hated every single moment of every single memory that told my orphan heart I was broken, different, and forever ruined.

"I hated every second of being profoundly affected by witnessing and living all the horrors that others did not have to experience.

"Why?

"Why me?

"Why them?

"Why us?"

Deep, painful questions I could only ask of God. Deep, painful questions left unvoiced, unspoken —and unheard, or so I thought. Deep, painful questions left unvoiced, unspoken, and unheard, yet loudly reverberating in every breath and action I took.

My confessions of my anger toward God about His unfairness led me to look at the scripture from the well-known 23rd Psalm:

"Yea, though I walk through the valley of the shadow of death, I will fear no evil, for Thou art with me" (v. 4).

This had been my father's favorite Psalm; it was written on the back of his funeral parlor cards when he died.

Now I sat and pondered the words "the valley of the shadow of death." What exactly does it mean to walk through this valley of the shadow of death?

What did it mean for me, and what would God ultimately mean these words to be for me?

These words had always seemed to refer to those who survive a brush with death or are currently fighting a battle with a deadly disease.

But what if "the shadow of death" is actually referring to the shadow cast on others watching loved ones die—standing by helplessly, willing to do anything asked of them, yet knowing intuitively and instinctively that there is nothing within their power that they can do to change what seems to be the inevitable death creeping ever closer and closer to their loved one?

Is "the shadow of death" what remains of our own once vibrant self, now exhausted, dazed, and emotionally spent once our loved one passes?

Is my now grieving, broken heart in reality this "valley of the shadow of death"?

With unanswered questions, I began to do the only thing I knew to do: run after God's answers—and in doing so receive the further, deeper, and more complete healing for my orphan heart that I still needed.

For many decades I had been an avid fan of the Trinity Broadcasting Network—known as TBN—as I preferred the deeply personal, real-world teaching of Bible teachers Joyce Meyers, Christine Caine, Alicia Brett Chloe, William Paul Young, and Pricilla Shirer, as well as Pastors Bishop T.D. Jakes, Steven Furtick, Joseph Prince, Jentezen Franklin, Creflo Dollar, Joel Osteen, Phil Munsey, Dr. Robert Morris and his son, Josh Morris. Additionally, I began to watch the Dr. Phil programs that specifically dealt with death, loss, and grief, and how it affected survivors and their families.

I knew if I did not dig deeper and face and admit who I was deep inside—deep in the broken places where all my hurts lived—I would be forever stuck and not completely healed; and with my broken places and my orphan heart, I would not be able to move forward into the full, happy, balanced life I envisioned for myself.

Joyce Meyer has long been a favorite Bible teacher, as I identified with and admired how she had healed of her childhood sexual abuse and her abnormal teenage years. I particularly liked her practical application of the Bible, and her teachings to be responsible for your own life now, not living a victim's existence of being frozen in past situations.

My niece gave me Joyce's book *Battlefield of the Mind* and I pored over it, reading it daily, using her book as a devotional. In addition, every single day started with me watching her daily program, *Enjoying Everyday Life*.

During the years when I worked as a trial paralegal, Joyce's program *Enjoying Everyday Life* was the start of my workday every single day, never any variation. Often, I would watch each daily program as many as seven times, repeating it right after it finished, taking notes, always finding new insight and healing in every word Joyce taught.

So many, many times when I felt defeated, lacking in my progress, or was hurting from new painful memories, I would say out loud, as Joyce often taught, "God is working on my behalf right now, right this minute, even if I don't see it or feel it."

Also, as Joyce taught, I would repeatedly remind myself that I had already made tremendous progress and I was continuing to make more progress, even if I didn't immediately see it or feel it.

Joyce's book and television show taught me to speak back to my paralyzing doubts and fears and inner self-defeating thoughts, and also to build myself up and encourage myself in the Lord, much as David, in his Psalms, had done when he felt discouraged.

I intentionally repeated to myself several times throughout the day that I was undefeatable, that there was nothing I could not accomplish; and I would say thank you to God for all the things I wanted and expected to see in my life.

"Speaking those things that are not as though they already are" (Romans 4:17).

William Paul Young, author of the best-selling book *The Shack,* has a television program called *Restoring the Shack.* On this program he unflinchingly looks at dark issues of grief, pain, and the underlying issues associated with the complications that arise when we need to forgive a person who has harmed us. He also gently, and with awareness and respect for the sensitive, painful areas of a grieving orphan heart, examines losing our loved ones and balancing, processing, and moving forward in those hard places in light of our loving God.

Daily, watching *Restoring the Shack,* I heard and saw myself in Paul Young's teaching and personal storytelling.

I quickly established a "playlist" of my daily Bible teachers' and pastors' programs.

As I mentioned, my day started with Bible teacher Joyce Meyer.

Next was Bishop T.D. Jakes, who also taught me to seek to be excellent in all I did. I was encouraged by Bishop Jakes' message about being exceptional. In his message he spoke of how Jesus was not accepted because He was Joseph's son. He emphasized how Jesus was intentionally belittled when He was asked, "Are you not Joseph's son?" Bishop Jakes went on, "Step out and be exceptional. If God has placed a dream in your heart, allow God to set the standard you live by."

One of Bishop T.D. Jakes' sermons that I vividly recall included having a gigantic birds' nest on the stage and Bishop Jakes teaching, "It is necessary to get pushed out of your nest; get pushed out of your comfort zone." This resonated, as I was learning many new skills at work and also balancing my graduate school classes and homework.

Additionally, Bishop Jakes encouraged me not to quit or lighten my class or work load. Bishop Jakes taught that every key that you hold and that you put in a lock—hoping and expecting a blessing, but the key won't turn—was practice for your future.

These words of my TV Bible teachers and pastors took root in my heart to not give up and to keep pushing forward, trusting in God's promise to heal my orphan's heart further.

In the spring of 2011, I started my Master's of Theology and Ministry degree at Fuller Theological Seminary, one of the top seminaries in the world. I was so honored to be attending the seminary. My spiritual mentor during this time was the Reverend Don Oliver, Ph.D., Chaplain and Director of Pastoral Care at Hoag Hospital in Newport Beach. I admire Dr. Oliver greatly, and he taught me valuable insights regarding the work of a chaplain—which I continue to implement today as a chaplain.

Bishop T.D. Jakes taught me the importance of understanding how one word or thought or idea from God could save years of hard work and ensure a much faster result.

I found Bishop T.D. Jakes' encouragement to be especially helpful, as I learned when I had a large term paper due or needed research for a particular problem, to stop and ask God for *His* help in giving me guidance in what I needed to see or research. Each time I asked for God's help, I would become very quiet and still—and almost immediately I would think of an idea or thought or previous project that would lead me to the much-needed solutions for my paper or project.

Of special help during this time when I was balancing so much was my best friend Gina Wilson, a kind, Godly woman who I had known since 2005. Gina would always seem to know exactly what I needed and without asking, Gina would continually send me articles, videos, and pastoral teachings about continuing to heal from past trauma that were particularly meaningful and helpful.

Another close friend, Rochelle SmallWare, was also a paralegal and a strong Christian, who countless times afforded me wisdom and Godly direction when I was at a crucial crossroads in both my personal and professional life.

I was now working full time as a senior nurse-paralegal for a medical defense firm, attending a graduate degree program full-time in the evenings and weekends, and also continuing to pursue my own continued emotional healing with my twice-weekly *Celebrate Recovery* meeting where I was a co-leader.

My days did not vary; I turned on my work computer, and instead of listening to music as my co-workers did, I started with Joyce Meyer's program; next would be Bishop T.D. Jakes, followed by Pastor Joseph Prince—who influenced me by his teachings on God's grace and communion, teaching, "When God restores, He never restores back to the original; God always restores *more* than we have lost. God always restores, either greater in quality or greater in quantity."

After I listened to Pastor Joseph Prince, I would put on Pastor Jentzen Franklin, the pastor whose sermon had started my healing journey back home to Buffalo, New York, when his sermon spoke of returning home to a gravesite to offer forgiveness.

I never tire of listening to Pastor Jentzen Franklin, as he also offers healing messages of all that God can and will do for us when we live within the boundaries of obedience to God.

One particularly helpful message was when Pastor Franklin taught, "If I will do what I can do, God will do what I can't do." Upon hearing his words, I decided I would run even harder after my healing for my orphan's heart and my education.

I knew I could show up with my homework prepared—and alert—to my graduate school classes and my *Celebrate Recovery* classes. I could share my answers; I could believe I was being changed; and I did believe that every single day, I was being healed of my orphan heart.

As I attended my Fuller Theological Seminary graduate classes in the evenings, I would often finish my homework after work, staying at my work desk, and then drive directly to school for my three-hour class, returning home close to 11:00 p.m. I would do more homework, and after getting a few hours' sleep, drive back to start work at 7:00 a.m. I remember napping in my car during my lunch hour and staying up all night doing my graduate homework, listening to Christian station TBN's lineup of my favorite pastors and Bible teachers, for the six years it took me to complete my Master's Degree in Theology and Ministry.

I soon added listening to Christine Caine both on television and on her videos. I would try to time my donations to TBN to coincide with receiving Christine Caine's materials, but if I could not accomplish that, I would find Christine's teaching someplace on one media or another and intently listen to her, always taking notes so I could go back and reference her vivid and helpful teaching. I was very, very moved by Christine's telling about learning she had been adopted, and upon seeing her birth certificate she saw that instead of a name she had seen listed only as a number, and how potentially devastating that discovery could have been to her.

Christine went on to say that despite that forlorn identification written on that piece of paper—her birth certificate—which could dictate a dismal life for her, she chose instead to believe what another piece of paper said when the Bible declared, "I formed you in your mother's womb and I knew you before you were born" (Jeremiah 1:5).

I so identified with Christine's choice to ignore her early label as I thought of my orphaned, homeless, penniless, uneducated, sad self—yet I decided I would choose instead to believe what God said in Genesis 1:1, "In the beginning, I created the heavens and the earth."

I knew that God had created me—not my early, traumatic years, and the labels I had not chosen for myself.

More and more, I clung to every word of the Bible teachers' and pastors' lessons as my personal life rafts and lights for my forward goals and plans.

Pastor Josh Morris taught, "It's a long process to get through; get through it anyway."

As Alicia Brett Chloe, author of *The Sacred Slow* teaches, "God seems to take issue with my clenched fist which held tightly to all my fears and abnormalities. They were my comforts; I needed them. I couldn't let go." So I began to look further at those issues I kept clenched in my fists, afraid to even let God's healing look at them, much less touch them.

Alicia shared how, as she read books that spoke to painful issues close to her own heart, "These books became lined with ink and tears." I found Alicia's words to be true for me, and I thought of the books I had read through dropping tears.

Pastor Leo Lusky spoke to my grieved heart when he spoke of the Saturday—the day between Good Friday and Easter morning. Saturday, when the stone that had sealed Jesus' lifeless body in the grave just sat there over the grave; when Saturday just sat there between the pain of the truth we knew and the promise of God of the better things to come.

I thought of what my Saturdays had been.

My Saturday was not riding to school with my dad anymore.

My Saturday was eating two scoops of mashed potatoes and gravy all alone in my high school cafeteria, always scared and always very sad.

My Saturday of being helpless to have stopped being separated from my sister and brothers.

As I listened and related to Pastor Leo Luskey I wondered, how do I turn off the pain of Saturday, that day of waiting between the pain and the promise?

He spoke with the empathy of knowing that the pain of the truth of the moments we've lived through is so very painful. He said, "I know it hurts so bad, and you don't think you can do it, but just breathe. The Holy Spirit is going to help you find grace until you can find a way to live again."

Shelia Walsh's TBN program, *Wednesdays in the Word*, had guest Michele Cushatt, who had three cancers and wrote her book *I Am*. Michele spoke, "We often equate the presence of pain with the absence of God. This is where our faith is tested; God is actually closer in moments of pain. We can only discover that closeness of God in that pain."

I found answers to my anger at God, and I found a true peace of heart and mind.

As I continued to listen to others' stories of grief and hope and joy restored, I was reminded of a song I particularly love by Mark Schultz titled "Remember Me," with the lyrics, "Child of wonder, child of God." I like the lyrics so very much, as they describe me in a simple way using six simple words.

As my life has been defined and directed by simple words—as many of our lives have been—these six words tell my story of heartbreak and grief and of hard, unimaginably hard work, yet always with God's hand on my life; knowing deep down in my soul that I am God's child.

I am not just one of the masses, but I belong to God; and as such, I have such a deeply rooted faith in God's ability to guide me to complete healing and restoration, I know none of what I've accomplished could have been done by chance or happenstance. My life has been intimately directed by God, as intimately and carefully directed by God as a laser focuses in on the exact place for its cause; that's been God's ever-providing and ever-guiding influence, direction, purpose, and plan, even when I sat blinded by tears from the mind-numbing and breathtaking events I endured in my life over which I had absolutely no control whatsoever.

I remember when America's space shuttle Challenger exploded shortly after take-off from Cape Canaveral, Florida. All of America watched in horror and disbelief as the explosion—starkly streaming white trails of smoke against the backdrop of the brilliant blue Florida sky, signaling the death of five of America's bravest astronauts—caused countless millions of people to earnestly ask in unison, "Why, God, why?" Pastor and New York Times best-selling author Max Lucado said in response to this question, "When we do not understand God's hand for us, we must trust in God's heart for us."

I decided, finally, that I will no longer ask God "why." I most likely will not ever know why I had to journey through my painful steps—seemingly alone.

Finally, I will rest on a conclusion which I have heard both Joyce Meyer and Christine Caine say. They have both said that while they hated the sexual abuse and the horrible things that they have experienced, they believe they have a closer walk with God because of those horrible events that they endured and ultimately triumphed over.

I agree with their sentiments—that while I would not wish what I have endured on anyone, I would not trade my walk with God, my closeness with God, and my love by God for anything.

If you too have an orphan heart, whether by natural or man-made choices or perhaps dysfunctional family circumstances, please stay and give God—and the healing power of Jesus Christ through His work on the cross—a chance to heal you and set you free, finally and completely, from all the hard bondages you find yourself in.

God says "You are fearfully and wonderfully made" in Psalm 139:14 and promises us, "I knew you before I formed you in your mother's womb. Before you were born I set you apart" (Jeremiah 1:5).

Think about that: when we were in our mother's wombs, God had a plan and a purpose for us. In spite of all the insanity I lived through God has kept me, and He's still keeping you—because I'm not more special than you are.

I say to you who share my affliction of having an orphan heart, the Bible says "Whosoever will, let him take the water of life freely" (Revelation 22:17). We, the owners of an orphan heart, can have all that God promises.

I decided I'm a "whosoever," and *I promise you're also a "whosoever."* God looked down—and when Satan tried his best to take us out and destroy us so completely that we would never again function normally, God said, "Not them! Not him! Not her, for they belong to me."

And yes, you do.

The horror that tragically attacked my family left a large trail of devastation, destruction, grief, pain, and damage.

Because horror is a lot like that.

But the God who loves us dearly, deeply, and fully, reached down and ever so gently lifted me out of the dark depths of despair—and consoled me, provided for me, guided me, and both redeemed my earthly family and placed me in His lovely family.

God has allowed me to not only to survive—but now, I thrive.

I promise you, if you choose to let God hold your hand as you face your own horrors, the horrors will lose their hold on your tomorrows. God will place them firmly in your past, where they belong, where they can no longer keep you captive with their chains of memories. Instead, you will drink freely of the abundant life offered to you when you are healed.

And you will yourself know a new freedom and a joy again in your life.

I know God can also heal your orphan heart if you let Him.

Because God heals like that, I've learned, when God heals our orphan hearts.

Epilogue

Restoration and Full Circles

Best friend Gina Wilson, my Master's Degree
Graduation from Fuller Theological Seminary, 2017

*"Go home and tell your friend what
God has done for you" (Luke 8:39).*

Many changes have occurred since *Celebrate Recovery*.

With my very first check of not needing every penny, I drove back to the Share Our Selves SOS Food Bank that used to give me a single large brown paper bag of food, which included a cellophane-wrapped piece of meat and on a really good day, a single long stemmed rose in my weekly brown bag of food. Smiling, I was beyond happy as I gave them a check for their Food bank along with a letter in which I explained I now no longer needed their weekly food items and explained I was deeply grateful for their years of help.

To my surprise and delight I received a form letter from the Share Our Selves SOS Food bank thanking me for my donation and a hand-written note at the bottom of the SOS form letter that said they were so happy for me and that I had made their day.

I recently took a friend to the county social services office. While I waited I thanked the worker at the window, telling her I now hold a Masters Degree and appreciated their work as county Food Stamps helped me meet my education and career goals. The worker called over several other workers to hear my story.

I no longer get fired from jobs. I started my job the same year I started *Celebrate Recovery*. I got my first raise in my entire life there and retired from that job, all while attending *Celebrate Recovery*.

On my last yearly review prior to my retirement, my managing attorney wrote: "Rosie shows exemplary character and does not involve herself in office gossip, and is well-known to help everyone, and is well-liked."

Thank you, *Celebrate Recovery*, for my new standards of work ethics.

I completed my Master's Degree of Theology and Ministry at Fuller Seminary in 2017. Dr. David Stoop was one of my professors at Fuller Seminary. Dr. Stoop's classes teaching the various stages of emotional growth taught me about my own stunted emotional growth and how to resolve it, and are to this day some of the best teachings I have ever received. Dr. Stoop's books on forgiveness, *Forgiving Our Parents and Forgiving Ourselves* and *Making Peace With Your Father,* have helped me immensely.

Additionally, I have met and continue to counsel with Dr. Jill Hubbard, a respected counselor whose personal counseling and books *Forgiving Our Fathers and Mothers: Finding Freedom from Hurt and Hate* and *Secrets Women Keep* have been valuable additional resources in helping me make peace with my past and live in my bright life of today.

I no longer need to be right, learning that others' behaviors come from their pain and not me. I'm a Billy Graham chaplain, and I maintain a seventy-five-pound weight loss. I am learning to have fun and relax, enjoying quiet free time with loved friends and family and even all by myself.

In *Celebrate Recovery* I've grieved and healed from being so consumed with keeping my promise to my dad for my family, I haven't yet married and have no children. That was a hard one. As I am a chaplain, my nephew and his fiancée requested I perform their wedding.

God has an interesting way of restoring all that's been taken. On New Year's Eve 2015, their daughter was born. I was unexpectedly honored as they named her AvaRose, after me. When they sent me her ultrasound my nephew said, "Now you have your little Rosie."

I *love* being an auntie, a sister, a friend—and yes, now, with *Celebrate Recovery*, I again love being a daughter. Tom and Teri Phipps, who loved me as a daughter when I was nineteen, homeless, and orphaned, have continued to love me now for forty-five years. They are continual fun, bright lights in my life, as are my older brother who was unavailable while I struggled, my three younger brothers, and my baby sister. My siblings all have given me the honor of being Auntie Rosie, also known as "the fun Auntie" and "the lipstick Auntie" to their children and now, to their adorable and fun grandchildren. It is my honor to be called my siblings' sister.

Gina Wilson continues to be the best friend I always dreamed of having offering valuable spiritual and practical advice that both makes me laugh and keeps me grounded. Rochelle SmallWare also continues providing a warm, God-centered friendship. Arnette Travis, continues to be amongst my most loved and trusted friends. Arnette is herself an author and well-known speaker who encouraged me to write this book. It's been, and still is, a very wonderful life.

When you fly, the oxygen mask wrinkly bag demonstration says, "Even if the bag does not fully inflate the oxygen is still flowing, and, when traveling with a small child, place mask over your face first, then over the child." I have learned that I needed to rescue and heal myself first.

I also learned, when I felt like God's healing wasn't working, that I needed to just stay, for God's healing was still flowing. When I was tired of coming, I stayed, for God's healing is still flowing.

My New York court papers said that my orphaned, uneducated, overwhelmed resume left me qualified for little more than homelessness, heartbreak, and a pretty dismal life.

But there was another paper written long ago, and it says, "In the beginning, God created."

That's the writing I have decided to choose—and the love which God offers, that I have decided to follow with my whole heart.

For the joy set before Him is why Jesus endured the cross. You'll be amazed at the freedom and joy that will be yours, if you just allow God to walk with you and heal your orphan heart.

Trust *Celebrate Recovery*, trust the process, trust God. More than anything, *trust yourself, trust* that you are good, *trust* that you are kind. *Trust* that your dreams *are* still available to you, that all of God's goodness and purposes are all still available to you.

Please continue believing in the HOPE of God, as God is able to heal our orphan hearts. Please let Him.

You deserve happiness, you deserve joy, and you deserve love.

You deserve to have—and can have—God heal your orphan heart.

Please choose to let Him.

Please choose life. Please choose love. Please choose joy.

Choose the happiness that awaits you when God heals your orphan heart.

Afterword

The Elephant in the Room

"Blessed are those who mourn, for they
shall be comforted" (Matthew 5:4).

I've always felt especially bad for my brothers. How could they—Daniel at ten years of age, Peter at eight years of age, and Curtis John Michael at five years of age—possibly understand, process, and make peace with watching their father die in front of them? How could they possibly normalize what they experienced? As difficult and heart-wrenching as that morning with my father was for me, I have often wondered: how in the world did my younger brothers make any sense of *their* worlds also being irreparably shattered in an instant?

Daniel, the oldest of my three younger brothers has always called our dad "my hero." He often says, "I had a great dad; I just only had him for ten years."

As odd and strange as it may sound, although my brothers, sister and I have lived together and continue to live geographically close to each other for almost fifty years now, none of us have ever had any kind of detailed, calm conversation regarding that fateful morning of our father's death and its aftermath; nor have we talked about, in any depth, our mother's death and all that followed in the ensuing years of being orphaned.

Sure, we've talked about some memories of hard times, fun times, and understandably confusing times, but we've never really talked about how we each *"felt"* about what happened to us and how we were each uniquely affected. But again, this realization takes me back to what I now understand—which is that extremely felt trauma, the kind of trauma that rocks you to the very core of your being, shocks your world, and kills every belief you held regarding your personal physical and emotional safety, is *not* a topic of conversation that one just pulls out as a conversation starter at their nightly dinner table.

I wish I had known and realized how deeply hurt my brothers were. I wish I had known how to offer some kind of inner peace and healing and comfort to my brothers. But I didn't. All I knew was to keep working and to try to keep all the visages of *normalcy* in their lives—yet never even thinking that their worlds were nothing even vaguely *close to normal.*

Over the years, I've learned that I did my best and that they and my sister did their best. All of us did the very best we could, with the limited tools and understanding we each possessed. All of us have succeeded in many areas, and not done as well as we would have liked to in other areas—much like the way life happens for everyone, even people that haven't gone through the tremendous grief and traumas our family has endured and survived.

I learned that the take-away is that we did endure, we did survive—and most importantly of all, we did thrive.

As you can also endure your pain, survive your pain—and with God's ample love, you can also thrive. I promise you can and you will. Maybe not in the ways you had dreamed about and hoped for. Maybe not with all the accomplishments you had dreamed and hoped for. But survival and endurance, in its purest form, is to simply take one breath at a time, savoring that breath and knowing you are alive—and a good life is still possible and a good life is still very achievable.

On a final note: I have begun to speak at alternative high schools, the very schools where I was expelled from because my attendance was so bad when I was sixteen and my mom was battling her cancer.

My friend Sonia Canaless Freeman invited me to speak at her school, and I enjoyed telling the bright students, "This is just your starting point, not your destiny."

I have lived the verse in Proverbs 13:12, "Hope deferred makes the heart sick, but when it comes, it is a tree of life."

I have known and lived hope deferred, and now I am experiencing hope like a tree of life.

I am immensely proud of my siblings and their accomplishments despite their almost unimaginable difficult beginnings.

Daniel Paul enjoys ownership of Fight Strong MMA gym in San Clemente, California, where he has trained athletes and champions in many sports for decades. Peter George became a licensed contractor and a licensed private pilot. John Michael is an accomplished artist, and enjoys fishing as often as he can. Peter George and John Michael still reside in southern California. Our baby sister Lisa Robin Michelle became a Nursery school assistant and a YMCA instructor and enjoys a thriving family life in Las Vegas.

Today, I am living proof of God's desire to heal our orphan heart, once again living a very wonderful life.

I still learn valuable lessons from attending *Celebrate Recovery*.

Upon writing this book, I unexpectedly discovered my memories still had the ability to move me to tears both in reliving the immense sadness, grief and unrelenting pain I had felt and also in simply reflecting on all the normal experiences held in the gentleness of simply joys of life that neither of my parents, my siblings nor I would ever know.

As I spoke to relatives and old family friends, I was finding out new, very sad facts about our family's dire circumstances after my father' death and sadness would again enveloped me. These moments continually caught me by surprise, but now, I just allowed myself the luxury of stopping and crying for a while. I had always been a person who though my eyes were red and swollen from crying, would lie and say, "I'm fine, just my allergies" because for decades I never felt safe saying I was drowning in feelings of sadness as there wasn't anybody there for me; I got used to figuring things out. But *Celebrate Recovery* had taught me not only God cares about my sadness, but others do too.

I've learned how helpful writing my feelings down on paper is, so in discovering how brutally painful and sad I was to even read my own early life story, even though I had lived it, I had taken pen and paper and written "This WAS HORRIBLE! This was really, truly HORRIFFIC and it REALLY WAS AWFUL to live through all of this. It REALLY, REALLY was!" I was surprised at the raw pain I still felt, all these decades later, yet relieved after I wrote out my pain and feelings.

Later, on this day of sadness, I'd told no one of my day of again crying while writing this book but had promised a friend we'd attend Bay Cities South *Celebrate Recovery* so I couldn't cancel. There, I did something I had not ever done. Instead of pretending I was just fine, I decided to confide in my friend Kevin Crowley, because I had come to know Kevin as a wise and compassionate friend.

I found myself surprised at the immense relief I felt talking to Kevin and in just admitting this book writing was not easy as my emotions that were so deeply scarred and long-buried were again reaching up to bring me great grief.

To my relief, Kevin wasn't shocked at all. Instead he commented I should add what I'd just told him to the end of my book, that I should detail how painful writing this book has been for me.

My first response inwardly was "Absolutely not, this is hard enough without telling the world it's still hard." Yet, later reflecting and praying, what Kevin proposed made a lot of sense, first because I came to *Celebrate Recovery* to face my fears and to tell my secrets in order to heal my Orphan heart. And second, even more importantly, through the years and ways I had sought healing, I had personally disliked when well-meaning friends and even professionals said I should just "get over old events" and presented healing as a once-and-for-all instantaneous fix that meant I'd never again feel a sad moment remembering the events.

I knew healing meant our painful events could still cause sad feelings in us, even cause us tears, but I needed in sharing my story, to convey the truth that my healing also meant these feelings would no longer dictate my life. I'd no longer be a prisoner to events over which I'd had no control. To write pretending I only thought happy thoughts now when I thought of my parents' deaths and subsequent events would be to lie to the very hurting people I was writing this book to help find their own way to healing.

I learned a couple good lessons that night speaking to Kevin.

I learned it's good to have wise and compassionate friends. Kevin certainly is and I am grateful for him and others that have advised me to bare my deepest hurts and pains.

I learned to not be ashamed of my emotions as they are God-given.

I've learned healing continues for me as it will for you even as the pain lessens. I saw demonstrated again, there's so much joy in just taking a chance and doing life a little bit different than the way I always done it.

That talk with Kevin reminded me of why I went to *Celebrate Recovery* to start with. I started *Celebrate Recovery* because I held a hope in the most private part of my orphan heart that I could find a way to not hurt and sabotage myself every single day; that I could learn to not be afraid every single day; that I could not be ravaged by fears, regrets and deep disappointments.

Speaking with Kevin also reminded me *why Celebrate Recovery* works, because the people there will gently walk you through your pain as they have walked through their own.

Today, I'm glad I did not hide how hard it's been to write this book. I'm glad I've shared my fears and my tears knowing God holds both dear in His heart and safe in His hands.

Because I know in my heart as you will learn in yours, God is gentle and shows us His special tender, loving kindness when He heals our orphan hearts.

Please let my story of healing my orphan heart become your story of God now healing your orphan heart.

Find again the joy you once knew.

This is your invitation.

My 5th birthday at my "happy house."
Buffalo, New York, 1958

About the Author

Rosie George Finocchi is an enthusiastic believer in Jesus Christ, and in the healing work achieved in her life through the Christ-centered *Celebrate Recovery* twelve-step recovery program, in which she still serves in a servant-leader position and travels, speaking of her own miraculous healing. Rosie George holds the record for most United States Figure Skating (USFS) and ISI (Ice Skating Institute) Adult National, Regional, and local gold medals, podium medals, and combined ISI gold medals and podium wins. She enjoys International and National competitive ice skating, roller blading and has been a Mixed Martial Arts assistant instructor, holding a brown-belt candidate designation in Mixed Martial Arts.

Rosie George is a devoted Pittsburgh Steelers fan, a licensed financial advisor, and licensed stock broker, an American Bar Association Senior trial paralegal, an IRS certified tax preparer, and a hospital chaplain also serving with the Billy Graham Rapid Response Team Chaplains.

Rosie George received her Master's Degree of Theology and Ministry from Fuller Theological Seminary and remains a Bible student. Her greatest joy comes from seeing God's healing of orphan hearts and joyful life restored.

Rosie George lives in Southern California, where she attends Cottonwood Church and enjoys her home, loving her large extended family, and her beloved friends.

Rosie's favorite titles are those of "Fancie Auntcie," fun friend and believer in Jesus Christ.